Ψάρι είναι αυτό μέσα στο αυτί σου;

Kalako sinulla on korvassa?

Che hai, un pesce nell'orecchio?

Что это у вас в ухе? Рыба?

Ĉu tiu estas fiŝo en via orelo?

?

Tu ce, ai peste in ureche?

☆▲ ❋✳◉▼ ☆ ◆❋▲❋ ☆■
❋▢◆▢ ✧✳▢ †

has gots fish in ur eer?!11

Translayshun
and da Meening
of stuffz

Что это у вас в ухе? Рыба?

אוזן

Kalako sinulla on korvassa?

Ψάρι είναι αυτό μέσα στο αυτί σου;

Is That a Fish in Your Ear?

ALSO BY DAVID BELLOS

Balzac Criticism in France, 1850–1900:
  The Making of a Reputation

Leo Spitzer, *Essays on Seventeenth Century French*
  Literature

Georges Perec: A Life in Words

Jacques Tati: His Life and Art

Romain Gary: A Tall Story

Is That a Fish in Your Ear?

David Bellos

Translation and the
Meaning of Everything

PARTICULAR BOOKS
an imprint of
PENGUIN BOOKS

PARTICULAR BOOKS

Published by the Penguin Group
Penguin Books Ltd, 80 Strand, London WC2R ORL, England
Penguin Group (USA) Inc., 375 Hudson Street, New York, New York 10014, USA
Penguin Group (Canada), 90 Eglinton Avenue East, Suite 700, Toronto, Ontario, Canada M4P 2Y3
(a division of Pearson Penguin Canada Inc.)
Penguin Ireland, 25 St Stephen's Green, Dublin 2, Ireland (a division of Penguin Books Ltd)
Penguin Group (Australia), 250 Camberwell Road, Camberwell, Victoria 3124, Australia
(a division of Pearson Australia Group Pty Ltd)
Penguin Books India Pvt Ltd, 11 Community Centre, Panchsheel Park, New Delhi – 110 017, India
Penguin Group (NZ), 67 Apollo Drive, Rosedale, Auckland 0632, New Zealand
(a division of Pearson New Zealand Ltd)
Penguin Books (South Africa) (Pty) Ltd, 24 Sturdee Avenue, Rosebank,
Johannesburg 2196, South Africa

Penguin Books Ltd, Registered Offices: 80 Strand, London WC2R ORL, England

www.penguin.com

First published 2011
004

The Acknowledgements on pp. 374–7 constitute an extension to this copyright page

Set in Caslon Pro 12/14.75pt
Typeset by Palimpsest Book Production Limited, Falkirk, Stirlingshire
Printed in Great Britain by Clays Ltd, St Ives plc

A CIP catalogue record for this book is available from the British Library

978-1-846-14464-6

www.greenpenguin.co.uk

ALWAYS LEARNING
PEARSON

In memory of my teachers

Contents

Prologue   1

1. *What* is a Translation?   4

2. *Is T*ranslation Avoidable?   7

3. Why Do *We* Call *It* 'Translation'?   21

4. *Things P*eople *Say* about *Translation*   34

5. *Fictions of the* Foreign: The Paradox of 'Foreign-Soundingness'   41

6. *Native* Command: Is Your *L*anguage Really Yours?   57

7. *M*eaning is *No* Simple Thing   67

8. *Words* ar*e Even* Worse   81

9. *Understanding* Dictionarie*s*   94

10. *The* My*th* of Literal Translation   103

11. *The* Issue *of T*rust: The Long Shadow of Oral Translation   118

12. Custom Cuts: Making Forms *F*it   133

13. *What* Can't *be* Said *Can't* be *Translated*: 149
     The Axiom of Effability

14. *How* Many *Words* Do W*e* Have *for* Coffee? 160

15. *Bibles* and *Bananas*: The Vertical Axis of 171
     Translation *R*elations

16. *Translation* Impacts 187

17. *The* Third *Code*: Translation as a *D*ialect 195

18. *No* Language is an *Island*: The Awkward 202
     Issue of L3

19. *Global* Flows: Centre and *P*eriphery in the 208
     Translation of Books

20. *A* *Q*uestion *of* Human *Rights*: Translation 224
     and the Spread of International Law

21. *Ceci n'est pas une traduction*: Language *P*arity 237
     in the European Union

22. *Translating* *N*ews 250

23. *The* Adventure *of* Automated *Language* 256
     Translation *M*achines

24. *A* Fish *in* Your *Ear*: The Short History of 268
     Si*m*ultaneous Interpreting

25. *Match* Me *If* You *Can*: Tra*n*slating **H**umour 283

26. *St*y*le* and *Translation* 291

27. *Translating* Literary *Texts*   302

28. *What* Translators *Do*   312

29. *Beating* the *Bounds*: What Translation is Not   322

30. *Under* Fire: Sniping at Tr*a*nslation   328

31. *Sa*m*eness*, Likeness *and* Match: Truths About Translation   332

32. Avatar: A *P*arable of Translation   337

    Afterbabble: In Lieu of an E*p*ilogue   339

    Caveats and Thanks   354

    Notes   356

    Permissions and Acknowledgements   374

    Index   378

Prologue

When I was an undergraduate a story went round among students in my college that a fellow called Harris had refused to teach translation classes on the grounds that he did not know what 'translation' was.

He'd challenged the Faculty Board to tell him what it was he was being asked to teach. Everyone knows what it is! they said. Translation has been taught here for centuries. But knowing how to perpetuate an academic tradition is not the same thing as knowing what you're doing. Harris could not possibly teach a subject his seniors were unable to define.

We thought it a great giggle: a junior don had used a philosophical conundrum to get out of a chore and tied the fuddy-duddies into knots.

Despite the tantalizing puzzle set by Roy Harris at the start of my adult life, I have dared to teach translation for several decades since then. I have also translated many books and become the Director of a Program in Translation and Intercultural Communication. So it's about time I tried to answer his question.

However, answers are best found when the question itself is well put. 'What is ... ?' doesn't normally provide a good prompt. It usually leads you headlong into hair-splitting disputes about the meanings of words.

The meaning of the word 'translation' is not without interest, of course, and I've devoted one chapter of this book to the issue. But it isn't as important as many other questions that arise just the same whatever word we use.

Here are some of those other questions: What can we learn from translation? What does it teach us?

Many others then spring to mind: What do we actually know about translation? What is it about translation that we still need to find out?

We also have to ask: What do people mean when they offer opinions and precepts about the best way to translate? Are all translations the same kind of thing, or are there different operations involved in different kinds of translating? Is translating fundamentally different from writing and speaking, or is it just another aspect of the unsolved mystery of how we come to know what someone else means?

This isn't a book that tells you how to translate, or how I translate. There are plenty of good books of those kinds; there's no need to add a lesser one to the pile.

Instead, it is made of stories and examples and arguments that circle round what seems to me to be the real issue – understanding what translation *does*.

I've tried to paint a big picture by exploring the role of translation in cultural, social and human issues of many kinds. To do so, I've used scholarly books and articles and exploited many erudite friends, but in many places I've also drawn on personal experience.

As I grew up in England and live in the United States, the point of view of this book is located unambiguously in the English-speaking world.

Because English is currently the dominant interlanguage of the world, English-speakers who aren't involved in translation have a harder time than most others in understanding what translation is. That's my main reason for writing about it.

Finding out what translation has done in the past and does today, finding out what people have said about it and why, finding out whether it is one thing or many – these inquiries take us far and wide, to Sumer, Brussels and Beijing, to comic books and literary classics, and into the fringes of disciplines as varied as anthropology, linguistics and computer science. What translation does raises so many answerable questions that we can leave the business of what it is to the side for quite some time.

1. *What* is *a* Translation?

Douglas Hofstadter took a great liking to this short poem by the sixteenth-century French wit Clément Marot:

Ma mignonne.	*Vitement,*	*Trop malade,*
Je vous donne	*Car Clément*	*Couleur fade*
Le bon jour;	*Le vous mande.*	*Tu prendras,*
Le séjour	*Va, friande*	*Et perdras*
C'est prison.	*De ta bouche,*	*L'embonpoint.*
Guérison	*Qui se couche*	*Dieu te doint*
Recouvrez,	*En danger*	*Santé bonne,*
Puis ouvrez	*Pour manger*	*Ma mignonne*
Votre porte	*Confitures;*	
Et qu'on sorte	*Si tu dures*	

He sent a copy of it to a great number of his friends and acquaintances and asked them to translate it into English, respecting as well as they could the formal properties that he identified in it:

> (1) 28 lines (2) of 3 syllables each (3) in rhyming couplets (4) with the last line being the same as the first; (5) midway the poem changes from formal (*vous*) to informal (*tu*) and (6) the poet puts his own name directly into the poem.[1]

Hofstadter, a cognitive scientist at Indiana University, got many dozens of responses over the following months and years. Each one of them was different, yet each one of them

4

was without doubt a translation of Marot's little poem. By this simple device he demonstrated one of the most awkward and wonderful truths about translation. It is this: any utterance of more than trivial length has no one translation. All utterances have innumerably many acceptable translations.

You get the same result with ordinary prose as you do with a poem. Give a hundred competent translators a page to translate, and the chances of any two versions being identical is close to zero. This fact about interlingual communication has persuaded many people that translation is not an interesting topic – because it is always approximate, it is just a second-rate kind of thing. That's why 'translation' isn't the name of a long-established academic discipline, even though its practitioners have often been academics in some other field. How can you have theories and principles about a process that comes up with no determinate results?

Like Hofstadter, I take the opposite view. The variability of translations is incontrovertible evidence of the limitless flexibility of human minds. There can hardly be a more interesting subject than that.

What is it that translators really do? How many different kinds of translating are there? What do the uses of this mysterious ability tell us about human societies, past and present? How do the facts of translation relate to language use in general – and to what we think a language is?

Those are the kinds of questions I explore in this book. Definitions, theories and principles can be left aside until we have a better idea what we are talking about. We shouldn't use them prematurely to decide whether or not the following version of Clément Marot's poem (one of many by Hofstadter himself) is good, bad or indifferent. It's the other way round. Until we can explain why the following version counts as a translation, we don't really know what we're saying when we utter the word.

Gentle gem,	From your oy-	Than fourteen,
Diadem,	ster bed, coy	Silv'ry queen –
Ciao! Bonjour!	Little pearl.	But no more
Heard that you're	See, blue girl,	'n twenty-four,
In the rough:	Beet-red ru-	Golden dream.
Glum, sub-snuff.	by's your hue.	How you'll gleam!
Precious, tone	For your aches,	Trust old Clem,
Down your moan,	Carat cakes	Gentle gem.
And fling wide	Are the cure.	
Your door; glide	Eat no few'r	

2. *Is* Translation *Avoidable?*

Translation is everywhere – at the United Nations, the European Union, the World Trade Organization and many other international bodies that regulate fundamental aspects of modern life. Translation is part and parcel of modern business, and there's hardly a major industry that doesn't use and produce translations for its own operations. We find translations on the bookshelves of our homes, on the reading lists for every course in every discipline taught at college, we find them on processed-food labels and on flat-pack furniture instructions. How could we do without translation? It seems pointless to wonder what world we would live in if translation didn't happen all the time at every level, from bilingual messages on cash machine screens to confidential discussions between heads of state, from the guarantee slip on a new watch we've just bought to the classics of world literature.

But we could do without it, all the same. Instead of using translation, we could learn the languages of all the different communities we wish to engage with; or we could decide to speak the same language; or else adopt a single common language for communicating with other communities. But if we baulk at adopting a common tongue and decline to learn the other languages we need, we could simply ignore people who don't speak the way we do.

These three options seem fairly radical, and it's likely that none of them figures among the aspirations of the readers of this book. However, they are not imaginary solutions to the many paradoxes of intercultural communication. All three paths away from translation are historically attested. More than that: the refusal of translation, by one or more of the means described, is probably closer to the historical norm on this planet than the culture of translation which seems natural and unavoidable around the world today. One big truth about translation that is often kept under wraps is that many societies did just fine by doing without.

The Indian subcontinent has long been the home of many different groups speaking a great variety of languages. However, there is no tradition of translation in India. Until very recently, nothing was ever translated directly between Urdu, Hindi, Kannada, Tamil, Marathi and so on. Yet these communities have lived cheek by jowl in a crowded continent for centuries. How did they manage? They learned other languages! Few inhabitants of the subcontinent have ever been monoglot; citizens of India have traditionally spoken three, four or five tongues. [1]

In the late Middle Ages, the situation was quite similar in many parts of Europe. Traders and poets, sailors and adventurers moved overland and around the inland seas picking up and often mixing more or less distantly related languages as they went, and only the most thoughtful of them even wondered whether or not they were speaking different 'languages', or just adapting to local peculiarities. The great explorer Christopher Columbus provides an unusually well-documented case of the intercomprehensibility and interchangeability of European tongues in the late Middle Ages. He wrote notes in the margins of his copy of Pliny in what we now recognize as an early form of Italian, but he used typically Portuguese place names – such as Cuba – to label his discoveries in the New World. He wrote his official correspondence in Castilian

Spanish, but used Latin for the precious journal he kept of his voyages. He made a 'secret' copy of the journal in Greek, however, and he also must have known enough Hebrew to use the *Astronomical Tables* of Abraham Zacuto, which allowed him to predict a lunar eclipse and impress the indigenous people he encountered in the Caribbean. He must have been familiar with lingua franca – a 'contact language' made of simplified Arabic syntax and a vocabulary mostly taken from Italian and Spanish, used by Mediterranean sailors and traders from the Middle Ages to the dawn of the nineteenth century – because he borrowed a few characteristic words from it when writing in Castilian and Italian.[2] How many languages did Columbus know when he sailed the ocean in 1492? As in today's India, where a degree of intercomprehensibility exists between several of its languages, the answer would be somewhat arbitrary. It's unlikely Columbus even conceptualized Italian, Castilian or Portuguese as distinct languages, for they did not yet have any grammar books. He was a learned man in being able to read and write the three ancient tongues. But beyond that, he was just a Mediterranean sailor, speaking whatever variety of language that he needed to do his job.

There are perhaps as many as 7,000 languages spoken in the world today,[3] and no individual could learn them all. Five to ten languages seem to represent the effective limit in all cultures, however multilingual they may be. Some obsessive individuals have clocked up twenty; a few champion linguists, who spend all their time learning languages, have claimed knowledge of fifty, or even more. But even these maniacal brain-boxes master only a tiny fraction of all the tongues that there are.

Most of the world's languages are spoken by very small groups, which is the main reason why a great number of them are near the point of collapse. However, outside the handful of countries speaking one of the half-dozen 'major' world languages, few people on this planet have only one tongue. Within the Russian Federation, for example, hundreds of languages are spoken – belonging to the Slavic, Turkic, Caucasian, Altaic and other language families. But there is hardly a member of any of the communities speaking these very diverse tongues who does not also speak Russian. Similarly, in India, there aren't many people who don't also have either Hindi, or Urdu, or Bengali, or English, or one of the half-dozen other interlanguages of the subcontinent. To engage with all but a tiny fraction of people in the world, you definitely do not need to learn all their first languages. You need to learn all their vehicular languages – languages learned by non-native speakers for the purpose of communicating with native speakers of a third tongue. There are about eighty languages used in this way in some part of the world. But because vehicular languages are also native to some (usually very large) group as well, and because many people speak more than one vehicular language (of which one may or may not be native to them), you do not need to learn all eighty vehicular languages to communicate with most people on the planet. Knowing just nine of them – Chinese (with 1,300 million users), Hindi (800 million), Arabic (530 million), Spanish (350 million), Russian (278 million), Urdu (180 million), French (175 million), Japanese (130 million) and English (somewhere between 800 and 1,800 million) – would permit effective everyday conversation, though probably not detailed negotiation or serious intellectual debate, with at least 4.5 billion and maybe up to 5.5 billion people, that is to say, around 90 per cent of the world's population. (The startlingly wide range of estimates of the number of people who 'speak English' reflects the difficulty we have in saying what 'speaking English' means.) Add Indonesian (250 million), German (185 million), Turkish (63 million) and Swahili (50 million) to make a baker's dozen,[4] and you have at your feet the entire American landmass, most of Europe from the Atlantic to the Urals, the great crescent of Islam from Morocco to Pakistan, a good part of India, a swathe of Africa and most of the densely populated parts of East Asia too. What more could you want?[5] *Exeunt* translators! Enter the language trainers! The cast would be more or less identical, so the net loss of jobs worldwide would most likely be nil.

If thirteen languages seems too hard to handle, why not have everyone learn the same one? The plan seemed obvious to the Romans, who made little attempt to learn the languages of the many peoples they conquered, with the sole but major exception of the Greeks. Barely a trace of interest has been found among Ancient Romans in learning Etruscan, Umbrian, the Celtic languages of what is now France and Britain, the Germanic languages of the tribes on the north-eastern borders of the empire, or the Semitic languages of the Carthage they deleted from the map and the colonies in the Eastern Mediterranean and Black Sea area. If you got taken over by Rome, you learned Latin, and that was that. The long-term result of the linguistic unification of the empire was that the written version of the Romans' language remained the main vehicle of intercultural communication in Europe for more than a thousand years after the end of the empire. Imperial blindness to the difference of others did a huge favour to Europe.[6]

Linguistic unification of the same order of magnitude has taken place in the last fifty years in most branches of science. Many languages have served at different times as vehicles of scientific advance: Chinese, Sanskrit, Greek, Syriac, Latin and Arabic from ancient times to the Middle Ages; then Italian and French in the European Renaissance and early modern period. In the eighteenth century, the advances made by Linnaeus in the description and classification of botanical species as well as Berzelius's research in chemistry made Swedish a language of science, and for about a hundred years it kept a respected place. English and French continued to be used for numerous disciplines, but German burst on to the scene in the nineteenth century with the new chemistry invented by Liebig and others; and Dmitri Mendeleev, the discoverer of the periodic table of the elements, helped to put Russian among the international languages of science before the end of the nineteenth century. Between 1900 and 1940, new scientific research continued to be published, often in intense rivalry, in Russian, French, German and English (Swedish having dropped off the map by then). But the Nazis' abuse of science between 1933 and 1945 discredited the language they used. German began to lose its status as a world science language on the fall of Berlin in 1945 – and many leading German scientists were of course whisked off to America and Britain in short order and functioned thereafter as English-speakers. French entered a slow decline, and Russian, which expanded in use after the Second World War and continued to be cultivated for political reasons during the remaining years of the USSR, dropped out of the science scene in 1989. So we are left with English. English is the language of science, worldwide; learned journals published in Tokyo, Beijing, Moscow, Berlin and Paris are either now entirely in English, or else carry English translations alongside foreign-language texts. Academic advancement everywhere is dependent on publications in English. Indeed, in Israel, it is said that God himself would not get promotion in any science department at the Hebrew University of Jerusalem. Why not? Because he has only one publication – and it was not written in English. (I do not really believe this story. The fact that the publication in question has been translated into English and is even available in paperback would surely overrule the promotions committee's misgivings.)

Despite this, efforts are being made to allow some languages to serve once again as local science dialects. A US-government-sponsored web service, for example, World-WideScience.org, now offers searches of non-English-language databases in China, Russia, France and some South American countries together with automatic retranslation of the results into Chinese, French, German, Japanese, Korean, Portuguese, Spanish and Russian. The asymmetry of sources and targets in this new arrangement gives an interesting map of where science is now done.

The reasons why English has made a clean sweep of the sciences are not straightforward. Among them we cannot possibly include the unfortunate but widespread idea that English is simpler than other languages.

However, you can't explain the history and present state of the language of science as the direct result of economic and military might either. In three instances, languages became science vehicles because the work of a single individual made advances that could not be ignored anywhere else in the world (Liebig for German, Berzelius for Swedish, Mendeleev for Russian). One language lost its role because of the political folly of its users (German). What we seem to have experienced is not a process of language-imposition, but of language-elimination, in a context where the scientific community needs a means of global communication among its members. The survivor language, English, is not necessarily the best suited to the job: it's just that nothing has yet happened to knock it out.

One result of the spread of English is that most of the English now spoken and written in the world comes from people who do not possess it natively, making 'English speakers' a minority among the users of the language. Much of the English now written by natural and social scientists whose native language is other is almost impenetrable to non-specialist readers who believe that because they are native English-speakers they should be able to understand whatever is written in English. So clumsy and 'deviant' is international scientific English that even non-native wits can have fun with it:

> Recent observations by Unsofort & Tchetera pointing out that *'the more you throw tomatoes on Sopranoes, the more they yell'* and comparative studies dealing with the gasp-reaction (Otis & Pifre, 1964), hiccup (Carpentier & Fialip, 1964), cat purring (Remmers & Gautier, 1972), HM reflex (Vincent *et al.*, 1976), ventriloquy (McCulloch *et al.*, 1964), shriek, scream, shrill and other hysterical reactions (Sturm & Drang, 1973) provoked by tomato as well as cabbages, apples, cream tarts, shoes, buts and anvil throwing (Harvar & Mercy, 1973) have led to the steady assumption of a positive feedback organization of the YR based upon a semilinear quadristable multi-switching inter-digitation of neuronal sub-networks functioning en desordre (Beulott *et al.*, 1974).[7]

Pastiche and parody notwithstanding, international scientific English serves an important purpose – and it would barely exist if it did not serve well enough the purposes for which it is used. It is, in a sense, an escape from translation (even if in many of its uses it is already translated from the writer's native tongue). Now if the natural and social sciences can achieve a world language, however clumsy it may sound, why should we not wish all other kinds of human contact and interchange to arrive at the same degree of linguistic unification? In the middle of the last century, the critic and reformer I. A. Richards believed with great passion that China could only become part of the concert of nations if it adopted an international language, BASIC, standing for 'British-American-Scientific-International-Commercial English'. (As its name suggests, it consists of a simplified English grammar and a limited vocabulary suited for technical and commercial use.) Richards devoted much of his energy in the second half of his life to devising, promoting, teaching and propagandizing on behalf of this utopian language of contact between 'East' and 'West'. He was in a way following in the footsteps of Lejzer Zamenhof, a Jewish intellectual from Bialystok (now Poland), who had also invented a language of hope, Esperanto, which he believed would rid the world of the muddles and horrors caused by multiple tongues. In the nineteenth century, in fact, international languages were invented in great number, in proportion to the rise of language-based national independence movements in Europe. All have disappeared for practical purposes, except Esperanto, which continues to be used as a language of culture by perhaps a few hundred thousand people scattered across the globe – but what they use it for most of all is not science or commerce, but to translate poetry, drama and fiction from vernacular languages for the benefit of other Esperantists around the world.

Modern Europeans seem to be haunted by a folk memory of the role of Latin in the Middle Ages and beyond. But Latin itself has continued to have a limited use as an international medium for the speakers of 'small' European languages. Antanas Smetona, the last president of Lithuania before it was overrun by Soviet and then Nazi armies in 1941, used Latin to make his last unsuccessful appeal for help from the Allies.[8]

From the other side of the Baltic Sea, a daily news bulletin in Latin is broadcast by web radio from Helsinki even now.

Language unification, if it ever comes, will probably not be achieved by Latin, Esperanto, Volapük or some yet to be invented 'contact vehicle', but by one of the languages that possesses a big head start already. It will probably not be the language with the largest number of native speakers (currently, Mandarin Chinese), but the one with the largest number of non-native users, which is English at the present time. This prospect terrifies and dismays many people, for a whole variety of reasons. But a world in which all intercultural communication was carried out in a single idiom would not diminish the variety of human tongues. It would just make native speakers of the international medium less sophisticated users of language than all others, since they alone would have only one language to think with.

Second or vehicular languages are learnt more quickly and also forgotten more easily than native tongues. Over the past fifty years, English has been acquired to some degree by countless millions across the continent of Europe and is now the only common language among speakers of the different native languages of Belgium, for example, or on the island of Cyprus. Russian, on the other hand, which was understood and used by the educated class across the entire sphere of influence of the USSR, from the Baltic to the Balkans and from Berlin to Outer Mongolia until 1989, has been forgotten very fast and, even when not forgotten entirely, is now usually left to one side for contact with foreigners. If language unification does proceed further in the twenty-first century, its course will be mapped not by the qualities or nature of the unifying language or of the languages it displaces. It will hang on the future course of world history.

Beyond multilingualism and language unification, the third path that leads away from translation is to stop fussing about what other cultures have to say and to stick to one's own. Isolation has been the dream of many societies and some have come close to achieving it. During the Edo period (1603–1868), Japan restricted contact with foreigners to a handful of adventurous Dutch, who were allowed to maintain a trading station on an island in Nagasaki harbour, and the Chinese. In Europe, Britain often seemed to wallow in 'splendid isolation' – *The Times* of 22 October 1957 famously ran a headline saying: 'FOG IN CHANNEL, CONTINENT CUT OFF' – but that was more pose than reality. Not so in the tiny land of Albania. Enver Hoxha, the country's Communist ruler from 1944 to 1985, first broke off relations with his nearest neighbour, Yugoslavia, in 1948, then with the Soviet Union in 1960, and then with Mao's China in 1976. Albania remained committed to total isolation for many years thereafter, and at one point in the early 1980s there were no more than a dozen foreigners (including diplomatic staff) in the whole country.[9] Televisions were tuned so as to disable the reception of broadcasts from outside the state; only those books that confirmed Albania's own view of its position in the world were translated (and there were not many of those); no foreign books were imported; commercial exchanges were as limited as cultural and linguistic contacts, and no foreign debts were contracted. On the very doorstep of Europe, just a short hop from the tourist sites of Corfu and the swankier resorts of the Italian Adriatic, Albania's half-century of voluntary isolation shows that relatively large groups of people are sometimes prepared to forgo all the supposed benefits of intercultural exchange.

The dream of isolation comes in many forms, but its recurrent shadow falls over the many stories that anthropologists have told us about pre-literate societies living in remote parts of the world. Barely pastiching scientific work of this kind, Georges Perec uses chapter 25 of *Life A User's Manual* to narrate the life of Marcel Appenzzell, a fictional pupil of the real Marcel Mauss, who set off to the jungle of Sumatra to establish contact with the Anadalams. After a debilitating journey through tropical forests Appenzzell finally encounters the tribe. They say nothing. He leaves out what he believes to be traditional gifts and falls asleep. When he awakes, the Anadalams have disappeared. They have left his gifts, up-ended their huts and walked away. He tracks them through the jungle, catches up with them and repeats his procedure, believing it to be the right way to establish communication with these 'pre-contact' people. But the result is the same. They leave. And so it goes on, week after terrible week, until the ethnographer grasps that the Anadalams do not want to engage in communication with him, or with anybody else. That is indeed their privilege. A people may choose autarchy in place of contact. Who are we to say that is wrong?

However, in Perec's telling of this story, the Anadalams exemplify not only pride and self-sufficiency, but also linguistic and cultural entropy. They possess a few metal tools they are no longer capable of fabricating themselves, suggesting they are drop-outs from a more developed civilization. Their language also appears to have had a large part of its vocabulary cut away:

> One consequence of this … was that the same word came to refer to an ever-increasing number of objects. Thus the Malay word for hunting, *pekee*, meant indifferently to hunt, to walk, to carry, spear, gazelle, antelope, peccary, *my'am* – a type of very hot spice used in meat dishes – as well as forest, tomorrow,

dawn, etc. Similarly, *sinuya*, a word which Appenzzell put alongside the Malay *usi*, 'banana', and *nuya*, 'coconut', meant to eat, meal, soup, gourd, spatula, plait, evening, house, pot, fire, silex (the Anadalams made fire by rubbing two flints), fibula, comb, hair, *hoja* (a hair-dye made from coconut milk mixed with various soils and plants), etc. . . . [10]

The reader can of course jump straight from this description of lexical entropy to the almost moral conviction that isolation is bad, for it leads (as the story shows) to the impoverishment and death of a language and the culture it supports, and ultimately to the extinction of a whole people. But Perec catches such sentimentality on the hop:

> Of all the characteristics of the Anadalams, these linguistic habits are the best known, because Appenzzell described them in detail in a long letter to the Swedish philologist Hambo Taskerson . . . He pointed out in an aside that these characteristics could perfectly well apply to a Western carpenter using tools with precise names – gauge, tonguing plane, moulding plane, jointer, mortise, jack plane, rabbet, etc. – but asking his apprentice to pass them to him by just saying 'Gimme the thingummy'.

Perec's tight-lipped carpenter may serve as a warning for people who too loudly lament the loss of language proficiency among (for example) today's teenagers and students. The carpenter's skill as a carpenter is unaffected by the form of words he uses to go about his trade because there is no relationship of cause and effect between linguistic entropy and cultural riches of most other kinds. The loss of a vocabulary, or its replacement by a less refined one, has no generalized impact on what people can do.

It would similarly be unwise to think that isolation causes languages to wither and die. Indeed, isolation may be the most fertile ground for the diversification and enrichment of forms of speech – the innumerable distinctive jargons created by clannish teenagers in every culture provide a good example of that.

Indeed, there are many richly rewarding activities we perform in contact with others, including others who speak different languages, that don't need any words at all.

My father once took a trip to Portugal. On unpacking his suitcase he realized he had forgotten to pack his bedroom slippers. He went out, found a shoe shop, selected the footwear he was lacking, got the assistant to find the right size (39 E), paid for his purchase, checked the change, expressed his thanks and gestured farewell, and went back to his hotel – all without uttering a word, in any language. Every user of a human language must have had or been close to having a language-free intercultural communication of a similar kind. We do use language to communicate, and the language that we use certainly has some bearing on what, with whom and how we communicate. But that's only part of the picture. It would be as artificial to limit our grasp of communication to written or even spoken language as it would be to restrict a study of human nutrition to the menus of restaurants in the Michelin guide.

3. *Why* Do *We* Call *It* 'Translation'?

Like speech and communication, words and things don't fill exactly the same space. But there's worse to come. Not all words have a meaningful relationship to things at all. C. K. Ogden, the famously eccentric co-author of *The Meaning of Meaning*, believed that much of the world's troubles could be ascribed to the illusion that a thing exists just because we have a word for it. He called this phenomenon 'Word Magic'. Candidates for the label include 'levitation', 'real existing socialism' and 'safe investment'. These aren't outright fictions, but illusions licensed and created by the lexicon. In Ogden's view, Word Magic is what makes us lazy. It stops us from questioning the assumptions that are hidden in words and leads us to allow words to manipulate our minds. It is in this sense that we need to ask: does 'translation' exist? That is to say, is 'translation' an actual thing we can identify, define, explore and understand – or is it just a word?

In English and many other languages the word for translation is a two-headed beast. 'A translation' names a product – any work translated from some other language; whereas 'translation', without an article, names a process – the process by which 'a translation' comes to exist. This kind of double meaning is not a problem for speakers of languages that possess regular sets of terms referring both to a process and to the product of that process (as do most Western European languages). Speakers of English, French and so forth are quite accustomed to negotiating such duplicity and can play games with it, as when they say *walk the walk* and *talk the talk*. More specifically, words derived from Latin that end in English in *-tion* nearly always name a process and a result of that process: 'abstraction' (the process of abstracting something) alongside 'an abstraction', 'construction' (the business of building structures) alongside 'a construction' (something built), and so on. In a related kind of word-use, the teacher of a *cordon bleu* cookery lesson hardly needs to explain that the French use the word *cuisine* to name the place where food is prepared (the kitchen) and the results of such preparation (*haute cuisine*, *cuisine bourgeoise*, etc.). Handling the different meanings of 'translation' and 'a translation' is therefore not a real problem. We should nonetheless keep in mind that they are not the same thing and always be wary of taking one for the other.

The difficulty with 'translation' is different. Many diverse kinds of text are habitually identified as instances of 'a translation': books, real estate contracts, car maintenance manuals, poems, plays, legal treatises, philosophical tomes, CD notes and website texts, to list just a few. What common property do they have to make us believe that they are all instances of the same thing that we label 'a translation'? Many language professionals will tell you that translating a manufacturer's catalogue is utterly different from translating a poem. Why do we not have different words for these different actions? There are other languages that have no shortage of separate words to name the many things that in English all go by the name of 'a translation'. Here, for example, are the main words that you have to talk about them in Japanese:

If the translation we are discussing is complete, we might call it a 全訳 *zen'yaku* or a 完訳 *kan'yaku*. A first translation is a 初訳 *shoyaku*. A retranslation is a 改訳 *kaiyaku*, and the new translation is a 新訳 *shin'yaku* that replaces the old translation, or 旧訳 *kyū yaku*. A translation of a translation is a 重訳 *jū yaku*. A standard translation that seems unlikely to be replaced is a 定訳 *teiyaku*; equally unlikely to be replaced is a 名訳 *meiyaku*, or 'celebrated translation'. When a celebrated translator speaks of her own work, she may disparage it as 拙訳 *setsuyaku*, 'clumsy translation', i.e. 'my own translation', which is not to be confused with a genuinely bad translation, disparaged as a 駄訳 *dayaku* or an 悪訳 *akuyaku*. A co-translation is a 共訳 *kyō yaku* or 合訳 *gō yaku*; a draft translation, or 下訳 *shitayaku*, may be polished through a process of 'supervising translation', or 監訳 *kan'yaku*, without it becoming a *kyō yaku* or *gō yaku*. Translations are given different names depending on the approach they take to the original: they can be 直訳 *chokuyaku* (literally 'direct translation'), 逐語訳 *chikugoyaku* ('word for word translation'), 意訳 *iyaku* ('sense translation'), 対訳 *taiyaku* ('translation presented with the original text on facing pages'), or in the case of translations of works by Sidney Sheldon, Danielle Steel, John Grisham and other popular American writers, 超訳 *chōyaku* ('translations that are even better than the originals', an invention and registered trademark of the Academy Press).[1]

English possesses a wide range of names for different kinds of flowers: one way of referring to the relationship between, say, 'tulip' and 'flower' is to call 'flower' a hypernym and 'tulip', along with 'rose', 'hydrangea', 'camellia', etc. the hyponyms of the term 'flower'. 'Hypernym' and 'hyponym' refer to relation-ships between words in a language, not to (botanical or other) relations between the things they refer to. So we could say that Japanese lacks a hypernym for all its various translation terms, whereas English has the hypernym, but no readily available set of hyponyms. But the very structure of such an argument takes us into dangerous territory. It sets up English as the

'Standard' or the 'Thinking Language' because it alone has the general term, and could easily accommodate new coinages to give the meanings of the Japanese terms – 'uptranslate', 'downtranslate', 'newtranslate', 'retranslate', 'cotranslate' and so on. But it is not so obvious how we could translate the general or abstract notion of 'translation' into Japanese, and so we would be predisposed to thinking of that language as deficient in precisely the respect in which it is richer than English.

In practice, Japanese speakers do have a way of translating the English term 'translation' into Japanese. The word *hon'yaku* is used for that purpose in Japanese translations of English-language works about comparative literature and translation theory, and also in the world of publishing and the international book trade. But its range of uses makes it an imperfect match for the word 'translation'. *Hon'yaku* covers translation from foreign (non-Japanese) languages into Japanese (or vice versa), sometimes more specifically translations from Europe or the United States, but not most other meaning of 'translation'. According to Michael Emmerich, 'those like myself who attempt to translate "translation" with the word *hon'yaku* are … subtly carrying out the type of translation known in Japanese as 誤訳 *goyaku*, or "mistranslation". *Hon'yaku* is more like a term of art, whereas we think that the English term 'translation' names something general of self-evident reality.

The Word Magic effect of a category-term is that it leads unwary users to believe that the category thus named really exists. One way of looking at this is to say that the category or class – any category or class – really does exist as a mental reality if a name for that category exists in the language. But that is not at all the same thing as saying that the category thus created is a reliable, useful, appropriate or truly meaningful way of talking about the world. The absence of a category-term clearly makes it harder (but not necessarily impossible) to think about what a set of entities distinguished by different words have in common. In the case that concerns us, we do have a single, very general word for translation whereas Japanese has many. That does not mean to say that in Japanese you cannot think about translation in general. But it does mean that European questions about the 'true nature of translation' when translated into Japanese tend to ask a question about an aspect of European culture (called 'translation', or *hon'yaku*), not about what *we* think the question really is – the nature of 'translation itself'.

You can't talk about it easily if you don't have a word for it, and that is why any intellectual inquiry invents a terminology for the things that exist, or need to be held to exist, within that particular field of specialization. But 'translation' is not an invented, technical or borrowed term like 'hydrogen', 'megabyte' or 'chiaroscuro'. It's a common noun and an ordinary, unmarked term available for general use. What exactly does it name?

The conventional way of tackling this question is to have recourse to etymology, the history of the word itself. 'Translate' comes from two Latin words, *trans*, meaning 'across', and the past form *latum* of the verb *ferre*, 'to bear'. The result of the word history is to give the term 'translate' the meaning of 'bear across' or 'bring over'. Several European languages have similar words from similar roots, such as German *übersetzen* ('to put across') or Russian переводить ('to lead across'). From the etymologies of these words come formula-like proclamations in course books on translation, encyclopaedias and so forth of the following familiar kind:

'Translation is the transfer of meaning from one language to another.'

That seems so obvious as to be not worth commenting upon. But the history of a word does not tell you much about its actual meaning. Knowing, for example, that 'divorce' comes from Latin *divortium*, 'watershed' or 'fork in the road', does not tell you what the word means now. Etymologies obscure essential truths about the way we use language and, among them, truths about translation. So let's be clear: a translator only 'carries [something] across [some obstacle]' because the word that is used to describe what he does meant 'bear across' in an ancient language. 'Carrying across' is only a metaphor, and its relation to the truth about translation needs to be established, not taken for granted. There are lots of other metaphors available in many languages, including our own, and they have just as much right to our attention as the far from solid conceit of the ferryman or trucker who carries something from A to B.

What if we used a word with a different set of historical roots? What if we had lost all trace of the history of the word? Translators would no doubt carry on translating, and the problems and paradoxes of their profession would not be altered one bit. But if we changed the word we used to talk about translation, large parts of contemporary discourse about the phenomenon would become meaningless and void.

In Sumerian, the language of ancient Babylon, the word for 'translator', written in cuneiform script, looks like this:

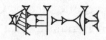

Pronounced *eme-bal*, it means 'language turner'. In classical Latin, too, what translators did was *vertere*, 'to turn' (Greek) expressions into the language of Rome. We still use the same image in English when we ask a solicitor to turn the small print on a contract into something comprehensible, or when a teacher asks a student to turn a sentence into German. *Tanimtok*, the word for 'translation' in Tok Pisin, the lingua franca of Papua-New Guinea, is also made of the same elements, 'turn' (*tanim*) and 'talk' (*tok*).[2] Of course, 'turning' is almost as slippery as 'carrying across', but because you can also turn milk into butter, a frog into a prince and base metal into gold, the history of translation (as well as the status and pay of translators) might have been significantly different in the West had the job always been thought of as a 'turning'.

There are two verbs in Finnish that translate 'translate', one, *kääntää*, being the same as the Finnish word for 'to turn' (as in Latin), the other, *suomentaa*, meaning 'to make Finnish' (just as *verdeutschen*, 'to make German', is one of the German ways of saying 'translate' (into German)). A witty Finnish writer took a German sight-poem by Christian Morgenstern called 'The Fish's Lullaby' and which looks like this:

Fisches Nachtgesang

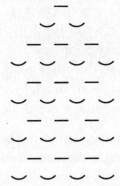

and 'turned' it into a Finnish poem that looks like this:

Kalan yölaula

Suom. Reijo Ollinen

The joke is that the (abbreviated) word used at the bottom to state that it has been 'translated by Reijo Ollinen' is not the one meaning 'to turn' (over) but the one meaning 'to Finnish-ise', suggesting that all you need to have a fish-dream in Finnish is to be turned upside down.[3]

In Ancient China, on the other hand, what you were called if you were employed as an official translator depended on which of the empire's borders you dealt with.

> Those in charge of the regions of the east were called *ji* (the entrusted; transmitters); in the south, *xiang* (likeness-renderers); in the west, *Didi* (they who know the Di tribes); and in the north, *yì* (translators/interpreters).[4]

The division of a translation bureaucracy into geographical parts may sound as if it had been invented by Borges, but it is not much stranger than our having separate terms like Sinologist, Arabist and Africanist for people working at different desks in the Foreign Office. But it seems fairly clear from the source quoted that the use of different names for the offices held by these language people did not give rise to the view that they were each doing something different. That's to say, before there was anything like a collective noun to describe them, the 'northers', 'southers', 'easters' and 'westers' were all understood to be doing the same kind of work.

However, as Buddhism made its way into China by means of translation, the notions connected to the word *yì* expanded beyond the original definition relating to government positions dealing with the languages of the north. Here, in chronological order, spread over several centuries of classical Chinese civilization, are explanations of the character *yì* given in word-lists and annotations of ancient texts:

1. Those who transmit the words of the tribes in the four directions.
2. To state in an orderly manner and be conversant in the words of the country and those outside the country.
3. To exchange, that is to say, to change and replace the words of one language by another to achieve mutual understanding.
4. To exchange, that is to say, to take what one has in exchange for what one does not have.[5]

The point here is not to engage with ongoing debates among Sinologists about the history and meaning of the sign now pronounced *fanyì* (an augmented form of *yì*) and which serves as the Chinese translation of 'translation', but simply this: in a culture more ancient than ours that has engaged with the practical and theoretical problems of translation with subtlety and erudition over several millennia, it occurred to no one to gloss 'translation' as 'the transfer of meaning from one language to another'.

'Turning', 'transmitting', 'speaking after', 'mouthing' and 'exchanging' are not necessarily more revealing or more accurate ways of understanding translation. But if you inherit any of these other ways of naming acts of interlingual communication, you do not even think of defining translation as 'the transfer of meaning from one language to another'. That standard English (and French, German, Russian . . .) definition is simply an extrapolation from the composition of the word that is used to name it. The definition tells us nothing more than the meaning of the word's etymological roots.

The metaphor of 'bearing across' has generated a wide range of words, thoughts, sayings and banalities that may have no more reality than the idea that translation 'transfers meaning' from A to B. Would we have ever thought up the idea of a 'language barrier' if our word for translator did not imply something like 'truck driver'? Would we have ever asked what it is that a translator 'carries across' the 'language barrier' if he or she were called a 'turner', 'tongue-man', or 'exchanger'? Probably not. The common terms of translation studies are metaphorical extensions – elaborations of the metaphor – of the etymological meaning of the term 'translation' itself.

But we cannot escape our own world. We do say 'translate', and we do think 'transfer', and because we think 'transfer', we have to find the complement or object of that verb. And in the mainstream tradition of Western thought about language, only one candidate has ever been thought suitable for the role: 'meaning'.

However, 'meaning' is not the only component of an utterance that can in principle and in practice be 'turned' into something else. Far from it. Things said are always said in some tone of voice, with some pattern of pitch, in some real context, with some kind of associated body-use (gestures, posture, movement) ... Written language is always presented in a particular layout, in some font or hand, in some physical medium (poster, book, back panel, or newspaper) ... However, most of the dimensions that an utterance necessarily possesses are not often treated as part of the translator's task. Like so much else, the boundaries of translation are best illuminated by a good joke.

Spanglish is a sentimental comedy film directed by James Brooks that depicts a language situation which is no doubt familiar to many readers of this book and probably as old as the history of human society itself. The heroine is a Mexican single mother who works as a maid for a prosperous American family. She speaks no English – but her ten-year-old daughter does. At a crucial moment, the mother needs to express her thoughts and strong feelings to her employers, so she enlists her daughter to act as translator.[6] The girl is linguistically well equipped to perform the task, but has no knowledge of current translation conventions. Instead of just translating the meanings of what her mother says, she replicates with gusto her mother's theatrical body-movements, in a time-lapse *pas-de-deux*. Speaking perfect English, she waves her arms, stamps her foot, raises the volume of her voice and modulates its pitch to imitate her mother's performance in Spanish. The sketch makes us laugh wholeheartedly. Why? Because only an intelligent but ill-educated child could imagine that's what translation is – for us.

Despite this, there are ways of re-enacting in another language some of the dimensions of an utterance that don't fall within the rather limited idea of meaning which makes translation less complex than it would otherwise be, but also much less fun. For example, take the sounds – and not the word-meanings – of a familiar rhyme:

Humpty Dumpty sat on a wall

and try to say those sounds – not their meanings – in French. Obviously, you can't do that exactly because French uses a different set of language sounds. But we can re-say them using those French sounds that most nearly approximate to the English sounds represented. We can then write them in a way that those approximately equivalent sounds would be written in French if they were the sounds of French words:

Un petit d'un petit
S'étonne aux Halles[7]

Is this a translation? Well, it might be if instead of translation we said 'mouthing' or 'after-speaking'. Sound translation (also called homophonic translation), of which this is an example, may have few practical uses at present, but in historical terms it is one of the main ways in which our vocabulary has grown. English-speakers have had contact over the centuries with dozens of other cultures, have listened to the words that they used, then said them again using the sound system of English, creating new words like 'bungalow', 'cocoa', 'tomato', 'potato' . . . and so on. Similarly, speakers of other languages having fruitful commercial and cultural contact with English-speaking peoples currently sound-translate all sorts of English terms, producing new words in Chinese (酷 *kù*, fashionable), French (*le footing*, jogging), Japanese (*smāto*, svelte), German (*Handy*, mobile phone) and so forth that English speakers understand imperfectly or not at all.

Loan words (and, more generally, the leakage of vocabulary, syntax and sounds between languages whose speakers are in contact with each other) are not usually thought of as relevant to the study of translation. Indeed, from a conventional point of view the probably universal device of repeating with approximation what you do not properly understand is the opposite of translation – which is to say something else in the place of what you do understand. On the other hand, linguistic borrowing between cultures in contact with each other is a fundamental fact of intercultural communication – and that is the very field of translation.

In reality, professional translators have frequent recourse to sound translation. The translator of Solzhenitsyn's unprecedented exposé of the Soviet gulag experience, *One Day in the Life of Ivan Denisovich*, had to decide what to say to refer to the inmates of the camps, who were called, and also called themselves, зеки (singular: зек, from заключенный, 'locked up') in Russian. He decided to call them *zeks*. *Zeks* is not a possible word of Russian. It is a sound translation of a Russian stem, altered in a way that marks it as an English plural. If translation is just the transfer of meaning from one language to another, then *zeks* is not a translation at all, and it is not English either. But that clearly will not do. Translation involves many things that don't fit common definitions. It is much more interesting to expand our understanding of translation than to reject the work of Solzhenitsyn's translator on the grounds that it is incompatible with the dictionary. That would be to throw out the baby *instead of* the bathwater.

4. *Things* People *Say* about *Translation*

It's a well-known fact that a translation is no substitute for the original.

It's also perfectly obvious that it is wrong. Translations *are* substitutes for original texts. You use them in the place of a work written in a language you cannot read with ease.

The claim that a translation is no substitute for an original is not the only piece of folk wisdom that isn't true. We happily utter sayings like 'crime doesn't pay', or 'it never rains but it pours', or 'truth will out' that fly in the face of the evidence – Russian mafiosi basking on the French Riviera, British drizzle and family secrets that never get out. Adages of this sort don't have to be true to be useful. Typically, they serve to warn, console or encourage other people in particular circumstances, not to establish a theory of justice, a weather forecasting system, or forensic science. That's why saying a translation is no substitute for the original misleads only those who take it to be a well-known fact. It's truly astounding how many people fall into the trap.

When you say 'crime doesn't pay' to a teenager caught filching a DVD from a market stall, it does not matter whether you believe this to be true or not. You are trying to steer the young person towards acceptance of the eighth commandment, and using a conventional phrase in the service of that moral aim.

Similarly, a schoolteacher who has just caught his students reading *The Outsider* in English when they were supposed to be preparing their lessons by reading Camus's novel in French may well admonish them by saying in an authoritative tone of voice: 'A translation is no substitute for the original.' The students know it's not true because they have just been caught using the translation as a substitute for the original. But they also understand that the teacher used a piece of folk wisdom to say something else that really is true – that only by reading more French will they improve their language skills. The teacher means to spur them into greater assiduity, not to speak the truth about translation.

Students eventually graduate and get jobs, and soon enough some of them start writing book reviews. In those circumstances, when they have to write about a work of foreign literature translated into English and are lost for a phrase to use, they may parrot the warning they first heard at school. In common with all things people say and write, however, the force of the saying that 'a translation is no substitute for an original' is completely altered when the context of utterance is changed.

In its new context, it means that the writer of the book review possesses sufficient knowledge of some original to be able to make a judgement that its translation is not a substitute for it. Whether or not the reviewer really has read the original work, the assertion that the translation does not constitute a substitute for it puts the reviewer in charge.

Using the adage in this way obviously affects the meaning of the word 'substitute'. If, for example, I said that 'instant coffee is no substitute for espresso made from freshly ground beans', I would be wrong, in the sense that the purpose of instant coffee is to serve as a substitute for more laborious ways of making the drink; but also right, as long as the word 'substitute' is understood to mean 'same', 'as good as' or 'equivalent'.

Instant coffee is clearly not the same as espresso; many people regard it as not as good as espresso; and because preferences in the field of coffee are matters of individual taste, it is not unreasonable to treat powdered coffee as not equivalent to espresso. We do often say all these more explicit things about coffee. But it is not so straightforward when it comes to translation.

People who declare translations to be no substitute for the original imply that they possess the means to recognize and appreciate the real thing, that is to say, original composition as opposed to a translation. Without this ability they could not possibly make the claim that they do. Just as an inability to distinguish two types of coffee would deprive you of any possibility of comparing them, so the ability to discriminate between 'a translation' and 'an original' is a basic requirement for anyone who wants to claim that one of them is not the same as, equivalent to, or as good as the other.

In practice, we look at the title page, back-panel copy or copyright page of a book or the by-line at the bottom of an article to find out whether or not we are reading a translation. But in the absence of such giveaways, are readers in fact able to distinguish, by the taste on their linguistic and literary tongues, whether a text is 'original' or 'translated'? Absolutely not. Countless writers have packaged originals as translations and translations as originals and got away with it for weeks, months, years, even centuries.

Fingal, an Ancient Epic Poem in Six Books appeared to great acclaim in 1762. For many decades, it was held to give precious insight into the ancient culture of the original inhabitants of Europe's north-western fringe. Figures as eminent as Napoleon and as learned as the German philosopher Herder were entranced by the authentic folk poetry of the 'Gaelic Bard'. But they were wrong. The story of Ossian hadn't been invented by Celtic rhapsodes at all. It was written in English by a minor poet called James MacPherson.

Horace Walpole had a shorter run. In the introduction to the first edition of *The Castle of Otranto* (1764) he claimed his novel was but a translation of an Italian work first published in 1529, and he promised to make it available if his work met with any success. It did – in fact, it was a best-seller and spawned a whole genre of writing called 'Gothic horror'. A second edition was needed, and so the author had to eat humble pie. He could not produce the Italian original, for there was none. He too had written his 'translation' in English.

Even grander deceptions speckle the history of many literatures. *The Letters of a Portuguese Nun*, first published in French in 1669, purports to be a translation, even though the original was never produced. This exquisite, spiritual text fascinated readers for three centuries and was translated from French into many other languages – one version was done into German by the poet Rainer Maria Rilke, who never even suspected that he had been taken for a ride. The letters had in fact been written in French by a friend of Jean Racine, Guilleragues. The hoax was not unravelled until 1954.[1]

A more recent example of pseudo-translation in French is provided by Andreï Makine, whose first three novels, published between 1990 and 1995, were presented as works translated from Russian by the fictional Françoise Bour. In 1995 *Le Monde* revealed that they were French originals and thus cleared the way for Makine's fourth novel, *Le Testament français*, to win the Goncourt Prize, which is only awarded to writers of French.

Pseudo-translations can be hard to kill off once they have come to life. In Soviet Russia, the poet Emmanuel Lifshitz felt he could express himself more fully by writing as if he were someone else – as James Clifford, an Englishman who did not exist. Originally printed in *The Batum Worker*, the twenty-three poems purportedly translated from English were reprinted in Moscow with a short biography of the poet that tried to give the game away in its closing sentence: 'Such could have been the biography of this English poet, who grew up in my imagination and who has materialized in the poems whose translation I ask you to consider.'[2] But even clues as big as that can be missed by readers who really want to believe they can tell the difference between originals and translations. Lifshitz did not include the Clifford poems in collections of his own verse, and that is perhaps why James Clifford lived on in literary circles as a well-known English poet for many years. In conversation with Lifshitz, Yevgeny Yevtushenko mentioned how well he remembered the melancholic Englishman – a true eccentric.[3]

Examples of the reverse process, passing off translations as original works, are probably just as numerous. Three novels by the multilingual writer-diplomat Romain Gary that were purportedly composed in French (*Lady L.*, 1963, *Les Mangeurs d'étoiles*, 1966, and *Adieu Gary Cooper*, 1969) had actually been written and published in English (as *Lady L*, 1958, *The Talent Scout*, 1961, and *The Ski Bum*, 1965, respectively) then secretly translated by a senior editor at Gary's French publishing house. How many translations have been misrepresented as originals and never rumbled? It can't be the case that every deception of the kind has already been unmasked.

Authors have many reasons for wanting to pass off original work as a translation and a translation as an original. Sometimes it helps to get through censorship, sometimes it is to try out a new identity. It can serve individual or collective fantasies about national or linguistic authenticity, and it can be done just to pander to a public taste for the exotic. What all such deceptions underscore is that reading alone simply does not tell you whether a work was originally written in the language you are reading it in. The difference between a translation and an original is not of the same order as the difference between powdered and percolated coffee. It's more than just an idea. But it is not at all easy to demonstrate.

The idea that a translation is not a substitute for an original work must also be subjected to another critique. If the adage were true, then what would users of a translation get from reading a translation? Not the real thing, obviously. But they would not even get a substitute for it – not even the literary equivalent of powdered coffee. Asserting the irreplaceable nature of a literary original condemns those who cannot read the language in question to the consumption, not of Nescafé, but of dishwater. No opinions would be worth holding except by those who read works in the original.

Yet the examples of Cervantes (*Don Quixote* claims to be translated from the Arabic), Walpole, MacPherson, Gary, Guilleragues, Makine, Clifford and countless others demonstrate that nobody can be certain that what he has read *is* an original.

Ismail Kadare tells another story about the indistinction of original and translated texts in his memoir-novel, *Chronicle in Stone*. As a ten-year-old, he was entranced by a book he'd been given by an uncle. With its story of ghosts, castles, murder and betrayal, it appealed to him immensely, especially as it seemed to explain some of what had been going on around him in the fortress-city of Gjirokastër over the preceding years of war and civil strife. The book's title? *Macbeth*, by William Shakespeare. Young Ismail could see Lady Macbeth down the street, wringing her hands on the balcony, washing away the terrible

things that had happened in her home. He had no idea that
the play had originally been written in English. In childish
fascination with a text he reread many times, Kadare copied
out the unsuspected translation by hand, and nowadays, when
asked by interviewers which was the first book he ever wrote,
he always answers, with only half a smile, *Macbeth*. To this day,
Kadare has not learned to speak English, but he counts *Macbeth*
beth as the founding experience of his own life in literature.
Whatever the quality of the translation that so inspired him,
it clearly did not have the effect of dishwater. It was more like
an elixir.

Why then do people still say that a translation is no substitute for an original? The adage might conceivably be of use
to people who consciously avoid reading anything in translation, as it would justify and explain their practice. But since
there is no reliable way of distinguishing a translation from
an original by internal criteria alone, such purists could never
be sure they were sticking to their guns. And even if by some
stroke of luck they did manage to keep clear of all but original
work in their reading, they would end up with a decidedly
peculiar view of the world – if they were English readers, they
would have no knowledge of the Bible, Tolstoy or *Planet of*
the Apes. All the adage really does is provide spurious cover
for the view that translation is a second-rate kind of thing.
That's what people really mean to say when they assert that a
translation is no substitute for original work.

5. *Fictions* of *the* Foreign: The Paradox of 'Foreign-Soundingness'

For most of the last century reviewers and laymen have customarily declared in order to praise a translation to the skies that it sounds as if it had been written in English. This is hollow praise, since the self-same community of reviewers and laymen has often shown itself unable to tell when an alleged translation *was* written in English. All the same, the high value placed on naturalness and fluency in the 'target' or 'receiving' language is a strong feature of the culture of translation in the English-speaking world today. But there are contrarian voices. If a detective novel set in Paris makes its characters speak and think in entirely fluent English – even while they plod along the Boulevard Saint-Germain, drink Pernod and scoff a *jarret de porc aux lentille*s – then something must be wrong. Where's the bonus in having a French detective novel for bedtime reading unless there is something French about it? Don't we want our French detectives to sound French? Domesticating translation styles that eradicate the Frenchness of Gallic thugs have been attacked by some critics for committing 'ethnocentric violence'.[1] An ethics of translation, such critics say, should restrain translators from erasing all that is foreign about works translated from a foreign tongue.

How then should the foreignness of the foreign best be represented in the receiving language? Jean d'Alembert, a mathematician and philosopher who was also co-editor of

Diderot's *Encyclopédie*, came up with an ingenious answer in 1763:

> The way foreigners speak [French] is the model for a good translation. The original should speak our language not with the superstitious caution we have for our native tongue, but with a noble freedom that allows features of one language to be borrowed in order to embellish another. Done in this way, a translation may possess all the qualities that make it commendable – a natural and easy manner, marked by the genius of the original and alongside that the added flavour of a homeland created by its foreign colouring.[2]

The risk of this approach is that in many social and historical circumstances the foreign-soundingness of a translation – just like the slightly unnatural diction of a real foreigner speaking French (or English, or German ...) – may be rejected as clumsy, false or even worse.

In fact, the most obvious way to make a text sound foreign is to leave parts of it in the original. Such was the convention in England in the Romantic era. In the earliest translation of the novel now known in English as *Dangerous Liaisons*, for instance, characters refer to and address each other by their full titles in French (*monsieur le vicomte, madame la présidente*) and use everyday expressions such as *Allez!, parbleu!* and *ma foi!* within sentences that are in other respects entirely in English.[3] Similarly, in recent translations of the novels of Fred Vargas, the lead character, Jean-Baptiste Adamsberg, retains his French rank of *commissaire* in charge of a clutch of *brigadiers*, but he talks to them in English.[4] Following the same logic of selective foreignism, German officers in most Second World War movies made in Hollywood speak natural English interrupted at regular intervals by *jawohl, Gott im Himmel* and *Heil Hitler*.

The device may be taken much further, in popular as well as classical works. The dubbed Italian version of *Singin' in the Rain*, though it performs miracles of lip-synch in the translation of witty patter, leaves the sound-track of the title song in the original English. A famous modern production of *King Lear* in Chinese has Cordelia speaking Shakespeare's lines – she speaks the truth to her father in the true language of her speech.[5]

In general, however, translations only simulate the foreign-soundingness of foreign works. In fact, the challenge of writing something that sounds like English to speakers of other languages can even be met by not writing English at all.

English is heard around the world in pop songs, TV broadcasts and so on by millions of people who do not understand the words of the lyrics, jingles and reports. As a result there are large numbers of people who recognize the phonology of English – the kinds of sounds English makes – without knowing any English vocabulary or grammar. Some forty years ago, an Italian rock star performed a musical routine in which he pretended to be a teacher of English showing his class that you do not need to understand a single word in order to know what English sounds like. Sung to a catchy tune, Adriano Celentano's *Prisencolinensinainciusol ol rait* is a witty and surprising simulation of what English sounds like – without being in English at all. However, the transcription of 'anglo-gibberish' in textual form represents English-soundingness only when it is vocalized (aloud, or in your head) according to the standard rules for vocalizing *Italian* script. *Prisencolinen sinainciusol ol rait*, which can be found on many currently available websites and in some cases with one of its possible transcriptions, is a specifically Italian fiction of the foreign.

It is equally possible to produce gibberish that sounds foreign to English ears. A famous example is the song sung by Charlie Chaplin in *Modern Times* (1936). Having got a job as a singing waiter, the hapless fellow finds himself on the restaurant dance floor with the band thumping out a French music-hall tune, 'Je cherche après Titine' – but he does not know the words. Chaplin dances, mimes, looks perplexed. Paulette Goddard, in the wings, mouths the word 'Sing!' Our lip-reading is confirmed by the inter-title: 'Sing! Never Mind the Words!'

Chaplin then launches into a ditty in Generic Immigrant Romance, which for English-speakers only can be represented thus:

Se bella giu satore	*Sa montia si n'amura*
Je notre so cafore	*La sontia so gravora*
Je notre si cavore	*La zontcha con sora*
Je la tu la ti la toi	*Je la possa ti la toit*
La spinash o la bouchon	*Je notre so lamina*
Cigaretto Portabello	*Je notre so consina*
Si rakish spaghaletto	*Je le se tro savita*
Ti la tu la ti la toi	*Je la tossa vi la toit*
Senora pilasina	*Se motra so la sonta*
Voulez-vous le taximeter?	*Chi vossa l'otra volta*
Le zionta su la sita	*Li zoscha si catonta*
Tu la tu la tu la oi	*Tra la la la la la la*

That sounds like French – or Italian, or perhaps Spanish – to an English-speaker with no knowledge of the languages, only a familiarity with what French (or Italian or Spanish) sounds like. The verses have no meaning and only a few of the words are actual words of French (Italian, Spanish). The point is this:

you do not have to make any sense at all to sound foreign. For the ancient Greeks, the sound of the foreign was the unarticulated, open-mouthed blabber of *va-va-va-*, which is why they called all non-Greek-speakers *varvaros*, that is to say, barbarians, 'blah-blah-ers'. To sound foreign is to mouth gibberish, to be dim, to be dumb: the Russian word for 'German' is немец, from немой, 'dumb, speechless', and in an older form of the language it was used for any non-Russian-speaker.

However, since the 1980s a number of modern European classics have been retranslated into English and French by translators whose avowed intention was to make familiar classics like *Crime and Punishment* or *The Metamorphosis* sound more foreign – although they certainly did not wish to make them sound dumb.

Nineteenth-century translators frequently left common words and phrases in the original (but mostly when the original was French), but this device is rarely used by contemporary retranslators into English, however 'foreignizing' they may seek to be. When Gregor Samsa wakes one morning and finds that he has turned into an insect overnight, he does not exclaim *Ach Gott!* in any modern English version; nor does Ivan Fyodorovich say *Это вот как* in any available translation of *The Brothers Karamazov*. Had these novels been written in French and translated into English by the conventions of the 1820s, we can be fairly sure that Gregor Samsa would have said *Oh mon Dieu!* and Ivan Fedorovich would have said *Alors, voilà* in the English translation.

Things have changed, not in French, German or Russian, but in English. In the language culture of today, English-language readers are not expected to know how to recognize conversational interjections like 'Good God!' or 'Well, now' when spoken in German or Russian; whereas within the language culture of Victorian and Edwardian Britain, educated readers were familiar with French expressions of that kind.

A genuine educational and social purpose can be served by maintaining items of the source text in the translation. It allows readers to acquire what they had not learned at school, or to refresh their memory of half-forgotten lessons. Retention of the original expression in narrowly delimited and self-explanatory speech situations such as greetings and exclamations provides readers with something they might well want to glean from reading a translated work: the vague impression of having read a novel in French. When reading French was an important mark of cultural distinction, this could be a very satisfying feeling indeed.

Selective or 'decorative' foreignism is only available in translation between languages with an established relationship. For many centuries, French was a requirement of advanced education in the English-speaking world and bits of French were therefore part of the educated English-speaker's general linguistic resource. What those fragments of the other language signified was simply, 'This is French!' together with the pleasing corollary, 'I know some French!' The effect on the reader's self-esteem was hardly diminished if the exact meaning of phrases like *parbleu* and *ma foi* had been lost. When a mastery of French was the hallmark of the educated classes, part of the point of reading a French novel in translation for those whose education had not been quite so complete was to acquire the cultural goods that the elite already possessed. The more French was left in the translation of work from French, the better the reader's needs and wants were served.

You can't do that with Russian or German any more. These languages are taught to only tiny groups of students nowadays. Knowledge of either or even both has no relation to cultural hierarchies in the English-speaking world – it just means you are some kind of a linguist, or maybe an astronaut or an automobile engineer.

What could represent 'Russianness' or 'Germanness' inside a work written in English? Conventional solutions to this conundrum are no more than that – cultural conventions, established within the English-language domain by historical contact, patterns of immigration and popular entertainments such as Cold War dramas like *Dr Strangelove*. But if we were to take d'Alembert's recommendation as our guide, then we would try to make Kafka and Dostoevsky sound like the foreigners that they surely were . . . by having them write English 'embellished' with features not native to it.

In German and Russian, of course, Kafka and Dostoevsky, however unique their manners of expression may be, do not sound foreign to native readers of those languages. Foreignness in a translation is necessarily an addition to the original. In Chaplin's gibberish as in retranslations of literary classics, foreignness is necessarily constructed inside the receiving tongue. As a result, the 'foreign-soundingness' of a translation seeking to give the reader a glimpse of the authentic quality of the source can only reproduce and reinforce what the receiving culture already imagines the foreign to be

Friedrich Schleiermacher, a distinguished nineteenth-century philosopher and the translator of Plato into German, hovered around this fundamental paradox in his much-quoted paper on 'The Different Methods of Translating'. He's usually understood to have taken his distance from fluent, invisible or 'normalizing' translation when he said that 'the goal of translating even as the author himself would have written originally in the language of the translation is not only unattainable but is also in itself null and void'.[6] But that famous statement can also be understood the other way round: that it would be just as artificial to make Kafka sound like a 'stage German' writing English as it would be to make Gregor Samsa sound as if he had turned into a beetle in a bedroom in High Barnet.

Why should we want or need Kafka to sound German in any case? In German, Kafka doesn't sound 'German' – he sounds like Kafka. But to the ear of an English-speaker who has learned German but does not inhabit that language entirely naturally, everything Kafka wrote 'sounds German' to some degree, precisely because German is not quite that reader's home tongue. Making Kafka sound German in English is perhaps the best a translator can do to communicate to the reader his or her own experience of reading the original.

For Schleiermacher, in fact, apart from 'those marvellous masters to whom several languages feel as one', everybody 'retains the feeling of foreignness' when reading works not in their home tongue. The translator's task is 'to transmit this feeling of foreignness to his readers'. But this is a peculiarly hard and rather paradoxical thing to do unless you can call on conventions that the target language already possesses for representing the specific 'other' associated with the culture of the language from which the source text comes.

Foreign-soundingness is therefore only a real option for a translator when working from a language with which the receiving language and its culture have an established relationship. The longest and most extensive rapport of that kind in the English-speaking world in general is with French. In the USA, Spanish has recently become the most familiar foreign tongue for the majority of younger readers. English therefore has many ways to represent Frenchness, and American English now also has a panoply of devices for representing Spanishness. To a lesser degree, we can represent Germanness, and, to a limited degree, Italianness as well. But what of Yoruba? Marathi? Chuvash? Or any one of the nearly 7,000 other languages of the world? There is no special reason why anything within the devices available to a writer of English should 'sound just like Yoruba' or give a more authentic representation of what it feels like to write in Chuvash. We just have no idea. The project of writing translations that preserve in the way they sound some trace of the work's 'authentic foreignness' is only really applicable when the original is not very foreign at all.

On the other hand, translated texts can teach interested and willing readers something about the sound and feel and even the syntactic properties of the original. So can originals – Achebe's *Things Fall Apart* introduces elements of African languages, and Chatterjee's *English, August*, gives you a good start on Hindi and Bengali vocabulary. But when foreignness is not thematized – not made the explicit subject of the story – some prior knowledge of the original language is essential for a foreign effect to arise. In order to even notice that this sentence from German a foreignizing translation is have you to know that in German subordinate clauses at the end their verbs put. Otherwise it is comical, clumsy, nonsensical and so forth – not 'German' at all.

Modern Times and Adriano Celentano play entertaining games with literal foreign-soundingness in sung and spoken speech-sounds. A recent translation of *Metamorphosis* could of course be sounded out in the reader's head in a non-native phonology. Gregor Samsa's first words in direct speech –

> 'Oh God,' he thought, 'what a gruelling job I've picked! Day in, day out – on the road.'

– would then be taken as a written representation of sounds more recognizably transcribed as:

'Och Gott,' e saut, 'vot a kruling tschop aif picked! Tay in, tay out – on ze rote.'

This is surely very silly: no translator ever intends his or her work to be sounded out with a stage accent. It nonetheless forces us to ask a real question: if that is not what is meant by foreign-soundingness in the translation of a foreign text, then what exactly is foreign-soundingness? What allows us to judge whether the following passage retains some authentic trace of the Frenchness of Jacques Derrida, or whether it is just terribly hard to understand?

The positive and the classical sciences of writing are obliged to repress this sort of question. Up to a certain point, such repression is even necessary to the progress of positive investigation. Beside the fact that it would still be held within a philosophizing logic, the ontophenomenological question of essence, that is to say of the origin of writing, could, by itself, only paralyse or sterilise the typological or historical research of *facts*.

My intention, therefore, is not to weigh that prejudicial question, that dry, necessary and somewhat facile question of right, against the power and efficacy of the positive researches which we may witness today. The genesis and system of scripts had never led to such profound, extended and assured explorations. It is not really a matter of weighing the question against the importance of the discovery; since the questions are imponderable, they cannot be weighed. If the issue is not quite that, it is perhaps because its repression has real consequences in the very content of the researches that, in the present case and in a privileged way, are always arranged around problems of definition and beginning.[7]

We know that the content of this hard-to-follow extract isn't related to whether it 'sounds like' English or not – Celentano's song has shown us already that you can make completely meaningless concatenations sound like perfect English if phonetic English-soundingness is all you want to achieve. However, one detail that marks it as a translation from French is the anomalous use of the word 'research' in the plural, matching a regular usage of a similar-looking word in French, *recherches*. Obviously, that can be seen only by a reader who knows French as well as English: the foreignness of 'researches' is not self-evident to an English-only speaker, who may well construct quite other hypotheses to account for it, or else accept it as a special or technical term belonging to this particular author. But if the bilingual reader also has some additional knowledge of French philosophical terminologies, then the word 'positive' preceding 'researches' becomes transparent. A bilingual reader can easily see that 'positive researches' stands for *recherches positives* in the source. What that French phrase means is another issue: it is the standard translation of 'empirical investigation' into French.

We could say that 'positive researches' is a poor translation of a standard French phrase that the translator seems to have treated as something else; or else we could see it as a trace of the authentic sound of the original. Indeed, unless an English phrase *is* perceptibly anomalous, we would not be able to see it as containing any trace of not-English. But it is equally clear that we would not be able to see the 'authentic Frenchness' of the phrase if we had no knowledge of French.

Back-translation of the foreignism 'positive researches' into a number of other languages, among them Modern Greek, would produce the same result, that is to say, would allow its meaning to be identified as 'empirical investigation'. Without the information that the work in question has been translated from language A, foreignizing translation styles do not themselves allow the reader to identify which foreign language A is.

Foreignizing translation styles bend English into shapes that mirror some limited aspect of the source language, such as word order or sentence structure. But they rely for their foreignizing effect on the reader's prior knowledge of the approximate shape and sound of the foreign language – in the quoted case of Spivak's translation of Derrida, specific items in the vocabulary of the foreign tongue.

Imagine a novel translated from a language like Hindi, where there are three ways of saying 'you': *tu*, *tum* and *ap*, corresponding to the intimate, the friendly and the formal. Alternation between the three forms of address is a significant part of the way the characters of our imaginary novel relate to each other. Could a translator create a linguistic anomaly in English that corresponds to this triple division of 'you'? Yes, of course. But would we know that it was a mark of Hindi? Not without a translator's footnote – because we do not know any Hindi.

Since the majority of translations take place between languages spoken by communities that have quite a lot to do with each other, culturally, economically or politically, formal and lexical borrowings from the source have often been used to represent the foreignness – and the prestige – of texts imported from abroad. In the sixteenth century, for example, many works of literature and philosophy were brought from Italian into French, just as many Italian craftsmen were imported to beautify palaces and castles across the land. The translators of that era wrote French with a wealth of Italian words and turns of phrase, because they felt that their readers either did or really should know the words and phrases they imported. More than that: they thought French would be positively improved by being made a little more like Italian.

And in fact the process of making French more like Italian has continued down to the present day. The *caban* (pea-jacket) and the *caleçon* (underpants) in your closet and, if you're lucky, the *canteloup* and the *caviar* in your refrigerator, like a huge number of other ordinary, scholarly, refined and delicious things, are all named in French by words taken from Italian, and for the majority of them the taking was first done by translators.[8]

A similar kind of lexical enrichment took place in the nineteenth century when German-speaking peoples sought to constitute themselves as a distinct and increasingly unified nation. German translators consciously imported a quantity of words from Greek, French and English not only to make European classics accessible to speakers of German, but also to improve the German language by extending its range of vocabulary. The issue as they saw it was this. French and English were international languages already, propped up by powerful states. That was why non-native speakers learned French (and, to a lesser extent, English). How could German ever be the vehicle of a powerful state unless non-natives learned to read it? And why should they learn to read it unless it could easily convey the meanings that arise in the transnational cultures held to represent the riches of European civilization?

In today's world translators into 'small' languages also often see their task as defending or else improving their own tongues – or both at the same time. Here's a letter I received just the other day from a translator in Tartu:

> My mother language, Estonian, is spoken by about a million people. Nevertheless I am convinced that *Life A User's Manual* and my language mutually deserve each other. Translating

Perec I want to prove that Estonian is rich and flexible enough
to face the complications that a work of this kind brings along.

Translation can clearly serve national purposes – but also their
opposite, the cause of internationalism itself. A contemporary
writer of French who uses the pen-name Antoine Volodine
has formulated in striking terms why he wishes to use his
native language as if it were a foreign tongue. For Volodine,
French is not just the language of Racine and Voltaire. Because
translation into French has been practised for a very long time,
French is also the language of Pushkin, Shalamov, Li Bai and
García Márquez. Far from being the privileged vector of
national identity, history and culture, 'French is a language that
transmits cultures, philosophies and concerns that have nothing to do with the habits of French society or the francophone
world.'[9] It is not that French is by its nature or destiny an
international language: on the contrary, only the practice of
translation into French makes the language a tool of internationalism in the modern world. Thanks to its long history of
translation from foreign languages, French is now a possible
vehicle for an imaginary, infinitely haunting literature that
Volodine would like to consider absolutely foreign to it.

It would therefore be quite wrong to see the progressive inter-
penetration of English, French, German and Italian together
with terms and phrases from the ancient source tongues, Latin
and Greek, and (in the writings of Volodine) Russian and Chinese too, as the sole product of what is now called globalization.
In any case, globalization does not spread only English into
other languages and cultures: it could just as well be exemplified
by the spread of pizza-language and the vocabulary of pasta into
corner stores and fast food joints the world over. It is also the
result of long efforts by translators to raise their national lan-

guages to international status. They did not necessarily seek to make their translations sound authentically foreign. Indeed, if that is what they were really trying to do, their success has made mincemeat of the ambition, because the words they imported or mimicked have now become part of the receiving language to such an extent that they are no longer foreign at all.

No less than 40 per cent of all the headwords in any large English dictionary are imports from other languages. A foreignism, be it a word, a turn of phrase or a grammatical structure that is brought into our marvellously and infuriatingly malleable tongue by a translator seeking to retain the authentic sound of the original, has its path already mapped out. Either it will be disregarded as a clumsy, awkward or incomplete act of translation, or it will be absorbed, reused, integrated, and become not foreign at all.

However, contemporary efforts to produce translations into English that keep something authentically foreign about them are not strictly comparable to the kind of translators' campaigns in centuries past that made German more like English, French more like Italian, Syriac more like Greek, and so forth. The foreignizers of today are not struggling to make English an international language, because English is the international language of the present. To some degree, they are seeking to enrich English with linguistic resources afforded by languages that are distant from it. 'One subliminal idea I started out with as a translator was to help energize English itself,' Richard Pevear stated in an interview in *The New Yorker*.[10] That creative, writerly project rests on a wish to share with readers some of the feelings that Pevear has when reading a Russian novel. He has also often said that he is not a fluent speaker of the language and relies on his partner to provide a basic crib that he then works into a literary version.[11] Something similar may be true of other proponents of awkward and foreign-sounding translation styles. The project of writing translations that do the least 'ethnocentric violence' to the original thus runs the risk of dissolving into something different – a representation of the funny ways foreigners speak.

The natural way to represent the foreignness of foreign utterances is to leave them in the original, in whole or in part. This resource is available in all languages and has always been used to some degree in every one of them.[12]

It is not easy to represent the foreignness of foreign languages in complete seriousness. It takes the wit of Chaplin or Celentano to do so for comic effect without causing offence.

What translation does in the first place is to represent the meaning of a foreign text. As we shall see, that's quite hard enough.

6. *Native* Command: Is Your Language Really Yours?

Translators traditionally and now almost by iron rule translate from a foreign language into what is called their mother tongue. In translation studies jargon this is called L1 translation, as opposed to L2 translation, which is translation out towards a learned or other tongue. But what exactly is a mother tongue?

We all start with a mother and it seems obvious that we first learn language in her arms. The language that your mother speaks to you is therefore what you are 'born into', which is all that can be meant when instead of 'mother tongue' we call it a native language.

It is an axiom of language study that to be a native speaker is to have complete possession of a language; reciprocally, complete possession of a language is usually glossed as precisely that knowledge of a language that a native speaker has. In spite of the obvious fact that speakers of the same language use it in infinitely varied ways and have often quite different vocabularies and language habits at the levels of register, style, diction and so forth, we proceed on the assumption that only native speakers of (let us say) English know English completely and that only native speakers of English are in a position to judge whether any other speaker is using the language 'natively'.

We also know, from observation and self-observation too, that native speakers make grammatical and lexical mistakes, and find themselves lost for words from time to time. In what is now a conventional view of language use, the slips and stumbles in the speech of a native speaker are themselves part of what it means to possess the language natively. Teachers of foreign languages are expert in distinguishing between mistakes that language learners make and those that are characteristic of native speech; and for a native speaker of any language, there are some kinds of errors made by others that sound not just wrong, but not native. But let us put these practical and effective uses of the distinction between 'native' and 'non-native' aside. Other, much more difficult issues are involved in using terms like 'mother' and 'native' to name the way we are more or less at home in the language we call our own.

We do not have to learn our mother tongue from a mother. It can be acquired just as effectively from siblings, from an au pair or from the kids next door. What matters for normal human development is that there be a language available in our immediate environment in infancy, for no child invents a language by itself, without input from outside. We acquire our first language from whatever sources are available in our infant environment. Some children do it faster than others, some acquire wider vocabularies than others, but all children normally achieve communicative competence within a relatively narrow time-band, between the ages of one and three. But the language that is acquired in those early stages of development may or may not turn out to be the one in which as adults we feel most at home. Great numbers of people the world over are not particularly skilled users of the language taught to them by their infant environment. In many circumstances, formal education replaces the infant language with one that goes on to be used in adult life as the operative means of communication.

From the disappearance of Latin as a spoken language in

around the sixth and seventh centuries CE until the age of Descartes, Newton and Leibniz, no mother ever spoke Latin to her child, and no child was ever born into a Latin-speaking home. However, Latin was learned by young males of the higher social classes throughout Christianized Europe for well over a thousand years. Throughout that long period Latin was the language in which all educated Europeans operated in thought, formal speech and writing, for purposes as varied as diplomacy, philosophy, mathematics, science and religion. The language was taught by means of writing, and it was also spoken – in schools, monasteries, churches, chancelleries and law courts – as the verbalization of a written idiom. All speakers of Latin in the period of its use as the primary form of communication had at least one other mother tongue, but these vernaculars were not used as tools for elaborated thinking or expression. But if a clear distinction can be made between the language learned from your mother and the language in which you operate most effectively for high-born males in Western Europe between 700 and 1700 CE, the very concepts of 'mother tongue' and 'native speaker' need to be looked at again.

Examples of the difference between 'first learned language' and 'operative language' can be found almost anywhere. I can find several in my own family. My father learned to speak in Yiddish, the language of his mother and of his environment in London's East End some ninety years ago. Once he started going to school, he acquired English. There is no question that he could soon do far more with it than he ever could with his mother tongue. Similarly, the mother of my children spoke Hungarian as an infant, but acquired French when she moved to France at the age of five. Neither of these cases involved the loss of the mother tongue. Newton, Descartes and Leibniz also remained everyday speakers of their 'native languages', respectively, English, French and German.

In many modern cases, the mother tongue that is supplanted by a learned language for higher-level activities remains only 'mother's tongue', used exclusively for interaction with the older generation. Yiddish and Hungarian remained for my two relatives the way they spoke with their mothers and served almost no other purpose in adult life. That is fairly typical of first-generation immigrants in countries like France, Britain and the USA, many of whom possess a mother tongue that is stuck at the state of sophistication achieved around the age of five. But that was certainly not true of Descartes or Newton, who also wrote in French and English respectively; it may well not be true of many millions of other bilingual speakers in the world today.

Throughout our lives we retain more or less strong emotions about the language in which we first learned songs, nursery rhymes, games and playgroup or family rituals. These are foundational experiences, and the language in which they were experienced must surely be for ever lit by the warm glow of our earliest reminiscences. But it does not automatically follow that the language of our earliest memories has any special importance as a language for what we may go on to become, or for what we take to be our personal identity.

When the first-learned language is overlaid by a language of education, it ceases to be at the forefront of an individual's development. What is learned in the second but increasingly first-like language are the foundational techniques of writing and counting, as well as all-important systems like the rules of cricket and hockey, alongside song lyrics and the bruising business of social interaction outside the family circle. All this sudden learning can of course be translated back into a first language, especially if the family environment supports parallel development and parents or siblings take the time to teach the child how to express all these new things in the family idiom; but without such support, few children would bother to do something so manifestly pointless (pointless, because unrelated to the social and personal uses of the newly acquired skills).

One problem with using the expression 'mother tongue' to name the language in which an adult operates most comfortably is that it confuses the history of an individual's acquisition of linguistic skills with the mystery of what we mean by the 'possession' of a language. But it also does something more insidious: it acts as a suggestion that our preferred language is not just the language spoken to us by a mother, but is, in some almost mystical sense, the mother of our selfhood – the tongue that made us what we are. It is not a neutral term: it is burdened with a complex set of ideas about the relationship between language and selfhood, and it unloads that burden on us as long as we take the term to be a natural, unproblematic way of naming our linguistic home.

We may all be born with the potential to acquire a language and a need to do so – with what some linguists have called a 'language-acquisition device', hard-wired in our brains. But in practice, we are not born into any particular language at all: all babies are languageless at the start of life. Yet we use the term 'native speaker' as if the contrary were true – as if the form of language acquired by natural but fairly strenuous effort from our infant environment were a birthright, an inheritance and the definitive, unalterable location of our linguistic identity. But knowing French or English or Tagalog is not a right of birth, even less an inheritance: it is a personal acquisition. To speak of 'native' command of a language is to be just as approximate, and, to a degree, just as misleading, as to speak of having a 'mother tongue'.

The curious ideology of these language terms is brought into clearer focus by British and American universities which, when seeking to appoint someone as a professor of languages, conventionally state that 'native or quasi-native competence' is required in the language to be taught. What can 'quasi-native' possibly mean? In practical terms it means 'very, very good'. Implicitly, it means that you can be very good at French or Russian or Arabic even if it is not your birthright. But the most obvious implications of the formula are, first, that a distinction can be made between those who were 'born into' the given language and those who were not; and, secondly, that for the purposes of high-level instruction in the language this distinction is of no consequence. But that creates a curious problem. If the latter holds, how can the former be true?

Language scholars distinguish between sentences that are grammatically and lexically 'acceptable' and 'unacceptable' by appealing to the intuitive judgements of 'native speakers'. 'Native speaker competence' is the criterion most commonly invoked for determining what it is that the grammar of a language has to explain. Now it may seem obvious that 'Jill loves Jack' is a sentence of English and that 'Jill Jack loves' is not, and that a grammar of English should explain why the first is acceptable and second is not. But to ground the boundaries of what is and is not English on the judgements of native speakers alone creates a somewhat mind-bending circularity to the whole project of writing a grammar. How do we judge in the first place whether the English spoken by some individual is 'native' or not? Only by appealing to the grammar, itself established by reference to the judgements of 'native speakers' themselves. Yet there is no regular way for distinguishing unambiguously between native and non-native speakers of any tongue. Most often we don't even use any formal tests, we just take people's word for it. And, as a result, we often make mistakes.

That is to say, speakers of English cannot reliably ascertain whether another person speaking the language acquired it in the cradle, or at school, or by some other means. And we are even less able to separate the 'natives' from the 'others' when it comes to written expression. I am sometimes mistaken for French when speaking the language. But I am not a 'native speaker' in the commonly accepted meaning of the word: I learned French at school, from a mild-mannered teacher called Mr Smith. When French people exclaim with surprise, 'But I thought you were French', I still blush with pride, like the good schoolboy I was. But what such flatterers really mean is not that I speak 'native French', but that they took my speech to indicate a particular nationality. Nationality is of course one of the few things that most people acquire by birth – either because of the nationality of their parents ('by right of blood', *jus sanguinis*) or because of where they were born ('by right of soil', *jus soli*).[1] The relatively short history of the European nation-state founded on linguistic uniformity has resulted in a fairly profound confusion of language with nationality, and of 'native speaker competence' with country of origin.

The passport you hold doesn't have anything to do with your competence as a translator; nor does the language that you learned in your infant environment. What matters is whether you are or feel you are at home in the language into which you are translating. It doesn't really help to call it 'native', and it helps even less to insist that you can only translate into a 'mother' tongue. The paths by which speakers come to feel at home in a language are far too varied for the range of their abilities to be forced into merely two slots ('native' and 'non-native'), however broad or flexible the definitions of those slots may be.

Knowing two languages extremely well is generally thought to be the prerequisite for being able to translate, but in numerous domains that is not actually the case. In the translation of poetry, drama and film subtitles, for example, collaborative translation is the norm. One partner is native in the 'source-text language', or L1, the other is native in the 'target language', or L2; both need competence in a shared language, usually but not necessarily L2. Also, the target language translator needs to be or to believe he is in expert command of the language of the genre – as a playwright, as a poet, as a skilled compressor of meanings into the very restricted format of subtitles, and so on. Even in the translation of prose fiction, there are celebrated translation teams – Richard Pevear and Larissa Volokhonsky, for example, who together have produced new English versions of many classic works of Russian literature. A different form of collaborative transmission is involved in my own work with the novels of Ismail Kadare, who writes in Albanian, a language I do not possess beyond phrase-book level. I work from the French translations done by the violinist Tedi Papavrami and then raise my own queries with both Papavrami and with Kadare himself, through the medium of French, which he speaks well enough to discuss allusions, references, questions of style, and so on.

In cultures other than those of Western Europe the prejudice against translating into a language that is not native is less profound, and in some places it is rejected outright. For many decades, Soviet Russia insisted that the speeches of its UN delegates be interpreted not by native speakers of the other official languages, but by Russian speakers who were expert interpreters and translators into Spanish, French, English, Arabic and Chinese. The translators' school in Moscow developed a theory – or a cover story – to justify this politically motivated practice, according to which the essential skill of an interpreter is her complete comprehension of the original.[2] Most professionals disagree, regarding unreflecting fluency in the target language as the real key to getting away with the almost unimaginably brain-taxing act of simultaneous interpretation – but for more than forty years the Russian booths at the UN relied almost exclusively on what are called 'L2 interpreters', who coped with the job very well.[3]

L2 translation – writing in a language that is not 'native' – is also quite widespread for languages that do not belong to the small group of Western tongues with established traditions of teaching each other's languages in schools and long-standing two-way translation relations. Few 'native' writers of English, French, Spanish or German are fluent readers of Tamil, Tagalog, Farsi or Wolof, and among them fewer still wish to devote their time to translation. For writers in these and most of the other languages of the world, the only way to get an international hearing is to put the work into a world language learned at school or else through emigration or travel. The effort often backfires. L2 translations from contemporary China and Albania are notoriously dreadful. Many of the sillier examples of translation mistakes in commercial material and tourist signage are visibly produced by L2 translation. But it would be futile to insist that the iron rule of L1 translation be imposed on all intercultural relations in the world without also insisting on its inescapable corollary: that every educational system in the world's eighty vehicular languages devote significant resources to producing seventy-nine groups of competent L1 translators in each cohort of graduating students. The only alternative to that still utopian solution would be for speakers of the target languages to become more tolerant and more welcoming of the variants introduced into English, French, German and so forth by L2 translators working very hard indeed to make themselves understood.

7. *Meaning* is *No* Simple *Thing*

Whether done by a speaker of L1 or L2, an adequate translation reproduces the meaning of an utterance made in a foreign language.

That sounds straightforward enough. It corresponds entirely to the service that contemporary translators and interpreters claim to provide. But it doesn't provide an adequate understanding of what translation is because the meaning of an utterance is not a single thing. Whatever we say or write means in many ways at once. The fact is, utterances have all sorts of 'meanings' of different kinds. The meaning of meaning is a daunting topic, but you can't really study translation if you leave it aside. It may be a philosophical can of worms – but it's an issue that every translation actually solves.

There is obviously more to meaning than the meaning of words, and here's a simple story to show why. Jim is out hiking with friends. He wanders away from the group and finds himself in thick woods. He's lost his bearings entirely. Then the smell of coffee reaches his nose. What does that mean? It means that camp is not far away. It's a real and important meaning to Jim – but it has nothing to do with words.

The kind of meaning that things have just by themselves is called symptomatic meaning. Smells, noises, physical sensations, the presence of this or that natural or manufactured object have symptomatic meanings all the time. In daily life we pick up a thousand clues of that kind every day but retain only those that endow our world with the meanings we need.

In like manner, anything said also has symptomatic meaning from the simple fact of it having been said. If I go into a coffee shop and order an espresso, what does that mean? As a symptom, it means I speak English, that the barista does too, and so forth. That's obvious. Most of the time, the symptomatic meaning of an utterance is just too obvious to be noticed. But not always.

The Great Escape, a film made by John Sturges in 1964, tells the almost-true story of a mass break-out from a prisoner-of-war camp in Germany. The leader of the plot, Squadron Leader Bartlett, has good language skills in French and German and teams up with MacDonald, who has only English, to get from the tunnel exit to the Channel coast. Camouflaged as a pair of French businessmen, they are in line to board a bus that will take them further on. There's a security check. Bartlett bluffs his way through in very plausible French and German. He has already begun to get inside the bus when the canny policeman wishes the pair of them 'Good luck' – *in English*. MacDonald, still on the step, instinctively turns round, smiles and blurts out, 'Thank you' – and that's the end of his great escape. It's not the linguistic meanings of the policeman's expression or MacDonald's response that catch the fugitives out, but the symptomatic meaning of the language used.

It is not possible to reproduce the symptomatic meaning of the use of a given language in a language other than the one being used. You can't use Finnish, for example, to re-create the force of 'speaking-in-English-when-escaping-from-a-German-prison-camp'. In the French-language version of the film, 'good luck' and 'thank you' stay in English – French audiences are expected to recognize the sounds of English and to know the symptomatic meaning of using English in war-time Germany. But in versions intended for audiences for whom spoken

English, French and German just have the sound of 'Average West European', the overall meaning of the sequence can't be saved by not translating the spoken sentences (as in French) or by translating them, since the use of any language other than English would miss the point. Some other layer or channel of communication has to be added, such as a subtitle or surtitle. The supplementary stream would give a metalinguistic description of the utterance, such as 'The German policeman is speaking English', or 'The authorities use the native language of the fugitive, who foolishly replies in like manner.' Would that count as translation? It surely must, since its purpose and real effect is to provide rapid access to the meaning of a work in a foreign language. But it doesn't fit the simple definition of translation given at the start of this chapter. The subtitle doesn't reproduce the meaning of the utterance made in another tongue. It just gives you the information you need to grasp not so much what is actually said, but what is going on in the saying of it.

Understanding anything always involves relating what is said (MacDonald's 'Thank you') to the meaning of its having been said. That's the basic framework of all acts of communication. The trouble is that the relationship of what's been said to what the saying of it means is unstable, and often extremely murky. After all, the English fugitive would have been caught out in exactly the same way whatever he had said in reply to the German policeman's 'Good luck!' if he had said it in English. In that specific context, 'Thank you', 'Get lost!' and 'You're a real gentleman' could be said to have the same meaning, and you could prove that outrageous assertion by showing that they would have to have identical subtitles in Chinese.

To return to the parable of Jim lost in the woods with his partner Jane, one of the pair might say on smelling the welcome aroma of coffee brewing nearby, 'Aha! I smell coffee!' or else 'Can you smell what I smell?' or 'Can *you* smell coffee too?' These are different sentences having what linguists would call different sentence meanings, but in that context they all have the same force – namely, that the camp is near at hand, that they are not lost, that they should rejoice, etc. In translation the differences between these sentence meanings hardly matter. What matters here is to preserve the force of the utterance, and knowing how to do that in another language is the translator's main skill. Levels of formality in conversation as well as customs and rules about how men and women may relate to each other when lost in the woods vary quite widely between languages and the cultures that they serve. For the story of Jim and Jane, the translator's job is to express the force of the utterance in those particular circumstances in forms appropriate to the target language and culture. Whether or not the chosen form of words corresponds to the sentence-meaning of the sentence that Jim uttered is beside the point.

Of course, Jim could have communicated the meaning he attached to his having smelled a particular smell not in words, but with a smile, a twitching of his nostrils, a wave of his hand. In many circumstances such as these, non-verbal communication can have pretty much the same force as an utterance. It's an awkward fact for translation studies, but the truth is that meaning does not inhere solely to words. When it comes to knowing what something means and what meaning has been received, there is no clear line to be drawn between language and non-linguistic forms of communication – in the story of Jim and Jane, between smiling, twitching, waving and speaking. There's no clear cut-off point, but only a shifting and ragged edge between language use and all the rest.

Symptoms and non-verbal complements to verbal expression lie on or just over the edge of the field of translation, which covers only utterances that have linguistic form – but there's always more to an utterance than just its linguistic form. That's why there's no unequivocal way of saying where one mode or type or level of meaning ends and another begins. If you turn off the sound-track of the bus-trap sequence in *The Great Escape*, you see a man in a leather coat saying farewell to two guys in mufti, one of whom returns his good wishes and then, inexplicably, tries to run away. You would have understood nothing. But if you just listen to the sound-track, without seeing the context in which someone says 'Good luck' with a slight German accent, you would probably have understood even less. The context alone doesn't tell you what the utterance means unless you can hear the utterance as well; conversely, the utterance alone doesn't contain nearly enough information to allow you to reconstruct the context. You have to have both.

Film is a useful tool for exploring the myriad ways in which meaning happens. What we understand from a shot or sequence is formed by different kinds of information made available by various technical means. The angle of the camera and the depth of field, the decor, the characters' clothing, facial gestures and body movements, the accessories displayed, the sound effects and background music that have been superimposed all affect the meanings we extract from a sequence or shot. In the most accomplished films, no single stream can be separated from all the others. They work in concert, and their timing is integral to the meaning that they build. Each stream of meaning is one part of the context which gives all other streams their power to mean, and necessarily affects the specific meanings that they have.

What is reasonably clear from film is also applicable to human communication in general, including the blandest and simplest of sentences uttered. For translation, and for us all, meaning *is* context.

The expression 'One double macchiato to go' – an expression I utter most mornings, around 8 a.m. – means what it means when uttered in a coffee shop by a customer to a barista. The situation (the coffee shop) and the participants (customer and barista) are indispensable, inseparable parts of the meaning of the utterance. Imagine saying the same thing at 2 a.m., in bed, to your partner. Or imagine it said by a trans-Saharan cycling fanatic on arrival at a Touareg tent-camp. The words would be the same, but the meaning of their being said would be entirely different. Symptomatically, it might be that you were having a nightmare, or that dehydration had driven the cyclist out of his mind. Any piece of language behaviour, even a simple request for a coffee, acquires a different meaning when its context of utterance is changed.

The point is worth repeating: what an utterance means to its utterer and to the addressee of the utterance does not depend exclusively on the meaning of the words uttered. Two of the key determinants of how an utterance conveys meaning (and of the meaning that it effectively conveys) are these: the situation in which it is uttered (the time, the place and knowledge of the practices that are conventionally performed by people present in such a time and place); and the identities of the participants, together with the relationship between them. The linguistic meaning of the words uttered is not irrelevant (a double macchiato is not the same drink as a skinny wet cap) but it's only a fragment of all that's going on when something is uttered. It may be the only fragment that can be seen to be translated, but it falls far short of constituting the entirety of what has been said.

In a classic contribution to the study of language, the philosopher J. L. Austin pointed out that there are some types of English verbs that don't describe an action, but *are* actions just by the fact of being uttered. 'I warn you to stay away from the edge of the cliff' is a warning because the speaker has said 'I warn you'. There are quite a number of these performative verbs in English, though they do not all function in exactly the same way. But many difficulties arise in trying to treat promising, warning, advising, threatening, marrying, christening, naming, judging and so forth as a special class of verb. For one thing, few of them constitute the act that they name unless various non-linguistic conditions are met. 'I name this vessel *The Royal Daffodil*' has its proper force (that is to say, really does grant that name to some real vessel) only if the person authorized to launch the ship utters it at the actual launching while the rituals associated with the launching of ships are performed at the same time – the champagne bottle cracking open against the bow, the chocks being removed, and so forth. Said in some other circumstance, by a man sitting in a deckchair on Southend Pier, for example, it doesn't constitute the action of naming a ship at all. Austin calls these necessary concomitants to the successful performance of the action of a performative verb its 'conditions of felicity'. Of course, there are many ways a 'performance' can be undermined or abused by tampering with the conditions of felicity it requires. But that doesn't alter Austin's vital point that the force of an utterance isn't exclusively a function of the meaning of the words of which it seems to be composed. The non-linguistic props and surroundings of a linguistic expression – this person, speaking in the presence of that other, at this time and in that place, and so on – are what really allow language-users to do things with words.

Many actions can be carried out with words without using any of the verbs that allegedly 'perform' the action. I can promise to marry someone by saying 'Sure I will' in response to a plea, and that's just as binding as saying 'I promise.' I can warn somebody with an imperative – 'Stay away from the cliff!' – just as I can threaten someone by asking them to step outside in a particular tone of voice. The force of an utterance is not related solely to the meanings of the words used in the utterance. In many instances, it is hard to show on linguistic evidence alone that they are related at all.

Intentional alteration of one or more of the basic contextual features of an utterance usually turns a meaningful expression into some kind of nonsense. But the reverse can also be achieved: nonsense can be made to make sense by supposing some alternative context for it. At the start of his revolutionary work *Syntactic Structures* (1957), Noam Chomsky cooked up a nonsense sentence in order to explain what he saw as the fundamental difference between a meaningful sentence and a grammatical one. 'Colorless green ideas sleep furiously' was proposed as a fully grammatical sentence that had no possible meaning at all. Within a few months, witty students devised ways of proving Chomsky wrong, and at Stanford they were soon running competitions for texts in which 'Colorless green ideas sleep furiously' would be not just a grammatical sentence, but a meaningful expression as well.

Here's one of the prize-winning entries:

> It can only be the thought of verdure to come, which prompts us in the autumn to buy these dormant white lumps of vegetable matter covered by a brown papery skin, and lovingly to plant them and care for them. It is a marvel to me that under this cover they are labouring unseen at such a rate within to give us the sudden awesome beauty of spring flowering bulbs. While winter reigns the earth reposes but these colourless green ideas sleep furiously.[1]

Nowadays the expression 'colourless green ideas' could perhaps refer to the topics of negotiation at the Copenhagen Climate Summit of December 2009; to say that they 'slept furiously' may be no more than to name the paltry outcome of the conference. The point of this is not just to say that people play with language and often make mincemeat of authoritative generalizations about it. It is this: no grammatical sentence in any language can be constructed such that it can never have a context of utterance in which it is meaningful. That also means that everything that can be said or written – even nonsense – can (at some time or another) be translated. *Verdi idee senza colore dormono furiosamente.*

To translate utterances that perform a conventional action by the fact of being uttered – greeting, ordering, commanding and so on – requires the target language to possess parallel conventions about things you can do with words. But there are significant differences between cultures and languages in how people do things with words. A promise may be a promise the world over, but the conditions of felicity as well as the forms of language that are appropriate to the making of a promise may vary greatly between, for example, Japan and the USA. It's not the linguistic meaning of 'I promise, cross my heart and hope to die' that needs to be translated if the aim is to make a similar commitment in the target language. Once again, the expression uttered (in speech or writing) is not the sole or even the primary object of translation when the force of an utterance is what matters, as it always does.

These considerations don't affect just the set of verbs that Austin called performatives. The range of things you can do with words goes far beyond the promising, warning, knighting, naming and so on that attracted the philosopher's attention, and it would be better to see those not-so-special verbs of

English as only one way of grasping a more general aspect of language use. When I say, 'How are you?' to an acquaintance I run across, I am performing the social convention of greeting with an utterance that is conventionally attached to it. Whether I use a performative verb (as in 'Salaam, your highness, I greet you most humbly') or not (as in 'Hi!'), the expression that constitutes the action of greeting has a meaning only by virtue of the kind of action I am performing with it. 'Greeting' could be thought of as a kind or register or genre of language use. It's not hard to see that translating 'How are you?' into any other language is to translate the convention of greeting, not to translate the individual items 'how', 'are' and 'you'. But what is widely understood as appropriate for the kind of language use that tourist phrase books always include is no less appropriate in many other translation contexts. A knitting pattern that does not follow target language conventions for knitting patterns is completely useless, just as a translated threat of retribution that does not conform to the conventions of threatening in the target culture is not a threat, or a translation.

In the summer of 2008 the *Wall Street Journal* ran a hot story under the headline:

GOP VEEP PICK ROILS DEMS

To make sense of this you need a lot of knowledge of American political events in the run-up to the last presidential election, including the conventional nicknames of the two main parties, as well as familiarity with the alphabetical games played by editors on night desks in Manhattan. Should we pity the poor translators the world over who needed to reproduce the bare bones of the story in double-quick time? Not really. The meaning of the words in that headline are not important.

What's important is that it works as a headline. Like any head-line in the English-language press, 'GOP Veep Pick Roils Dems' is explained by the story that follows it in less com-pressed language. The task of the translator – if indeed it is the translator, not the editor, who performs this function – is to understand the story first and only then invent an appropriate headline within the language of headlines holding sway in the target culture. '*Le choix de Madame Palin comme candidate républ-icaine à la vice-présidence des États-Unis choque le parti démocrate*' conforms quite well to French headline-writing style, for example, and is a plausible counterpart to the *Wall Street Jour-nal*'s nutshell quip. The original and its translation must conform to the general conventions of headline-writing in their respective cultures, because headline-writing is just as much a genre – a particular kind of language use restricted to particular contexts – as promising, christening, threatening and so forth.

How many genres are there? Uncountably many. How do you know what genre a given written sentence is in? Well, you don't, and that's the point. No sentence contains all the infor-mation you need to translate it. One of the key levels of information that is always missing from a sentence taken sim-ply as a grammatically well-formed string of lexically acceptable words is knowledge of its genre. You can only get that from the context of utterance. Of course, you know what that is in the case of a spoken sentence – you have to be there, in the context, to hear it spoken. You usually know quite a lot in the case of written texts, too. Translators do not usually agree to work on a text without being told first of all whether it is a railway timetable or a poem, a speech at the UN or a fragment of a novel (and few people read such things in their original languages either without being told by the cover sheet, dust-jacket or other peritextual material what kind of thing they are reading). To do their jobs, translators have to know what job they are doing.

Translating something 'from cold', 'unseen', 'out of the blue' or, as some literary scholars would put it, 'translating a text in and for itself' isn't technically impossible. After all, students at some universities are asked to do just that in their final examinations. But it is not an honest job. It can only be done by guessing what the context and genre of the utterance are. Even if you guess right, and even granted that guessing right may well be the sign of wide knowledge and a smart mind, you are still only playing a game.

Many genres have recognizable forms in the majority of languages and cultures: kitchen recipes, fairground hype, greeting people, expressing condolences, pronouncing marriage, court proceedings, the rules of soccer and haggling can be found almost anywhere on the planet. The linguistic forms through which these genres are conducted vary somewhat, and in some cases vary a great deal, but as long as the translator knows what genre he is translating and is familiar with its forms in the target language, their translation is not a special problem. Problems arise more typically when the users of translation raise objections to the shifts in verbal form that an appropriate translation involves. Translators do not translate Chinese kitchen recipes 'into English'. If they are translators, they translate them into kitchen recipes. Similarly, when a film title needs translating, it needs translating into a film title, not an examination answer.

It's Complicated is a romantic comedy starring Alec Baldwin and Meryl Streep, playing characters who have a romantic fling in sun-drenched Santa Barbara despite having been divorced for some years. The complications alluded to in the title include Baldwin's slinky and suspicious young wife, her five-year-old son with uncannily acute ears, as well as the three children of the re-found lovers' original marriage, now aged between eighteen and twenty-five. Can the two parents really get back together again? As Baldwin says in his closing lines, in a sentimental scene on the swing-seat in the front garden: 'It's complicated.' As a sentence abstracted from any context of utterance, 'It's complicated' can be adequately represented in French by *C'est compliqué*. That would get full marks in a school quiz.

In the context of utterance as it occurs in the film, Baldwin's resigned, evasive and inconclusive 'It's complicated' can also be plausibly rendered in French by the same sentence: *C'est compliqué*. But the French release of the movie itself is not titled *C'est compliqué*. The distributors preferred to call it *Pas si simple!* ('Not so simple!').

It's not that the meaning is very different. Nor is it because the context of utterance alone changes the meaning: film titles, by virtue of being titles, have, in a sense, no context at all. Titles of new works announce and constitute the context in which the work's meaning is to be construed. Title-making, in other words, is a particular use of language – a genre. As in any other genre, a translated title only counts as a translation if it performs its proper function, that is to say, if it works as a title in the conventions of title-making that hold sway in the target language. That's no different from saying that the most important thing about the translation of a compliment is that it fulfils the function of the kind of language behaviour that we call a compliment.

In languages and societies as close as French and English, it's often the case that sentences having much the same shape and similar verbal content in the two languages fulfil the same

genre-functions as well. But not always. The task of the translator is to know when to step outside.

In contemporary spoken French, *compliqué* has connota-
tions that English 'complicated' does not. Its sense in some
contexts may verge on 'over-sophisticated' and 'perverse'. A
more likely way of suspending a decision, of getting off a hook,
of lamenting the unstraightforwardness of life, is to say: it's
not so simple. Of course, you could say that in English too, in
the right context. But could it be a film title? 'Not so simple!'
doesn't work nearly as well, and that's no doubt why the original producers of the movie didn't use it. In French it works
just fine and avoids the unwanted additional suggestions of
perversity that cloud *C'est compliqué*. Judgements like these
don't only call for 'native speaker competence' in the translator.
They rely on profound familiarity with the genre.

What it comes down to is this. Written and spoken expressions in any language don't have a meaning just like that, on
their own, in themselves. Translation represents the meaning
that an utterance has, and in that sense translation is a pretty
good way of finding out what the expression used in it may
mean. In fact, the only way of being sure whether an utterance
has any meaning at all is to get someone to translate it for you.

8. *Words* are *Even* Worse

In Russian, there are two words, голубой and синий, that mean 'blue', but they do not have the same meaning. The first is used for light or pale blue hues, the second for darker, navy or ultramarine shades. So both can be translated into English, subject to the addition of words that specify the quality of blueness involved. But you can't translate plain English 'blue' back into Russian, because whatever you say – whichever of the two adjectives you use – you can't avoid saying more than the English said. The conventions that hold sway among publishers and the general public do not allow translators to add something that is not in the original text. So if you accept those terms of the trade, you could quickly arrive with impeccable logic at the conclusion that translation is completely impossible.

Observations of this kind have been used by many eminent scholars to put translation outside of the field of serious thought. Roman Jakobson, a major figure in the history of linguistics, pointed out that сыр, the Russian word for 'cheese', cannot be used to refer to cottage cheese, which has another name, творога, in Russian. As he puts it, 'the English word "cheese" cannot be completely identified with its Russian heteronym'.[1] As a result, there is no fully adequate Russian translation of something as apparently simple as the word 'cheese'.

It's an indisputable fact about languages that the sets of words that each possesses divide up the features of the world in slightly and sometimes radically different ways. Colour terms never match up completely, and it's always a problem for a French speaker to know what an English person means by 'brown shoes', since the footwear in question may be *marron*, *bordeaux*, even *rouge foncé*. The names of fishes and birds often come in non-matching sets of labyrinthine complexity; similarly, fixed formulae for signing off letters come in graded levels of politeness and servility that have no possible application outside of the culture in which they exist.

These well-known examples of the 'imperfect matching' or anisomorphism of languages do not really support the conclusion that translation is impossible. If the translator can see the sky that's being called blue – either the real one or a representation of it in a painting for example – then it's perfectly obvious which Russian colour-term is appropriate; similarly, if the cheese being bought at the shop is not cottage cheese, the choice of the Russian term is not an issue. If on the other hand what's being translated is a sentence in a novel, then it really doesn't matter which kind of Russian blue is used to qualify a dress that only exists in the reader's mental image of it. If the specific shade of blue becomes relevant to some part or level of the story later on, the translator can always go back and adjust the term to fit the later development. The lack of exactly matching terms is not as big a problem for translation as many people think it is.

Pocket dictionaries contain common, frequently used words, and their larger brethren are fattened up with words used less often. Most of those additional words are nouns with relatively precise and sometimes recondite meanings, like 'polyester', 'recitative' or 'crankset'. It's trivially easy to translate words of that sort into the language of any community that has occasion to refer to synthetic fibres, Italian opera or bicycle maintenance. Large authoritative dictionaries thus create the curious illusion that most of the words in a language are automatically translatable by slotting in the matching term from the dictionary. But there's a huge difference between most of the headwords in a dictionary and the words that occur most often in the use of a language. In fact, just two or three thousand items account for the vast majority of word occurrences in all utterances in any language – and they aren't words like 'crankset', 'recitative' or 'polyester' at all.[2]

If translation were a matter of slotting in matching terms, then translation would clearly be impossible for almost everything we say except for our fairly infrequent references to a very large range of specific material things. Conversely, those many people who come up with the false truism that translation is impossible certainly wish that all words were like that. A desire to believe (despite all evidence to the contrary) that words are at bottom the names of things is what makes the translator's mission seem so impossible.

The idea that a language is a list of names for the things that exist runs through Western thought from the Hebrews and Greeks to the man in the street by way of many distinguished minds. Leonard Bloomfield, a professor of linguistics who dominated the field in the United States for more than twenty-five years, tackled the problem of meaning in the course-book he wrote in the following way. Let us take the word 'salt'. What does it mean? In Bloomfield's book, the token 'salt' is said to be the label of sodium chloride, more accurately (or at least, more scientifically) designated by the symbols NaCl. But Bloomfield was obviously aware that not many words of a language are amenable to such simple analysis. You can't get at the meaning of words like 'love' or 'anguish' in the same way. And so he concludes:

In order to give a scientifically accurate definition of meaning for every form of a language we should have to have a scientifically accurate knowledge of everything in the speaker's world . . . [and since this is lacking] the statement of meanings is the weak point in language study.[3]

Indeed it is, if you go about it that way.

I still find it bewildering why a man of Bloomfield's vast knowledge and intelligence should ever have thought that 'NaCl' or 'sodium chloride' constitute the meaning of the word salt. What they are is obvious: they are translations of 'salt' into different registers of language. But even if we revise Bloomfieldian naivety in this way, we are still trapped inside the idea that words (translated into whatever other register or language you like) are the names of things.

One well-known reason why so many people believe words to be the names of things is because that's what they've been told by the Hebrew Bible:

And out of the ground the Lord God formed every beast of the field and every fowl of the air and brought them unto Adam to see what he would call them; and whatsoever Adam called every living creature, that was the name thereof (Genesis 2:19).

This short verse has had long-lasting effects on the way language has been imagined in Western cultures. It says that language was, to begin with, and in principle still is, a list of words; and that words are the names of things (more particularly, the names of living things). Also, it says very succinctly that language is not among the things that God created, but an arbitrary invention of humankind, sanctioned by divine assent.

Nomenclaturism – the notion that words are essentially

names – has thus had a long history; surreptitiously it still pervades much of the discourse about the nature of translation between languages, which have words that 'name' different things, or that name the same things in different ways. But the problem doesn't really lie in translation, but in nomenclaturism itself, for it provides a very unsatisfactory account of how a language works. A simple term such as 'head', for example, can't be counted as the 'name' of any particular thing. It figures in all kinds of expressions. It can be used to refer to a rocky promontory ('Beachy Head', in Sussex), a layer of froth ('a nice head of beer') or a particular role in a bureaucratic hierarchy ('head of department'). What connects these disparate things? How do we know which meaning 'head' has in these different contexts? What does it mean, in fact, to say that we know the meaning of the word 'head'? That we know all the different things that it means? Or that we know its real meaning, but can also cope with it when it means something else?

One solution proposed to the conundrum of words and meanings is to tell a story about how a word has come to mean all the things for which it serves. The story of the word 'head', for example, as told in many dictionaries, is that once upon a time it had a central, basic or original reference to that part of the anatomy which sits on top of the neck. Its meaning was subsequently extended to cover other kinds of things that sit on top of something else – a head of beer, a head of department, would represent extensions of that kind. But as familiar animals with four feet instead of two have their anatomical heads not at the top, but at the front, 'head' was extended in a different direction to cover things that stick out (Beachy Head, or the head of a procession).

Some such stories can be supported with historical evidence, from written texts representing an earlier state of the same language. The study of how words have in fact or must be supposed to have altered or extended their meanings is the field of historical semantics. But however elaborate the story, however subtle the story-teller and however copious the documentary evidence, historical semantics can never tell you how any ordinary user of English just knows (a) that 'head' is a word and (b) all of the things that 'head' means.

From this it follows that the word 'head' cannot be translated as a word into any other language. But the meaning it has in any particular usage can easily be represented in another language. In French, for example, you would use *cap* for 'Beachy Head', *mousse* for 'head of beer', and *chef*, *patron* or *supérieur hiérarchique* to say 'head of department'. Translation is in fact a very handy way of solving the conundrum of words and meanings. That's not to say that anyone can tell you what the word means in French or any other language. But what you can say by means of translation is what the word means in the context in which it occurs. That's a very significant fact. It demonstrates a wonderful capacity of human minds. Translation *is* meaning.

Linguists and philosophers have nonetheless devised Houdini-like ways of extricating themselves from the self-imposed dilemma of having to account for what words mean *qua* words. 'Head' is considered a single word with a range of transferred or figurative meanings and can serve as an example of polysemy. Yet equally common words like 'light' are treated as a pair of homonyms – two different words having the same form in speech and writing – one of them referring to weight (as in 'a light suitcase'), the other to luminosity (as in 'the light of day'). The distinction between polysemy and homonymy is completely arbitrary from the point of view of language use.[4] Where the spelling is different but the sound the same, as in *beat* and *beet*, linguists switch terms and give them as examples of homophony. Yet more subdivisions can be made in the tendencies of words to drift from one meaning to another. A part can stand for a whole when you have fifty head in a flock, or the whole can stand for the part, as when you refer to a sailor walking into a bar as the arrival of the fleet. Sometimes there is or is said to be a visual analogy between the central meaning of a word and one of its extensions, as when you nose your car into a parking slot, and this is called metaphor; sometimes the extension of meaning is the supposed fruit of contiguity or physical connection, as when you knock on doors in your attempt to get a job, and this is called metonymy. The machinery of 'figures of meaning', taught for centuries as part of the now-lost tradition of rhetoric, is fun to play with, but at bottom it's eyewash. Polysemy, homonymy, homophony, metaphor and metonymy aren't terms that help to understand how words mean, they're just fuzzy ways of holding down the irresistible desire of words to mean something else. It would take a very imaginative language maven indeed to explain satisfactorily why the part of a car which covers either the engine or the luggage compartment is called a bonnet in the UK and a hood in the US. Despite the enthusiasm of the large throng of hobbyists who contribute to it, the semantics of words is an intellectual mess.

All the same, most languages have words for the same kinds of things and don't bother with words for things they don't have or need. They tend to have separate expressions for basic orientation – (up, down, left, right – but see p. 163 for languages that do not), for ways of moving (run, walk, jump, swim) and for directional movement (come, go, leave, arrive), for family relations (son, daughter, brother's wife and so on), for feelings and sensations (hot, cold, love, hate), for life events (birth, marriage, death, sickness and health), for types of clothing, food and animals, for physical features of the landscape and for the cardinal numbers (up to five, ten, twelve, or sixteen). Some have words for fractional numbers, such as the German *anderthalb* (one and a half) or the Hindi *sawa* (one and a quarter) – but I don't believe any has a separate item for the number 2.375. All languages used in societies that have wheeled vehicles have words for wheeled vehicles of various kinds, but none, as far as I know, has a single lexical item with the meaning 'wheeled vehicles with chrome handlebars', so as to refer collectively to bicycles, tricycles, tandems, mopeds, motorcycles, prams and lawnmowers. French may have single words for 'the whole contents of a deceased sailor's sea-chest' (*hardes*) and 'gravelly soil suitable for growing vines' (*grou*), but in practice all sorts of real and possible things, classes of things, actions and feelings don't have names in most languages. English, for instance, does not possess a designated term for the half-eaten pitta-bread placed in perilous balance on the top of a garden fence by an overfed squirrel that I can see right now out of my study window, but this deficiency in my vocabulary doesn't prevent me from observing, describing or referring to it. Conversely, the existence in Arabic of *ghanam*, a word that means sheep and goats without distinction, does not prevent speakers of Arabic from sorting the sheep from the goats when they need to. Just because English does not have a one-word or phrasal counterpart to French *je ne sais quoi* or German *Zeitgeist* in no way prevents me from knowing how to say what these words mean. Far from providing labels for 'all the things in the world', languages restrict their word-lists to an ultimately arbitrary range of states and actions, while also having means to talk about anything that comes up. The peculiar flexibility of human languages to bend themselves to new meanings is part of what makes translation not only possible, but a basic aspect of language use. Using one word for another isn't special, it's what we do all the time. Translators just do it in two languages.

One formerly fashionable way of avoiding the insoluble problem of fixing the meaning of a word was to imagine it as the compound product of sub-linguistic mental units, or 'features' of meaning. Take the three words house, hut and tent. They can all be used to refer to dwellings of some sort, but they refer to three different kinds of dwelling. The task of distinctive feature analysis was to find the minimal semantic constituents that would account for the meaning-relations between these three semantically related terms. All three are 'marked' with the feature [+dwelling], but only 'house' also has the two features [+permanent] and [+brick]. 'Tent' would be marked [−permanent][−brick] and 'hut' could be marked [+permanent][−brick]. How wonderful it would be if all words in the language could be decomposed into atoms of meaning in this way. The meaning of a word would then be fully specified through the list of the distinctive features that mark it. If you could show that it was possible to account for the differences in the meanings of all the words in a language by the distribution of a finite set of semantic features, then you could go further still. You would be in a position to build a great Legoland of the mind, in which all possible meanings could be constructed out of irreducible, binary building blocks of sense.

To map some area of vocabulary (let alone a whole language) using only such elementary features of meaning is an enticing prospect, but it runs up against a fundamental problem: what criterion to use to establish the list of the elementary semantic features themselves. Common sense no doubt dictates that ± /animate] and ± /female] are among the distinctive features relevant to the meaning of the term *woman* and that ± 'chrome-plated' is not. But common sense appeals to our total experience of the non-linguistic world as well as to our ability to find a way through the language maze: it is precisely the kind of fuzzy, vague and informal knowledge that distinctive feature analysis seeks to overcome and replace. Despite the usefulness of binary decomposition for some kinds of linguistic description and (in far more complex form) in the 'natural language processing' that computers can now perform, word-meanings can never be fully specified by atomic distinctions alone. People are just too adept at using words to mean something else.

Such quasi-mathematical computation of 'meaning' is equally unable to solve an even more basic problem, which is how to identify the very units whose meaning is to be specified. To ask what a word means (and translators often are asked to say what this or that word means) is to suppose that you know what word you are asking about, and that in turn requires you to know what a word is. The word 'word' is certainly a familiar, convenient and effective tool in the mental kit box we use to talk about language. But it is uncommonly hard to say what it means.

Computers must know the answer, because they count words. That's no consolation to us, however. What computers know about words is what they've been told, which comes down to this: a word is a string of alphabetic characters bounded on left and right by a space or one of these typographical symbols – / ' ? ! : ; , .[5] Computers don't need to know what a word means to carry out the operations we ask of them. But we do! And if in some instance we really don't, then we try to find out from a dictionary, from an acquaintance, or from listening to how other people speak. But all kinds of problems remain. In languages like English the identification of words is more art than science. Publishers have their own style sheets with rules for deciding whether couples have break-ups or break ups or breakups; but ordinary people also want to know if 'to break up' should be counted as one, two or three words. Yet nobody can really say.[6]

English prepositional verbs provide unending employment for language experts who want to determine what a word is. They come in three or four parts. Sometimes they stay together – 'Did you remember *to take out* the bins?' – and sometimes they don't – 'I promised *to take* my daughter *out* to see a film'. Does that mean that 'to take out' is a word – or three – or two different words – 'to take out' and 'to take . . . out' – (or six) that look the same? Compilers of alphabetical dictionaries adopt practical solutions, but not the same ones, leaving the underlying question – what word is this? – unresolved. Teachers of English as a second language know the best answer to the question of how many words there are in a prepositional verb. If you want to know how to use the language properly – don't ask.

Given the labyrinthine complexity of the variable terminologies and conflicting expert solutions to the conundrum of establishing what the word-units are in perfectly ordinary English expressions, it seems fairly obvious that an ordinary user of a language like English doesn't need to know what a word is – or what word it is – in order to make sense. Wordhood is often a useful notion, but it is not a hard-edged thing.

Other languages undermine the wordness of words in a variety of different ways. German runs them together to make new ones. *Lastkraftwagenfahrer* (truck driver) is of course a single word in ordinary use, but it can easily be seen as two words written next to each other (*Lastkraftwagen* plus *Fahrer*, truck plus driver), or as three words run together (*Last* plus *Kraftwagen* plus *Fahrer*, freight plus motor vehicle plus driver), or as four (*Last* plus *Kraft* plus *Wagen* plus *Fahrer*, freight plus power plus vehicle plus driver). Hungarian also melds what we think of as many separate words, but in a different and equally elegant way. What a computer would count as a three-word expression, *Annáékkal voltunk moziban*, for example, would be expressed in English by around a dozen words: 'We were [*voltunk*] at the cinema [*moziban*] with Anna and her folk' (that's to say, friends or relatives or hangers-on, without distinction). That modest suffix *-ék* is all that is needed to turn 'Anna' into a whole group, and the 'glued-on' or agglutinated addition *-kal* says that you were part of it too. Indeed, at my younger daughter's wedding in London in 2003, in honour of her Hungarian grandparents I was able (after doing my homework) to raise a toast, *édeslányaméknak*, which is to say in one word 'to my dear daughter's husband, in-laws and friends'.

Classical Greek has no proper word for 'word'; moreover, in manuscripts and monuments from the earlier period Greek is written without spaces between words. But that does not automatically mean that Greek thinkers had no concept of a basic unit of language smaller than the utterance. There is evidence of word-dividers in Greek written in Linear B and Cyprian, ancient scripts that predate the Greek alphabet, and in various other ways a notion of 'basic unit' does seem to emerge even in a language that supposedly has no 'word' for the unit thus distinguished.[7] Even Hungarians recognize that some 'words' are more basic than others, that beneath the practically infinite welter of possible agglutinated and compounded forms lie nuggets that are the elementary building-blocks of sense. *Gyerek* is Hungarian for 'child', and though it may almost never occur in that form in any actual expression, it is nonetheless the 'root' or 'stem' corresponding to the English stem-word 'child'. Without an operative concept of the meaning-units of which a language is made, it would be hard to imagine how a dictionary could be constructed. And without a dictionary, how would anyone ever learn a foreign tongue, let alone be able to translate it?

9. *Understanding* Dictionaries

Translators use dictionaries all the time. I have a whole set, with the *Oxford English Dictionary* in two volumes and Roget's *Thesaurus* in pride of place, alongside monolingual, bilingual and picture dictionaries of French idioms, Russian proverbs, legal terminologies and much else. These books are my constant friends, and they tell me many fascinating things. But the fact that I seek and obtain a lot of help from dictionaries doesn't mean that without them translation would not exist. The real story is the other way round. Without translators, Western dictionaries would not exist.

Among the very earliest instances of writing are lists of terms for important things in two languages. These bilingual glossaries were drawn up by scribes to maintain consistency in translating between two languages, and to accelerate the acquisition of translating skills by apprentices. These still are the main purposes of the bilingual and multilingual glossaries in use today. French perfume manufacturers maintain proprietary databases of the terms of their trade to help translators produce promotional material for export markets, as do lathe manufacturers, medical specialists and legal firms working in international commercial law. These tools assist translators mightily, but they do not lie at the origin of translating itself. They are the fruits of established translation practice, not the original source of translators' skills.

Sumerian bilingual dictionaries consist of roomfuls of clay tablets sorted into categories – occupations, kinship, law, wooden artefacts, reed artefacts, pottery, hides and copper, other metals, domestic and wild animals, parts of the body, stones, plants, birds and fish, textiles, place-names and food and drink, each with its matching term in the unrelated language of Sumer's Akkadian conquerors.[1] As they are organized by field, they correspond directly to today's SPDs or 'special purpose' dictionaries – 'Business French', 'Russian for the Oil and Gas Industries', 'German Legal Terminology' and so forth. Some of them are multilingual (as are many of today's SPDs) and give equivalents in Amoritic, Hurritic, Elamite, Ugaritic and other languages spoken by civilizations with which the Akkadians were in commercial if not always peaceful contact.[2] From Ancient Mesopotamia to the late Middle Ages in Western Europe, word-lists with second-language equivalents went on serving the same purposes – to regularize translation practice and to train the next generation of translators. Characteristically, they mediate between the language of conquerors and the language of the conquered retained as a language of culture. What did not arise in the West at any time until after the invention of the printed book were general or all-purpose word-lists giving definitions in the same language. The Western monolingual dictionary – the 'general purpose' dictionary or GPD – is a late by-product of the ancient tradition of the translator's companion, the bilingual word-list, but its impact on the way we think about a language has been immense. The first real GPD was launched by the French Academy in the seventeenth century (volume 1, A–L, appeared in 1694); the first to be finished from A to Z was Samuel Johnson's dictionary of the English language, which came out in 1755.

These monuments mark the invention of French and of English as languages in a peculiar, modern sense. Once they had been launched, every other language had to have its own GPD – failing which, it would not be a real language. It wasn't just rivalry that sparked the great race to produce national dictionaries for every 'national language'. The need to compile self-glossing lists of all the words in a language also expressed a new idea of what kind of a thing a language was, an idea taken directly from what had happened in English and French.

The Chinese tradition is entirely different.[3] Its rich history of word-lists is essentially linked to the tradition of writing commentaries on ancient texts, not at all with the business of translating foreign languages, in which traditional Chinese civilization seems to have had as little interest as did the Greeks. Early Chinese dictionaries were organized by semantic field and gave definitions roughly like this: *If someone calls me an uncle, I call him a nephew* (from the *Erh Ya*, third century BCE). It was not easy to find a word in the *Erh Ya*, and many of the definitions given were too vague to be useful in the way we would now want a dictionary to be. It was a tool for cultivating knowledge of more ancient texts, so as to maintain refinement in speech and script. The second kind of glossary of classical Chinese arose in the first century CE and it listed characters organized by their basic written shapes, or 'graphic radicals'. These works gave no clues as to how the words should be pronounced, and their purpose was mainly to assist the interpretation of ancient written texts. The third type of early Chinese lexicon was the rhyme dictionary – handbooks for people who needed to know what rhymes with what, because rhyming skills were tested in examinations for the imperial civil service. It was not until the seventeenth century that a device for classifying Chinese characters in a way that made them easily retrievable was devised by the scholar Mei Ying-Tso, a few years before Jesuit missionaries produced the first

Western-style bilingual dictionaries of Chinese (into Latin, then Portuguese, Spanish and French). Traditional Chinese dictionaries, lexicons and glossaries do not list 'all the words of the language' in the way that Western dictionaries seek to do: they list written characters and they organize them either by semantic field, or by written forms, or by sound. Their profound difference perhaps makes clearer the extent to which Western dictionary-making is also a 'regional' tradition arising from the particular nature of the script that we have.

What is a dictionary for? The utility of a bilingual glossary is obvious. But what is the purpose of a monolingual one? A GPD seems to imply that speakers of the language do not know it very well, as if English, to take the first real example, were to some degree foreign to speakers of English themselves. Why else would they need a dictionary to translate the words of the language for them? The conceptualization of anything as grand and comprehensive as the *Dictionnaire de l'Académie* involves treating the written form of a spoken language as a thing that can be learned and studied not by foreigners, but by native speakers of that language. It's a peculiar idea. By definition, what a monolingual dictionary codifies is precisely the ability to speak that users of the dictionary possess.

The second presupposition of general purpose dictionaries is that a list of all the word-forms of a language is possible. We have become so accustomed to GPDs that it takes a moment to realize just what an extraordinary proposition that is. We may grant that dictionaries are always a little bit out of date, that even the best among them always miss something we would have liked to see there – but we should stop to take such thoughts a step further. To try to capture 'all the words of a language' is as futile as trying to capture all the drops of water in a flowing river. If you managed to do it, it wouldn't be a flowing river any more. It would be a fish-tank.

Once Latin had ceased to be a spoken language, it became possible to list all the word-forms occurring in Latin manuscripts. That was done many times over, just as Roman scholars had compiled lexicons of words in Homer's Greek, and Buddhist monks had listed all the words in sacred Sanskrit texts.[4] The monolingual dictionary of modern times treats French, or English, or German as if it was Latin – and that was the point. It raises the vernacular to the level of the language of the scholars. It proves that speaking English requires and also shows as much cultivation as using Latin. The monolingual dictionary was in the first place a two-pronged weapon for the improvement and the assertion of the common man.

'Improvement' and 'assertion' may seem to go hand in hand, but those locked hands are really engaged in an arm-wrestling match. The first alphabetical lists of words in vernacular languages were extensions of traditional language-teaching tools: Robert Estienne's *Les Mots français selon l'ordre des lettres ainsi que les fault escrire & tourner en latin*, first published in 1544, helped French-speaking children learn the rudiments of their language of culture, namely Latin, but incidentally gave them a tool for writing the vernacular correctly. (Spelling in French was quite variable in the sixteenth century. As Estienne was a printer, he had a stake in the standardization of the written language.) Over the following century, as both English and French absorbed more words from each other and from classical languages, alphabetical listings of technical, philosophical and foreign words became quite popular. In 1604, a Coventry schoolmaster, Robert Cawdrey, brought out a work whose lengthy title explains the social and cultural basis for dictionary-making ever since: *A Table Alphabeticall of hard usual English wordes, with the interpretation thereof by plaine English words, gathered for the benefit & help of Ladies, gentlewomen, or any other unskilful person. Whereby they more easilie and better understand many hard English wordes, which they shall heare or read in the Scriptures, Sermons, or elsewhere, and also be made able to do the same aptly themselves.*

The step from compiling such socially useful works for the improvement of the undereducated classes to making dictionaries of *all* words may seem natural. It could be accounted for by the spread of literacy, the growth of the book trade, an obsession with the making of more and more specialized glossaries, and the wish to bring all this language-lore together in one place. But that would be a retrospective illusion. Intellectually, there is a huge gulf between works, however extensive, that lay down the meanings of 'hard' or technical or foreign terms to help less well-educated folk, and an attempt to list all the words that are spoken by the speakers of a given language. To make that leap you have to think of the language you speak as a finite entity. 'The English language' has to be conceptualized not as a social practice, but as a thing in itself. That is why the history of the English dictionary is the history of the invention of 'a language' in the sense that we now understand that word.

Dictionaries alone aren't responsible for the thingification of natural languages, but they crystallized a peculiar modern view of what it means to have a language. The spread of the printed book is also a major factor in the converging circumstances and technologies that gave us the ideas which have dominated modern language study ever since, and profoundly affected our understanding of what translators do.

GPDs, from Samuel Johnson's to Webster's and from

Brockhaus to Robert, list the words that are part of the language. In so doing they also tell us that the language we speak is a list of words. From its origin in the Hebrew Bible, the nomenclaturist understanding of what a language is was given a huge, definitive boost by the emergence of the modern typographical mind.

Which words are entitled to be listed in a dictionary that gives not a field-restricted set of words, but the words of a whole language? Well, the words that people use. All of them? To the extent that is even possible, GPDs forfeit their historical claim to be instruments of improvement. That's the arm-wrestle. Laying down what words mean and how they should best be used, as was Cawdrey's laudable plan, runs directly counter to the wider project of listing all the words people actually use with the varied meanings they may give to them. That's why monolingual reference dictionaries have grown so impractically large. The solution to that problem is vividly illustrated by the career of one of Perec's fictional characters:

> Cinoc . . . pursued a curious profession. As he said himself, he was a 'word-killer': he worked at keeping Larousse dictionaries up to date. But while other compilers sought out new words and meanings, his job was to make room for them by eliminating all the words and meanings that had fallen into disuse.
>
> When he retired . . . he had disposed of hundreds and thousands of tools, techniques, customs, beliefs, sayings, dishes, games, nicknames, weights and measures . . . He had returned to taxonomic anonymity hundreds of varieties of cattle, species of birds, insects and snakes, rather special sorts of fish, kinds of crustaceans, slightly dissimilar plants and particular breeds of vegetables and fruit; and cohorts of geographers, missionaries, entomologists, Church Fathers, men of letters, generals,

Gods & Demons had been swept by his hand into eternal obscurity.[5]

GPDs of any language, and quite especially those using an alphabetical script, are always of potentially infinite size, because no language can have fixed boundaries in time or space, and there can be no ultimate, definitive division of a social practice into a finite set of components. To escape from this dilemma while pursuing the broad project of mapping a particular language, Peter Mark Roget devised his *Thesaurus* ('treasure' in Greek), which uses not the arbitrary order of the alphabet, but the natural order of the world as its organizing principle. He established six general classes of 'real things', which are not material things, but ideas: Abstract Relations, Space, Matter, Intellectual Faculties, Voluntary Power, and Sentient and Moral Powers. These he divided into categories, then broke down each category into lesser groups of ideas, and only at this point does he list all the words and expressions that may be used to communicate the idea. 'Sentient and Moral Powers', for example, incorporates the category of 'Personal Affections', one of whose groups is constituted by 'Discriminative Affections', among which figures the sub-group 'Aggravation'. That's where you find a raft of words and phrases including 'anger', 'ire', 'fury', 'to get up someone's nose', 'to piss someone off' and 'to get someone's goat' – a long list of synonyms all of which express some quality or variety of aggravation. Roget's *Thesaurus* is an extraordinary achievement. Its structure harks back to those Sumerian word-hoards on clay tablets, sorted by thematic category, but as it contains very few words like 'polyester', 'crankset', or 'recitative', it offers no support at all to those who would like to see a language as a list of the names of things. Rather, it displays to a spectacular degree the sheer redundancy of the vocabulary set that we have, with dozens of words giving only minutely different shades of meaning for almost exactly the same thing (*anger, ire, fury* . . .). Roget shows language to be a rich, illogical and complicated tool for making fine and often arbitrary distinctions – for discriminating, separating out and saying the same thing in different ways.

The thesaurus was not designed as a resource for translators, but it serves translation in two distinct and equally important ways. The first is eminently practical. Browsing Roget's lists of quasi-synonyms and cognate words helps a writer – who may also be a translator at that point – to identify a term to express a more precise shade of meaning than the word that first came to mind. In the second place, however, a thesaurus says on every page that *to know a language is to know how to say the same thing in different words*. That is precisely what translators seek to do. Roget's wonderful *Thesaurus* reminds them that in one language as well as between any two, all words are translations of others.

10. *The* Myth *of* Literal *Translation*

With bilingual dictionaries to get them started and Roget's *Thesaurus* to help them polish their work to a nice finish, translators ought not to find it too hard to tell us what the words on the page really mean. In practice, however, it's the words on the page that hang like a dark veil over what a piece of written language means. Words taken one by one obscure the force and meaning of a text, which is why a word-for-word translation is almost never a good job. This isn't a new insight: arguments against literal translation go back almost as far as written translation itself. [1]

After immersing himself for several years in the history of translation, George Steiner discovered that it consisted very largely of repeated arguments over this same point. 'Over some two thousand years of argument and precept,' he wrote with perceptible frustration, 'the beliefs and disagreements voiced about the nature of translation have been almost the same.' [2]

When Don Quixote's favourite bedtime book, *Amadis de Gaula*, appeared in French, for example, the translator gave his patron two reasons for not having stuck to the literal meanings of the Spanish words:

> I beg you to believe I did it both because many things appeared to me to be inappropriate for people in courtly circles with respect to the customs and standards of our day, and on the advice of some of my friends who saw fit for me to free myself

from the usual punctiliousness of translators, precisely because [this book] doesn't deal with material where such pernickety observance is necessary.[3]

These twin justifications for 'free' translation – literal translation just isn't appropriate for the target audience and isn't suited to the original either – were familiar themes in the sixteenth century, as they had been for many centuries already. In fact, few commentators on translation have ever come out in favour of a literal or word-for-word style. Literal translation is precisely what translators in the broad Western tradition don't do. But if literal translation is not a widespread practice, why do so many translators feel a need to shoot it down – often with overwhelming force? Octavio Paz, the Mexican poet and man of letters, stated the standard view in more recent times: *No digo que la traducción literal sea imposible, sino que no es una traducción*: 'I'm not saying a literal translation is impossible, only that it's not a translation.'[4]

How far back does it go? There are references to the issue in the writings of Cicero (106–43 BCE) and Horace (65–8 BCE), but a long sentence written by St Jerome, the first translator of the Bible into Latin and subsequently the patron saint of translators, can be taken as the first full formulation of the lop-sided dispute between 'literal' and 'free'. In 346 CE, when he was near the end of his labours, Jerome wrote a letter to his friend Pammachius to counter the criticisms that had been made of the translations he had done so far. He said this about how he had gone about his task:

Ego enim non solum fateor, sed libera voce profiteor me in inter-pretatione Graecorum absque scripturis sanctis ubi et verborum ordo mysterium est non verbum e verbo sed sensum exprimere de sensu.

A provisional translation would give the following sense: 'Thus I not only confess but of my own free voice proclaim that apart from translations of sacred scriptures from the Greek, where even the order of the words is a *mysterium*, I express not the word for the word but the sense for the sense.'

Jerome's expression *verbum e verbo*, ' the word . . . from the word', can be considered synonymous with 'literal' translation, and his *sensum exprimere de sensu*, 'to express the sense from the sense' corresponds to the idea of 'free' translation. Jerome proclaims that he doesn't do 'literal' except when translating 'sacred scriptures from the Greek'. That seems clear until you realize that the exception clause drives a cart and horses through the main claim, because what Jerome did throughout his long life was to translate sacred scripture, more than half of which he translated from Greek.

Jerome also says he abandons 'sense-for-sense' translation not just when translating scripture from Greek, but specifically *ubi et verborum ordo mysterium est*, 'in those places where the order of the words is even a *mysterium*'. As the meaning of the word *mysterium* is uncertain, there's no final agreement as to what Jerome was really talking about. At the root of Western arguments about how best to translate lies a mystery-word that nobody is quite sure how to translate.

In late Latin written by Christians, *mysterium* most often means a holy sacrament. Jerome's sentence therefore seems to recommend sticking to the exact order of the words of the Greek New Testament because its word order is sacred. Louis Kelly understands Jerome to be saying:

> Not only do I admit, but I proclaim at the top of my voice, that in translating from Greek, except from Sacred Scripture,

where even the order of the words is of God's doing, I have not translated word for word, but sense for sense.[5]

This reading supports the view that Jerome is not really defending 'sense for sense' translation, as he first seems to be doing, but 'word for word'. But why would Jerome treat Greek word order as sacrosanct and not do the same for the scriptures he translated from Hebrew and Aramaic? The 'Greek exception' doesn't make a lot of sense if holiness is the dominant reason for mimicking the word order of the source.

However, Jerome may have meant something else by *mysterium*. He may have wanted to explain his approach to an issue that confronts every translator at some point: what to do with expressions that you don't understand. It's a real problem for all translators, because every utterance ever made in speech or writing has something blank or fuzzy or uncertain about it.

In ordinary speaking, listening and reading, we cope with the gaps in various ways. An impenetrable phrase may be treated as a transmission error – a mispronunciation, a typo, a scribal glitch. We have no trouble replacing it with what we instantly guess to be the true form, and in spoken interaction we do this automatically, without noticing the corrections that we bring to what we hear. When reading, we use the context to prompt a meaning that fits. Where the context isn't good enough to allow this, we just skip it. We skip-read all the time! Nobody knows the meanings of all the French words in *Les Misérables*, but that's never stopped anyone from enjoying Hugo's novel. However, translators are not granted the right to skip. That's a serious constraint. It hardly arises in most kinds of language use; it's one of the few things that sets a problem for translation that is almost unique to it.

Jerome was working with many different sources, but his

main text for the Old Testament was the Greek Septuagint, translated from now lost Hebrew sources several centuries earlier. According to legend, it had been commissioned around 236 BCE by Ptolemy II, the Greek-speaking ruler of Egypt, for his new library in Alexandria. He had sent men to Judea to round up learned Jews who understood the source text, then wined and dined them and set them up at on Pharos, the 'lighthouse island' to get down to work. There were seventy (or seventy-two) participants in this foundational translation workshop, which is why the text they produced is called the Septuagint – a way of writing (not translating) the Greek word meaning 'seventy'.

The Seventy wrote not in the language of Homer and Sophocles, but in *koiné*, the popular spoken language of the Hellenistic cultures dotted around the Middle East. They also wrote it in a peculiar way, perhaps because *koiné* was their vehicular language and not completely native to them. So it would hardly be surprising if some words, phrases and sentences in it baffled St Jerome seven centuries later. One tell-tale sign of the Seventy's difficulty with Greek is the way they handled Hebrew words referring to Jewish religious mysteries. For example, they represented Hebrew כרובים as Χερουβὶμ, which is not a translation, but just the same word sounded out in a different alphabet. Jerome followed style – he wrote out approximately the same sounds in Latin script, making *cherubim*. English Bible translators have done the same, giving us a Hebrew masculine plural form (*-im*) for a concept that has stumped all translators since the third century BCE. In addition, the transfer of letters through three scripts and four languages has altered the sound of the word almost beyond recognition, from *kheruvím* to 'cherubim'.

This way of dealing with an untranslatable by not translating it while making it pronounceable (sound translation, homophonic translation: see above, p. 32) could be considered the primary, original meaning of the term literal translation. It represents a foreign word by putting in place of the letters of which it is made the corresponding letters of the script of the target language. But we do not call that literal translation nowadays – we call it transliteration. And it probably wasn't what Jerome had in mind in the famous passage from his letter to Pammachius.

What then did Jerome mean by *mysterium*? Here's an alternative translation of the mystery passage by a canon of Canterbury Cathedral:

> For I myself not only admit but freely proclaim that in translating from the Greek (except in the case of the holy scriptures where even the order of the words is a mystery) I render sense for sense and not word for word.

To put it in a slacker style, 'I only translate word for word where the original – even its word order – is completely impenetrable to me.' That is of course what translators have always done. For the most part, they transmit the sense; where the sense is obscure, the best they can do – because unlike ordinary readers they are not allowed to skip – is to offer a representation of the separate words of the original. This may even explain the style of the translation of the extract quoted on page 50. Maybe Derrida's translator, far from trying to sound foreign, was simply baffled.

What then is a literal translation? Not a substitution of letters, since we call that transliteration. A one-for-one substitution of the separated written words? Maybe. When confronted with a decidedly loose French translation of *The Jumping Frog of Calaveras County*, Mark Twain decided to back-translate his story into English using a single-word substitution device intended as the opposite of his French translator's overuse of rephrasing.

The Frog Jumping of the County of Calaveras

It there was one time here an individual known under the name of Jim Smiley; it was in the winter of '49, possibly well at the spring of '50, I no me recollect not exactly. This which me makes to believe that it was the one or the other, it is that I shall remember that the grand flume is not achieved when he arrives at the camp for the first time, but of all sides he was the man the most fond of to bet which one have seen, betting upon all that which is presented, when he could find an adversary; and when he not of it could not, he passed to the side opposed.[6]

This schoolboy prank mocks French, French grammar, the school teaching of French and so forth. But the main thing it demonstrates is Octavio Paz's point: 'literal translation' is not impossible, but it is not a translation. You can only understand the target text if you can do a reverse substitution of the words of the source and read the French through its representation in English. In other words, to make any sense of 'The Frog Jumping' you have to know French, whereas the whole purpose of translation of any kind is to make the source available to those readers of the target who do not know the source language. A translation that makes no sense without recourse to the original is not a translation. This axiom incidentally explains why the meaning of 'cherub' will for ever remain a speculation.

The term 'literal' also hides other mysteries. It is used to refer not only to a translation style that barely exists, but to say something about the way an expression is supposed to be understood.

The distinction between the literal and figurative meanings

of words has been at the heart of Western education for more than two millennia. The literal meaning of an expression is supposed to be its meaning prior to any act of interpretation, its natural, given, standard, shared, neutral, plain meaning.

However, when we say 'It was literally raining cats and dogs last night', we mean the adverb 'literally' in a figurative sense. Studies of large corpora of recorded speech have shown that the majority of the uses of 'literal' and 'literally' in English are figurative; similar results would no doubt be extracted from written texts in all European languages.[7] This is a curious irony, because expressions that mean one thing and its opposite were a thorn in the flesh of precisely those Greek thinkers who invented the distinction between literal and figurative in the first place. But language is like putty. The figurative use of 'literal' is one among a thousand cases of expressions meaning this and its opposite, depending on what you use them to mean.

'Literal' is an adjective formed from the noun *littera*, meaning 'letter' in Latin. A letter in this sense is a written sign that belongs to a set of signs some subsets of which can be used to communicate meanings. Speech communicates meaning, writing communicates meaning – but letters on their own do not have any meaning. That's what a letter is – a sign that is meaningless except when used as part of a string. The expression 'literal meaning', taken literally, is a contradiction in terms, an oxymoron and a nonsense.

What we probably meant in the distant past when we asserted that something was 'literally true' in order to emphasize that it was really true, true to a higher degree than just being true, was that it was among those rare things that were worthy of being 'put into letters', of being written down. All the uses of 'literal' with respect to meaning and translation implicitly value writtenness more highly than oral speech.

They are now among the surviving linguistic traces of the fantastic change in social and cultural hierarchies that the invention of writing brought about. They carry the shadow of the early stages of literacy in the Mediterranean Basin between the third and first millennia BCE, when alphabetic scripts first arose together with the texts which through translation and retranslation have shaped and fed Western civilization ever since. That is presumably why the same words and the same terms still persist in debates about how best to translate.

Yet even in the modern era we do not always know quite what we mean when we claim that something is literally true, and even less when we call a translation a literal one.

Towards the end of the nineteenth century a Franco-Egyptian mountebank with a medical degree and a talent for social climbing and free composition in French published a new version of *The Arabian Nights*. It was a commercial and cultural success, feeding a wave of interest in the Sexy Orient among the élite, and it impressed many writers of the day, including Marcel Proust. The translator, Joseph-Charles Mardrus, knew Arabic and he used some Arabic texts as the basis of his rewriting of the collection of ancient Eastern tales which he titled, in a daring Arabism in French, *Les Mille Nuits et Une Nuit*, with a subtitle as clear as can be: *Traduction littérale et complète du texte arabe*, 'The Thousand Nights and One Night. A Complete and Literal Translation of the Arabic Text'.[8]

The subtitle is less a description than an assertion of status. Calling the work 'complete' is obviously intended to give it a higher value than previous versions – but why should 'literal' have seemed to Mardrus an effective way of enhancing the status of his work?

It wasn't a slip: Mardrus's preface emphasizes and magnifies the meaning of his subtitle:

> 'Only one honest and logical method of translation exists: impersonal, barely modulated literalism ... It is the greatest guarantee of truth ... The reader will find here a pure, inflexible word-for-word version. The Arabic text has simply changed alphabet: here it is in French writing, that's all ...'⁹

Mardrus was not a conventional translation theorist, and scholars of Middle Eastern languages claimed that he was not a translator either. A professor of Arabic at the Sorbonne demonstrated that there were no textual sources for many passages and stories in Mardrus's entertaining and readable compilation. But Mardrus was a personage on the Parisian cultural scene and would not suffer such slings and arrows without returning fire. Friends came to his defence: André Gide argued that despite the demonstrations of Professor Gaudefroy-Demombynes, Mardrus's work was 'more authentic than the original'.¹⁰ The translator's own riposte built on Gide's extraordinary claim. Academic critics learned Arabic in the classroom, not from living in the Middle East.

> To carry out a translation of this kind properly, to give a definitive reflection of the Arabic mind and its genius [...] you must be born and you must have lived in the Arabic world; [...] to translate decently the spirit and the letter of stories of this kind, you must have heard them spoken out loud in a local accent, with ethnic gestures and appropriate intonation by storytellers in full possession of their material.¹¹

His translation was therefore the 'literal' version of an essentially oral source. Mardrus's written word in French stands for the spoken word of Arabic culture. If academic critics insist on having a textual source for the authentic *Arabian Nights*, which he wrote, well, no problem: 'One day, in order to please

M. Demombynes, I want to settle once and for all the Arabic text of *The Arabian Nights* by translating my French translation into Arabic.'

What stands out from this literary squabble is that the idea of what a literal translation consists of is culturally conditioned to a high degree. Mardrus wanted to say that his work was authentic, that it gave the true voice of the Arabic culture that he rightly or wrongly regarded as his special native privilege to possess. His solution to the argument – to manufacture a source to give textual scholars the evidence they demanded – may appear quite nutty, but it is not illogical from Mardrus's point of view.

What all other Western commentators mean by 'literal translation', on the other hand, is unrelated to authenticity, truthfulness, or plainness of expression. It really only refers to the written form of words, and even more particularly to the representation of words in an alphabetic script. When that technology for the preservation of thought was still relatively new, and for those many centuries when it was not widely shared and was used for a restricted range of needs and pursuits (law, religion, philosophy, mathematics, astronomy and, occasionally, the entertainment of the elite) it made sense to attach high prestige to the writtenness of written texts.

But in a world of near-universal literacy, that's to say, for the last two or three generations, where alphabetic script is used for entirely ordinary tasks (to label packaged food, to advertise underwear, and to write blogs, horror comics and pulp fiction), the fact that something is worthy of being written down in letters gives it no added value at all. 'Literal' isn't 'Word Magic' any more, it's just a hangover from the past. The terms of debate about translation and meaning need to be updated, and the long-lasting scrap between literal and free should now be laid to rest.

However, there is one important area where the transposition of meanings at the level of individual words is a valuable, inescapable tool: in school and, more particularly, in foreign language lessons.

There are many different ways of teaching languages. The Ottomans rounded up youngsters in conquered lands and brought them back as slaves to be trained as *dil oğlan*, or 'language-boys' in Istanbul. Modern direct methods are gentler but rely on the same understanding of how languages are best learned – through total immersion in a *bain linguistique*, a kind of baptism of the brain.

Throughout the period of learned Latin in Western Europe, immersion was not an option. There was no environment in which everybody spoke Latin as a native tongue, and so the language had to be taught by teachers, in classrooms, through writing. Reprising Roman methods in the teaching of Greek, the European language-teaching tradition was heavily skewed towards the use of translation as the means of imparting written skills in the foreign tongue, and also as a means of assessing students' progress towards that aim. The teaching of modern European languages in schools and universities got off the ground towards the end of the nineteenth century and borrowed its methods from the translation-based traditions in the teaching of Latin and Greek. It is generally reckoned to have been a disaster. However, if the aim of learning Latin (or French, or German) is to be able to read texts in that language fluently and also perhaps to be able to compose and thus to correspond with other users of Latin or French or German (whose native languages may be quite varied), then translation and composition skills are quite appropriate educational aims.

Translation-based language teaching is no longer in fashion, but its ghost still inhabits a number of misconceptions about what translation is or should be.

Teaching a foreign language when an actual linguistic environment is not available and in the absence of technologies that allow a linguistic environment to be simulated (television, radio, film, sound recording and the web) was obliged to rely on writing – on slates or on chalkboards, in exercise books or in print. With only those tools available it's not obvious how to explain that the expression

У меня большой дом

is to be understood as 'I have a big house' unless you also explain that it can be broken down into

At-me-big-house

and use this item-by-item representation of the foreign in English disguise to introduce basic grammatical features – the fact that Russian doesn't have a definite or indefinite article, for instance, that adjectives agree in number, gender and case with the nouns they qualify, that there is no place for the verb 'to be' in a Russian expression of this kind, and that possession may be expressed by a preposition before a personal pronoun, which has to be put into the appropriate grammatical case. Indeed, the grammar explanation I've just given is almost meaningless until you have seen it in action in a written expression and been told what each written item stands for.

Some people call this 'literal translation', but it would be better to adopt a distinct term for the parallel, item-by-item explication of an expression in a foreign language for the purpose of teaching how the foreign language works. 'Wording' is invaluable, and I don't think even the most direct of direct methods can do without it at some point. In fact, language learners taught by other methods always re-invent wording for themselves when grappling with a sentence just beyond the level of competence they have reached.

'Wording' gives you a first approach to the shape and order of the language you are learning. It helps not so much to translate as produce acceptable expressions in the foreign tongue. To translate into the foreign language, you learn first of all to put the source into foreign dress. You learn that 'My father has a big car' must first be translated into 'At father big car' before you can even start to slot in the Russian expressions that will add up to the sentence with the stated meaning.

Wording is neither a language nor a translation, just an uncommonly helpful intermediate stage in learning how to read and write in a foreign tongue. School translation into L2 also gives the instructor a means of checking whether students have grasped and remembered the shape and order of the language. It's not a test of an abstract grammar point, but of grammar in a context of use. That's how I learned languages at school. Given good teachers and keen students, it works.

But often it does not. Worse still, it often leaves ex-school students who failed the test pieces with a horror of doing translations, and sometimes a lingering resentment of those who can.

Since the expansion of education in the nineteenth century down to the present day, facing-page printed translations of standard works in foreign languages have helped countless students improve their grasp of grammar and vocabulary, and allowed them also to read foreign works at greater speed and thus to understand them more completely. Some facing-page translation series, particularly of Latin and Greek, use techniques very close to wording and are often called cribs. Others aim at a more fluent target text, but the constraint of fitting paragraph to paragraph, if not quite line to line, limits the reorganization of material and rephrasing normally found in a literary translation. Penguin Parallel Texts, in the UK, and the series currently published by Folio in France, are of great use to foreign-language learners of Italian, Spanish, Russian and so forth, and also to people like me who were taught a language long ago and are glad to have some help when revisiting the key texts of youth.

Wording translation and facing-page translation (which almost always uses matching sentence length) are not 'bad' ways to translate. They are language operations with specific finalities, serving communicative and educational purposes proper to them and to nothing else. Translation is not just one thing; how best to do it depends on what you are doing it for.

However, wording is not what people mean when they call something a literal translation. The so-called literal translation of У меня большой дом is not 'at me big house', but 'I have a big house'. That's to say, all that is actually meant by calling something a literal translation is a version that preserves meaning in grammatical forms appropriate to the language of the translation. Octavio Paz was right to say that there is no such thing as a literal translation! It's just a translation – a plain, ordinary, actual translation of the source. The left-side player in the long and frustrating game of squash between 'literal' and 'free' doesn't really exist. It's just the shadow of another, more ancient world. But shadows can be quite frightening even when you know they don't exist.

11. *The* Issue *of* Trust: The Long Shadow of Oral Translation

There used to be many good reasons to mistrust translators. War, diplomacy, trade and exploration are activities where trust is both crucial and difficult to grant – and also the key fields in which translators work. If you don't know the language of your enemy or your partner, you depend entirely on the people who do – and there's nothing like dependency to foster resentment and fear.

The user's mistrust is a big issue in all kinds of translation, but its role ought to be rather different in the two main branches of language work, oral translation and the translation of written texts. Oral mediation – the translation of live speech, straightaway and *in situ* – has been around for much longer than writing. In all likelihood it's been a human language skill since the emergence of speech itself, tens if not hundreds of thousands of years ago. For up to 90 per cent of its history, translating, alongside language itself, has been an exclusively spoken affair. The inheritance of oral translating affects how we think about translation even now. Writing transformed and multiplied the uses of language, and naturally affected the ways in which it is possible to think and talk about it. We are now so thoroughly accustomed to the existence and use of script that it's hard to imagine what life is like for someone who does not know how to read or write. It's harder still to imagine living and speaking in a society in which nobody has an inkling that anything like writing could exist. But those are the circumstances in which translation first emerged, and where it stayed for tens of thousands of years. Indeed, the archaeological evidence that we have of the origins of script suggests that alphabetic writing emerged in multilingual cities and empires in the Middle East, where translation was already of paramount importance.[1]

The fundamental difference between oral cultures and those that have writing is that only in the latter can an utterance be brought to life a second time. In 'primary orality', language is nothing other than speech, and speech vanishes without a trace the moment it is done.[2] Translation likewise. You can check, evaluate, test, or trust a translation only when you have a means of returning to it later on.

This would be of purely antiquarian interest if everything had changed overnight upon the invention of script. But that was obviously not the case. The mental transformation that writing prompted did not happen all at once; in some respects, it did not begin to affect the vast mass of humanity until a few generations ago.[3] Residues of the older oral order persisted for millennia, and persist even now. They affect our feelings and fears about translation quite directly.

A clue to the enduring presence of orality in our now thoroughly typographical world is the way we still use the word 'word'. It does not always mean the hazy and problematic items you find printed as headwords in dictionaries. In fact, in much of our everyday use of language it means something else.

When I 'give you my word' that I'll do the washing-up tonight, I am not giving you a 'word' in the dictionary sense. I am making a promise, and grounding your trust in the promise thus made in the fact that the person speaking the promise is me.

'My word' is simply my saying of it. In this usage, 'word' is not a unit of speaking, but the act of speech itself. Similarly, when I call a friend 'a man of his word' I make no reference to his using some particular lexical item. I mean to say that whatever my friend undertakes to do by an act of speech is to be taken seriously, because it was he who said it.

In French, the distinction between 'word as act' and 'word as unit' is made clearer by the general use of *parole* for the first and *mot* for the second. In German, too, there is a trace of the fundamental divide in the meaning of the word 'word' in the two different plurals of *Wort* – *Worte* for acts of speech and *Wörter* for entries in a *Wörterbuch*.

There is of course a real connection between these two divergent associations of 'word'. Both of them name the smallest handy unit of speech. It's just that since the invention of alphabetic script we've grown completely accustomed to thinking that the true form of what we say is the way it looks when written down. 'Scriptism', as Roy Harris called the illusion that a language consists of things called words, has served us well for a few thousand years, but it has a downside as well. It makes it harder to understand what translation does.

The uses in many Western languages of words meaning 'word' to refer to acts of speech are perseverating traces of primary orality. The status of any utterance in a mental world without script derives mainly from the identity of the speaker, much less from the 'meanings' of the 'words' that are spoken. The concepts in scare quotes are probably not even thinkable without writing. The indeterminacy of the flow of speech and the dependence of meaning on the human context in an oral culture are pinpointed with affection and insight by Tolstoy, in his portrait of the illiterate peasant-philosopher Platon Karataev, in *War and Peace*:

Platon could never recall what he had said a moment before, just as he could never tell Pierre [Bezukhov] the words of his favourite song . . . He did not understand and could not grasp the meaning of words apart from their context . . . His words and actions flowed from him as smoothly, as inevitably and as spontaneously as fragrance exhales from a flower. He could not understand the value or significance of any word or deed taken separately.[4]

'Translating' in this kind of cultural circumstance calls for a special kind of trust. If the force of an utterance is intimately linked to the identity of the speaker, then it can't be conveyed by any other speaker. That fundamental rule has to be suspended for oral translation to come into existence, since it requires the listener to take the words of the translator as if they had been uttered by the speaker of a foreign tongue. Oral translation in a world without writing creates and relies on a fiction – perhaps the earliest fictional invention of all. The first great leap forward in the history of translation must have been when some two communities found a way of agreeing that the speech of the translator was to be taken as having the same force as the immediately prior speech of the principal.

It's not hard to account for the existence of bilinguals in early human societies: taking brides from different communities and taking slaves from vanquished enemies are ancient practices, and both of them can easily result in people who understand two different languages. But there's a great difference between bilingualism and translation. For the latter to exist, huge intellectual and emotional obstacles to taking the word of another for the word of the source have to be overcome. They can only be overcome by a shared willingness to enter a realm in which meaning cannot be completely guaranteed. That kind of trust is perhaps the foundation of all culture.

But that trust is never granted without reservation. To conduct the negotiation or the trade between two communities speaking mutually incomprehensible tongues, the principal relies on the translator and is in his power, just as the translator serves one master only and is entirely in his power. The situation is guaranteed to create anxiety, suspicion and mistrust.

The fear of imperfect or deceptive performance by an oral translator affects the translation protocols for private meetings between world leaders today. Each side brings along his or her own oral translator. When the British PM talks to the French president in confidential, face-to-face encounters, the person employed by HM Government speaks in French on behalf of the PM, and the French translator similarly speaks back the French president's words in English. Such two-handed, one-way speech translation, out of the mother-tongue and into the foreign, is never seen in public.[5] These arrangements hark back directly to the issue of trust in oral translation. Translators are no longer slaves, but states still have greater recourse against employees who have signed the Official Secrets Act than against a translator hired by the other side.

This costly double dose of oral interpreting is rare, but not solely because it is expensive. Outside of private head-of-state encounters, almost all speech by politicians, diplomats and public figures begins and ends its life on the page. Delegates at the United Nations General Assembly and Security Council, for example, read from prepared texts, and often the interpreters translating the speech simultaneously into English, French, Spanish, Russian, Chinese or Arabic have the relevant original text in front of them. All six language versions are recorded on tape and these recordings are used by the UN

Documentation Division to produce the 'Verbatim', the official written record of what was said. This allows translation errors to be trapped and corrected, but, more significantly, it allows delegates to edit what they actually said. The 'Verbatim', the final official repository of UN proceedings, is not actually verbatim at all – it's a rewritten version of a written text that passed through an untrusted oral stage in the interim. In large areas of national and international affairs, speech has now become a secondary medium, a by-product of writing. But this is a very recent state of affairs. Our thoughts and feelings about language and translation, together with many of the things we say about it, have much older sources.

Between the fifteenth and early twentieth centuries, the Ottoman Empire held in its not always steady sway mostly illiterate populations speaking a great number of different languages. Throughout these five centuries the administration of this vast and elaborate state was carried out in Ottoman Turkish – a partly artificial hybrid of Turkish, Persian and Arabic vocabulary held together by Turkish grammar, with some Persian syntax added on, written in an adapted Arabic script which was not particularly well suited to it. It was the official language of the court at Istanbul, but outside the circle of imperial grandees and civil servants Ottoman Turkish did not have many speakers. Its written form was of course used for the state's labyrinthine archives – by some accounts, the Ottomans even kept records of people's dreams.[6] However, one characteristic of Ottoman society was a paranoid suspicion of forgery, and as a result writing was not used for all purposes of state. Strong residues of orality – of a trust in personal speech over the impersonal technology of writing – affected the management of public affairs, and most especially its use of translators.

Ottoman society, like those of the Greeks and the Romans, made slaves of a significant proportion of its subjects, and it recruited translators from among the young boys sent back from the provinces to Istanbul as obligatory payment for the protection the empire provided. Most of these enforced bilinguals served the internal needs of the empire, since they spoke one of its regional languages and received an education in Ottoman Turkish. Its external translation needs for trade, war and diplomacy were mostly served by other means.

The Ottomans were Muslims and could therefore communicate with many of the peoples on the southern and eastern borders of the empire in Arabic, which was either a native or a vehicular tongue over a wide area. But contact with Western Europe was not so easy. In no region of the empire were any of the Western languages taught. Initially, therefore, the training of cadres who could handle relations with the West was farmed out to the Republic of Venice, which had long-standing ties with many parts of the Mediterranean that had fallen into Ottoman hands.

From the late fifteenth century on, Venice dispatched plenipotentiaries on two-year postings to Istanbul to run the *bailo*, which was something like a translator's school. It recruited adolescent apprentices called 'language-boys' – *giovanni di lingua*, a translation of the Turkish *dil oğlan* – across the Venetian and Ottoman territories, and turned them into loyal, Italian-speaking Venetian subjects capable of talking to the Turks. Many of the recruits came from the Greek-speaking Roman Catholic community that had settled in a quarter of Istanbul called Pera, or Phanari in Greek, and Phanariots eventually became a hereditary 'translation caste' within the stratified world of Ottoman society. By the early seventeenth century, the whole business of translation at the highest levels of the Ottoman state was in the hands of closely linked families of Phanariots, whose status was partly protected by the fact that many of them also held Venetian citizenship by inheritance. But they did not translate very much into or out of Greek: they were trained to translate Ottoman Turkish into Italian, and sometimes Arabic as well. They became richly rewarded grandees. Based in Istanbul, they sent their sons to Italian universities before bringing them back to continue the family trade.[7]

Diplomacy, spying and administrative intrigue were all part of the job done by these Ottoman translators, called *tercüman*. This Turkish term has come into English as *dragoman*, but in only slightly altered forms it can be found in dozens of other languages that had contact with the Turks. Azerbaijani *tərcüməçi*, Amharic *ästärg*ʷ*ami*, Dari *tarjomân*, Persian *motarjem*, Uzbek *tarzhimon* (таржимон), Arabic *mutarjim*, Moroccan Arabic *terzman* and Hebrew *metargem* (מתרגם) are all sound-translations of *tercüman*. But whether written as *dragoman* or as *tercüman*, the Ottoman word for translator is not a Turkish word at all. It is first found in a language spoken in Mesopotamia in the third millennium BCE, as a translation of the even more ancient Sumerian word *eme-bal*. Akkadian *targumannu* thus has a descendant by way of Turkish *tercüman* in an admittedly obsolete but still extant word of English – probably the only word with a stable meaning whose history can be traced in writing over a period of 5,000 years.[8] The spread of one of the most widely used root-words for 'translator' from one of the cradles of writing in Ancient Mesopotamia can hardly be bettered as evidence for the immensely greater antiquity of the practice of translation itself.

Top Ottoman dragomans became the equals of ambassadors. The first to be granted the title 'Grand Dragoman' by the

Sultan was appointed in 1661 under the reign of Küprölü Ahmed Pasha – the famous Albanian Grand Vizir Quprili whose many adventures are turned into fiction in the novels of Ismail Kadare.[9] A later Grand Dragoman, Alexander Mavrokordato, founded a dynasty that eventually acquired princely status. His direct descendants became the royal family of Romania.

Because they were diplomats and negotiators using speech and not writing for the most delicate matters, dragomans dealt with their written tasks along lines more characteristic of oral translation. Dragomans altered the pasha's language to put it in a form best suited to performing the act that the principal intended. They did this in order to remain faithful to the Sultan – for disloyalty was punishable by death, if not worse. Far from being 'free', the dragomans' reformulation of the words of the source expressed subservience to their principal's intention. Despite appearances to the contrary – substantial amounts of contraction, expansion and recasting – dragomans stuck rigidly to their brief, which was not to translate the Sultan's words, but his word.

For example, when Sultan Murad II granted permission for English merchants to trade in the Ottoman lands, his original letter in Turkish refers to Queen Elizabeth as 'having demonstrated her subservience and devotion and declared her servitude and attachment' to the Sultan. For onward communication to the English court the letter was translated by the Grand Dragoman into Italian, which was still the international language of the Ottoman Empire.[10] In Italian, however, the letter doesn't say nearly as much: it expresses the elaborate Turkish formula economically as *sincera amicizia*.[11]

Is this a 'free' translation or an 'unfaithful' one? I don't think either term is appropriate. The dragoman's occlusion of the words for 'subservience' and 'servitude' is not an expression of his freedom, but of the political and administrative constraints of his own position. He knows that his own master will never regard the Queen of England as a monarch of equal power; and as a seasoned diplomat he also knows that Elizabeth I cannot possibly accede to the expression of her 'servitude' to the Sultan, even in a conventional flourish.

Western embassies in Istanbul did not use the official court interpreters in the service of the Ottoman court, who were bound to be loyal to their sovereign. They employed less eminent, and mostly non-Muslim, bilinguals to be found in Istanbul. As they became less and less familiar with oral culture over the several centuries of Ottoman rule, Western diplomats increasingly described their Levantine intermediaries as unreliable and untrustworthy folk. In the first place, they grumbled, at least half of what they wrote and pretended to be translation 'from English' was pure invention, in the following style:

> Having bowed my head in submission and rubbed my slavish brow in utter humility and complete abjection and supplication to the beneficent dust beneath the feet of my mighty, gracious, condescending, compassionate, merciful benefactor, my most generous and open-handed master, I pray that the peerless and almighty provider of remedies may bless your lofty person, the extremity of benefit, protect my benefactor from the vicissitudes and afflictions of time, prolong the days of his life, his might and his splendour . . .

Also, every scrap of information they gleaned from translating for a foreign embassy was put up for sale. As one English ambassador put it, since these dragomans 'with large families live upon a small salary and are used to Oriental luxury, the temptation of money from others is with difficulty withstood by them'.[12]

It's easy to see why such dragomans should adapt their work to their audience – they were Ottoman subjects and stood to lose far more from displeasing the authorities than from misrepresenting their foreign employers:

> Fear tied their tongues: they would much rather risk their employer's displeasure than the brutal fury of an angry pasha ... At times, ingenious interpreters ... were known to improvise imaginary dialogues – to substitute speeches of their own inspiration for those really made.[13]

They were suspect in any case for the mere fact of working for a foreign embassy. Why double the risk by failing to address local potentates with the florid servility to which they were accustomed? Adding a few paragraphs of eternal devotion wasn't mistranslation. It was life insurance. 'All things considered, the wonder is not so much that Dragomans fulfilled their perilous task inadequately, as that they dared undertake it at all.'[14]

Fidelity was obviously a major issue for Ottoman dragomans, but it didn't mean what translation commentators in the West seem to mean by 'fidelity to the source'. Dragomans needed to prove that they were faithful to the Padishah or to the particular Ottoman grandee they were addressing.

It was the grandest of the Phanariot dragomans who paid the highest price for suspected disloyalty. In 1821, the Greek provinces of the Ottoman Empire rose up in revolt. Because they were Greeks as well as Catholics, Phanariot families in Istanbul came under immediate suspicion. Their leader, Grand Dragoman Stavraki Aristarchi, was hanged for treason. Why? Because, as had long been said in the Ottomans' international language, *Traduttore/traditore!* Translators are traitors anyway! This exotic adage has percolated into all Western languages, in Italian and in translation, and has become one of the most commonly touted pieces of expertise about translation in circulation. But save in quite exceptional cases it is wrong, and always was. The translation practice of the dragomans was generally subservient to an outstanding degree – subservient to the purpose of the original, and subservient to the dragomans' real masters. Treachery was what the masters feared, not what the translators performed. But even if Phanariots did on occasion make deals for themselves by misrepresenting their commissioners, the connection between 'translating' and 'treachery' is of no relevance to modern, thoroughly print-based societies. In a world where you can check the translation against the original, even when it has the form of speech (thanks to the sound-recording devices we have used for the past one hundred years) the principal grounds for the fear and mistrust of linguistic intermediaries that is endemic to oral societies no longer exist. Yet people go on saying *traduttore/ traditore* believing they have said something meaningful about translation. A thoughtful translator like Douglas Hofstadter still feels he needs to counter it with a pun in the title of his book, *Translator, Trader*.[15] We may now live in a sophisticated, wealthy, technologically advanced society – but when it comes to translation, some people seem to be stuck in the age of the clepsydra.

Traditional mistrust of oral interpreters in the Middle East affected Western tourists when visits to the region became practical and prestigious for individuals in the nineteenth century. Tourists had to rely on local intermediaries for contact with the authorities, and hereditary dragoman families turned themselves into guides, guest house brokers, and go-betweens for the purchase of antiquities and other delights. As they performed their tasks according to their own traditions of highly adaptive translation, they were despised and scorned. 'Dragomania', the fear and loathing of the intermediaries who ran rings around all but the most canny Western travellers, made a major contribution to the stereotype of the 'wily oriental gentleman' of colonial-era travelogues.[16]

The tropes of 'fidelity' and 'betrayal' in translation commentary do not come to us only from a vanished Ottoman past. In seventeenth-century France, several translators of the Greek and Latin classics thought it best to amend the originals to make them correspond more closely to the standards of politeness that ruled behaviour and writing at the Court of Versailles. Swear words and references to bodily functions were simply cut out, as were whole passages referring to drinking, homosexuality or the sharing of partners. Confident in the absolute rightness of the courtly manners of France, these translators tried to produce translations that were fitter for their target audience, and also (in their view) better and more beautiful works. They were saving the Greeks from themselves by editing out all those primitive blemishes. Purposefully and intentionally adaptive, these many classical texts refashioned for courtiers (or for children), were dubbed *les belles infidèles*, literally, 'beautiful unfaithful [ones] [feminine]'.

These two adjectives juxtaposed imply a missing noun between them, and the absent word is obviously *traductions*, 'translations'. At bottom, the phrase *les belles infidèles* only says 'beautiful free translations'. However, French adjectives preceded by an article ('a', 'the') can also be taken as nouns, just like 'the poor' or 'the unwashed' in English. So because its form is feminine and plural, *les belles* . . . can also mean '[the] beautiful women', and the whole phrase, *les belles infidèles*, read that way round, may be taken to say 'beautiful women who cheat'. This construction of the phrase allowed for the invention of another adage which has burdened translation commentary ever since. Translations, this saying goes, are like women. *Si elles sont belles, elles sont infidèles, mais si elles sont fidèles, elles ne sont pas belles* – 'If they are good-looking, you can't trust them to be faithful, and if they stick by their mates, it's because they're old frumps.' That's a fairly free translation by conventional standards, but it is exactly what the adage implies (while also being translatable in its other dimension as 'Aesthetically pleasing ones are adaptive and non-adaptive ones are just plain'. The shadow of such sexist nonsense falls even today upon a French publishing house with an otherwise admirable list of translated works – Les Belles Infidèles.

Sexist language has been the object of long and mostly successful campaigns in France as in the English-speaking world, but only rarely has it been observed that outside the context of politeness as it was understood in the French seventeenth century, *les belles infidèles*, whether used as a three-word catchphrase or in the longer adage which was built from it, is an insult to women. Most people let it pass because they think it is a statement about translation. It is not. It's about male anxiety – to the point of misogyny. It applies to translation, I suspect, only because, like other versions of the betrayal motif, it says just how frightening translation can seem.

Some critics have argued that a good translation is one that is faithful to its source. The corollary would be that a bad one counts as some kind of a betrayal, and therefore justifies to some degree the worn-out and disreputable clichés we've tried to demolish. The corollary would be plausible if we knew what we meant in saying that a faithful translation is a good one. Why indeed is the term 'faithful' applied to translation at all? True, a good spouse is a loyal one, and a decent spy is not a traitor. We also used to ask of servants and family retainers that they be faithful to their masters. But translators aren't married to their originals, nor do they work for the CIA. The repeated insistence on 'fidelity' as a criterion of quality in translation has certainly led many to describe themselves as servants of their originals. In so doing, they re-enact the historical and prehistoric origins of their profession – the exercise of skills possessed by slaves.

Slavery was abolished in Brazil in 1880. Time to move on.

12. *Custom* Cuts: Making Forms Fit

Chinese people love to pass around *shunkouliu* on oral grapevines. These are satiric rhythmical sayings, often consisting of quatrains with seven-syllable lines. The regularity of the form is audible and also visible in writing, because each Chinese character corresponds to one syllable. Here's a jingle of that kind:

辛辛苦苦四十年

一朝回到解放前

既然回到解放前

当年革命又为谁

Compact, patterned, dense, allusive, bitter and humorous ... translating a *shunkouliu* is a tall order. So why bother to try? Yet despite the odds, this barbed rhyme about New China's old guard can be tailored into a pleasing and meaningful shape in a language completely unrelated to its original tongue. Here's how it can be done, step by step.

1. Translated character for character
Hard hard bitter bitter four ten years
One morning return to untie release before
Already thus return to untie release before
Just-at year change fate in-fact for whom?

2. *Translated group for group*
   Strenuous, strenuous forty years
   One morning return to before Liberation
   Given that return to before Liberation
   In those days revolution in fact for whom?

3. *Explanation, sense for sense*
   An extremely strenuous forty years
   And one morning we [find ourselves having]
       returned to before Liberation
   And given that we've returned to before Liberation
   [We might ask] who, in fact, the revolution back in those
       days was for

4. *Plain translation*
   An extremely strenuous forty years
   And suddenly we're back to before Liberation
   And given our return to before Liberation
   Who, in fact, was the revolution for?

5. *Adding some rhythm*
   An extremely strenuous forty years
   And suddenly we're back to forty-nine,
   And since we've gone back to forty-nine
   Who, in fact, was it all for?

6. *Matching words to Chinese syllables*
   For forty long years ever more perspiration
   And we just circle back to before Liberation
   And speaking again of that big revolution
   Who, after all, was it for?

7. *Adding rhyme*
   Forty long years crack our spine
   Back we go to forty-nine
   Since we go to 'forty-nine
   Back then who was it all for?

8. *First polish*
   Forty years we bend our spine
   And just go back to forty-nine
   And having gone to forty-nine
   Whom back then was this for?

9. *Adaptation, with double rhyme*
   Blood sweat and tears
   For forty long years
   Now we're back to before
   Who the hell was it for?

10. *As a word rectangle (6 x 4)*
    We had sweat toil and tears
    For more than forty bloody years
    Now we're back to square one
    For whom was it all done?

11. *Isogrammatical lines (21 x 4)*
    Blood sweat and tears
    Over forty long years
    Now it's utterly over
    Who stole the clover?

12. *Sounded out in Chinese*
    Xin xin ku ku si shi nian
    yi zhao hui dao jie fang qian
    ji ran hui dao jie fang qian
    dang nian ge ming you wei shui

What's been done in the later versions of this translation is to exploit the flexibility of English to simulate artificially the patterned visual effect of a script whose appearance naturally represents patterned sound. Counting characters and spaces along the line isn't usually considered a translator's task, but it's really just one variant of the need in a whole variety of fields to make words fit shapes.

Strip cartoons are not redrawn when they are translated, and of the four colour plates used only the black/white one with the lettering is remade for international sales. The cartoon translator has to make his version fit physically into the bubble-spaces left blank by the three other plates. A very small amount of flexibility is provided by being able to alter the size of hand-drawn lettering – but limits are set by the requirement of legibility. The cartoon translator also has very little freedom to move meanings around between frames, since the captions must fit the picture, right down to the details of what the depicted characters are doing with their arms and hands. If you thought translating Proust might be difficult, just try *Astérix*:

This is the version invented by Anthea Bell, OBE, for the following original frame:

The 'Breton' cousin of the Gaulish heroes speaks a parody of schoolbook English in French, with word-for-word renderings of 'I say', 'a bit of luck' and 'shake hands'. Moreover, his name, *Jolitorax*, is a pun on 'fair chest', 'pretty thorax', which is not remotely funny in English. Anthea Bell deftly reinstates the caricatural nature of the representation of English in French by inserting 'Oh' and 'old boy', and she substitutes a rather better pun of her own for the name. Doing all that within the confines of a physical space that can only take so many letters makes this translation an exploit, a victory over language itself. But only slightly lesser feats are performed every day by professionals and amateurs the world over who translate Japanese manga into English or Belgian graphic novels into Portuguese, and so on. Graphic translation is much bigger business than literary fiction, and probably rivals the translation of cookery books in volume and turnover. Studying translated captions of works of this kind is an education in the flexibility of human languages and human minds. Nothing ever fits easily, but in the end a really surprising amount of form and content can be made to fit external constraints of non-linguistic (bubble size) and paralinguistic (gestural) kinds.

Subtitling is a smaller business, but the skills it engages are of the same kind. It has become conventional to regard average filmgoers as capable of reading only about 15 characters per second; and in order to be legible on a screen as small as a television set, no more than 32 alphabetic characters can be displayed in a line. In addition, no more than two lines can be displayed at a time without obscuring significant parts of the image, so the subtitler has around 64 characters including spaces that must be displayed for a few seconds at most to express the key meanings of a shot or sequence in which characters may speak many more words than that. The limits are set by human physiology, average reading speeds and the physical shape of the cinema screen. It's really amazing that it can be done at all.

A further constraint on subtitling is the convention that a subtitle may not bleed across a cut: if you have someone chatting to his neighbour on an aeroplane seat and then a cut to a shot of the plane landing, for example, the subtitle must disappear at or just before the cut, and the following caption may not appear before the next audio sequence begins. Consequently, a film has to be decomposed into the 'spots' in which subtitling may occur. The delicate job of 'spotting' (made a lot easier if the film distributor can provide a transcript of the voice track) may or may not be done by the translator hired to write the captions. Usually, at least two people are involved. It follows almost automatically from this that subtitles do not offer a translation of all the words spoken, and in particularly fast-talking films they can offer only a compression or a résumé.

Stringent formal constraints in film translation are believed to have had important retroactive effect on original work. Film-makers dependent on foreign-language markets are well aware of how little spoken language can actually be represented in writing on screen. Sometimes they choose to limit the volubility of their characters to make it easier for foreign-language versions to fit all the dialogue on the screen. Ingmar Bergman made two quite different kinds of films – jolly comedies with lots of words for Swedish consumption, and tight-lipped, moody dramas for the rest of the world. Our standard vision of Swedes as verbally challenged depressives is in some degree a by-product of Bergman's success in building subtitling constraints into the composition of his more ambitious international films. It's called the 'Bergman effect', and it can be observed in the early films of Istvan Szabó and Roman Polanski too.

The supposed Bergman effect in film may actually be only a 'keyhole' example of a much wider modern trend. Steven Owen has argued that some contemporary poets from China, for example, write in a way that presupposes the translation of their work into English – and that all writing in foreign languages that now aspires to belong to 'world literature' is built on writers' effective internalization of translation constraints.[1]

Subtitling into English is a very small part of the translation world because so few foreign films are screened in the USA. At present there are only two American companies that provide subtitling services (and neither of them do only that), and they rely on a loose network of translators whose main jobs are elsewhere. Paid derisory sums at piece rates, the tiny band of English-language subtitlers are among the least-loved and least-understood language athletes of the modern media world.

In many countries, dubbing is preferred. It is rarely done into English nowadays because American audiences insist on complete lip-synching, so that no trace remains of the foreignness of foreign-language films. To make a translation of speech such that when pronounced it matches the lip movements of the original speaker – measured in fractions of a second – is no trivial task. But it's not only the microseconds that count. The translated dialogue is also constrained by facial gestures and movements of the body, even when those are not the customary accompaniment of the words spoken in the target language. The writers of dubbing scripts are not just athletes, they are world-class gymnasts of words – but almost never credited with their achievements in the English-speaking world.

The popularity of English-language films worldwide means that most American and British films are dubbed in multiple versions for sale abroad. Dubbing skills are much more widely used and appreciated in German, Italian, Spanish and many other languages. One result of this asymmetry that is quite perceptible on screen is that perfect lip-synchronization is not always felt to be necessary by non-English-language audiences. American and Brazilian soap operas broadcast on Russian television channels frequently have voice tracks that bleed (when dialogue continues beyond the point at which the characters' lips stop moving) – but the voices of familiar actors are characteristically those of well-known 'dub stars' in the target tongue. Everyone in Germany knows the voice of 'Robert de Niro', for example, and knows also whose actual voice it is – that of Christian Brückner, a prize-winning star among audio-book readers too, nicknamed 'The Voice' in the German-language media press. Meryl Streep's German voice is that of Dagmar Dempe, for *all* her films; Gabriel Byrne has been voiced by Klaus-Dieter Klebsch throughout his career since 1981. German cinema-goers would be discombobulated if Russell Crowe, in his next blockbuster appearance, didn't have the voice that really is his – that of Thomas Fritsch.[2] The French voices of Homer and Marge Simpson, Philippe Peythieux and Véronique Augerau, have their pictures in newspapers.[3] In this respect as in others, English-speakers find in the language culture of almost any other country a truly foreign land.

In Palestine, Biblical Hebrew ceased to be a spoken language among Jews long before the Roman occupation. From perhaps as early as the fifth century BCE, Aramaic interpreters read out a translation of the words of the service *sotto voce*, just after or even while the rabbi was speaking or chanting the more ancient tongue. Eventually, the words of such Aramaic whisper-translations (called *chuchotage* in the modern world of international interpreters) were written down, mostly in small fragments, and these *targums* now provide precious linguistic and historical records for scholars of Judaism. For contemporary re-broadcasts of British and American television soaps and comedy programmes in East and Central European languages, the *targum* device – low-volume voice-over translation – has been reinvented. Lectoring, as it is now called, often astounds English-language visitors to Poland or Hungary. It doesn't make even a nod towards aural realism: a single voice speaks on behalf of all characters of both genders, and the original English-language sound remains clearly audible.

Lectoring is obviously cheaper and quicker to do than dubbing, as it requires a smaller team of translators and performers. The high volumes of English-language media imported into the smaller European countries would make it difficult to find all the linguistic trapeze-artists you would need to dub everything in lip-synch while the shows were still 'hot'. So lectoring is a rational solution – but its underlying justification is not economic at all.

As in the synagogues of Palestine and Syria long ago, lectoring is done for people who view the original language as endowed with prestige. English is nowadays seen as a cultural asset and an object of desire. Lectoring allows English-language learners to check that they have understood correctly, and to improve their English as they enjoy the film. The Hungarian viewer of *The Colbert Report* wants to experience authentic American comedy, and the lector – like an interpreter performing *chuchotage* at a high-level meeting of heads of state – serves primarily as a check on the viewer's grasp of the real thing. How much of Colbert's political satire can be truly grasped by a Hungarian viewer of a lectored episode is slightly beside the point: something gets through. Because the original has not been erased by translation, that something is better than naught.

Lectoring makes no attempt to fit form to form. But in a medium of much greater cultural distinction than TV and film even the wish to do so has been derided as futile and vain. Vladimir Nabokov is famous among students of translation for his thundering assault on the folly of trying to translate rhyme by rhyme. His notorious comments accompany his own annotated translation of Pushkin's novel in verse, *Eugene Onegin*. Any attempt to reproduce the wry, light, witty and rhythmical movement of the special form of the sonnet Pushkin used, Nabokov declared, was bound to misrepresent the poet's true meaning, and was therefore to be abhorred. Nabokov's views on poetry translation have coloured many arguments in the translation studies field with a peculiarly vituperative tone. What he said needs to be understood in context. It is unfortunate that Nabokov put his strong opinions in such absolute and radical terms as to distract attention from the real issues.

Attempts to render a poem in another language fall into three categories. (1) Paraphrastic: offering a free version of the original, with omissions and additions prompted by the exigencies of form, the conventions attributed to the consumer and the translator's ignorance. (2) Lexical (or constructional): rendering the basic meaning of words (and their order). This a machine can do under the direction of an intelligent bilinguist. (3) Literal: rendering, as closely as the associative and syntactical capacities of another language allow, the exact contextual meaning of the original. Only this is a true translation. (...) Can a rhymed poem like *Eugene Onegin* be truly translated with a retention of its rhymes? The answer is, of course, no. To reproduce the rhymes and yet translate the entire poem literally is mathematically impossible. [4]

This statement (mimicking and also reversing John Dryden's much earlier distinction between imitation, paraphrase and metaphrase) introduces Nabokov's own non-rhyming translation of Pushkin's novel, accompanied by an immensely long and learned, line-by-line commentary on the meanings of Pushkin's verses. The main work is not the translation at all, but Nabokov's appropriation of it through his inflated peritext. Master of style in two languages and a uniquely skilful crafter of translingual puns, Nabokov laid down his writer's mantle on the altar of Pushkin and adopted what he called 'the servile path'.[5] There's a profound reason for his frankly uncharacteristic modesty in this case. Who can rival Pushkin? No Russian can dream of doing such a thing – yet every Russian writer also dreams of unseating Pushkin from his throne. For the Russian writer that Nabokov still was twenty years after the adoption of English as his literary tongue, translating Pushkin was not a straightforward translation task.

Let's consider what the stakes were for Nabokov (but for no one else) in recasting Pushkin in English verse. It's safe to assume that Nabokov could have done so like no other had he let himself dare. He would have set himself up as Pushkin's rival. More than that: he would have written *Eugene Onegin* himself.

At much the same time as Nabokov started his plain prose version of Pushkin, Georges Perec read Herman Melville's story of a New York clerk, *Bartleby the Scrivener*. It seemed to him quite perfect, and he wished he had written it himself. But I can't do that! he explained in an interview, because Melville wrote it first.[6] The same sense of having been already out-written – of having been robbed in advance of a glory that could perhaps have been his – lies at the root of Nabokov's strange operation with Pushkin's sublime verse.

In fact, Nabokov had done some stanzas of *Onegin* into English verse in the 1950s already – but then turned around in fright. He could see he was not Pushkin. Later on, he adopted his servile path of pseudo-literal translation not because it was relevant to the study or practice of literary translation, but because it helped hide that embarrassing fact.

Nabokov's public lesson in poetry translation quoted above is threadbare and misleading. There are far more ways than three of translating fixed form. A 'paraphrase' is not the only alternative to a 'lexical' translation, and the latter can in no way even now be done directly by a machine. The 'literal' style Nabokov proposes and claims to use is just what anyone else would call plain prose. Nabokov's introduction to his exhaustive exploration of all the allusions and referential meanings of the words of Pushkin's novel tells us many interesting things (about Nabokov, about Russia, about language and style) but nothing about the translation of form.

Onegin has attracted many gifted translators, and there are several versions now available that give good approximations of Pushkin's verse. A second-hand copy of one of these, by Charles Johnson, published in 1977, fell into the hands of a polyglot Indian postgrad at Stanford around 1982, who was charmed and entranced by a whole novel in fourteen-line stanzas with alternating masculine–feminine rhymes in abab-ccddeffegg order and frequent use of enjambment. Vikram Seth decided to make this form his own. He composed a story of his own life in the same regular form. *The Golden Gate* – 'The Great California Novel' according to Gore Vidal – set Seth on the path to literary glory. Fifteen years later, *The Golden Gate* in its turn fell into the hands of an Israeli scholar, Maya Arad, who was entranced by the stanza form relayed to her by Seth from Charles Johnson's version of Pushkin, whose *Yevgeni Onegin* she then read in the original. She appropriated the form for her own novel in verse, *Another Place, a Foreign City*, published to great acclaim in Hebrew in 2003. Here is one of Arad's 355 stanzas translated into English by Adriana Jacobs. Though the rhymes have gone, old Onegin's zest for St Petersburg partying remains intact in twenty-first-century Tel Aviv:

Faster! Faster! No dawdling! Eat up!
Where will we go this time?
Who knows! The opera? The cinema?
The theater? Or a restaurant?
The city's riches seem endless
Until it loses consciousness.
Faster – draining every minute –
Until the hour hand strikes midnight.
Sleep? Too bad! We're still running
On full and the night is still young.
Let's go party! Let's find a club!
The night is tender and inviting.
December's here, can you believe?
It feels like spring in Tel Aviv!

If the formal constraints of *Eugene Onegin* can be used to tell stories of America and Israel, why can they not be used to equal poetic effect to tell the very story that Pushkin told? Nabokov claims this is 'mathematically impossible'. Mathematics has nothing to do with it. What he meant was that he wasn't going to try.

Gilbert Adair was faced with a challenge of no lesser 'mathematical impossibility' when he set out to translate Georges Perec's *La Disparition*, a novel written exclusively with French words and expressions that do not contain the letter *e*. Writing without the letter *e* is hard to do for more than a short paragraph because we are simply not accustomed to conceptualizing words in terms of the letters by which they are set down in writing. It takes time and effort to learn the trick – but once you have taught yourself to do it, you can say as much as Perec learned to say in French. And more! Adair decorated his translation, called *A Void*, with many quips and interpolations of his own, and replaced Perec's *e*-less parodies of famous French poems with *e*-less versions of well-known English-language verse:

> 'Sybil,' said I, 'thing of loathing – Sybil, fury in bird's
>   clothing!
> By God's radiant kingdom soothing all man's purgatorial
>   pain,
> Inform this soul laid low with sorrow if upon a distant morrow
> It shall find that symbol for – oh for its too long unjoin'd
>   chain –
> Find that pictographic symbol, missing from its unjoin'd
>   chain'
> Quoth that Black Bird, 'Not Again'

And my Black Bird, still not quitting, still is sitting, still is
   sitting
On that pallid bust – still flitting through my dolorous
   domain;
But it cannot stop from gazing for it truly finds amazing
That, by artful paraphrasing, I such rhyming can sustain –
Notwithstanding my lost symbol I such rhyming still sustain –
Though I shan't try it again!

Translators working in many languages in widely separated
cultural fields – manga, subtitles, political jingles, experimental fiction, poetry and popular verse – confront and overcome
stringent formal constraints. Moreover, the forms themselves
are often transported across historical, linguistic and cultural
space. These facts make it seem unwise to claim that anything
is impossible. The only impossible things in translation are
those that haven't been done.

A less prejudiced way of understanding the work that translators do is to look more closely at the effects of successful
matchings of strict form. Has Gilbert Adair improved Edgar
Allan Poe? How come that the very diluted version of the
Onegin stanza in Adriana Jacobs's translation of Maya Arad's
imitation of Vikram Seth's imitation of Charles Johnson's verse
translation of Pushkin resurrects something of the lightness
and joy of Onegin's youth? How has Anthea Bell made *Astérix*
even funnier in English than in French? And why did anyone
ever think that translating verse by verse was a dead end? The
truth is quite the opposite. When you have to pay attention to
more than one dimension of an utterance – when your mind
is engaged in multi-level pattern-matching pursuits – you find
resources in your language you never knew were there.

Of course there's never a match that is 100 per cent, because that's not the way of the world. Just as it would be silly to claim that high-quality tailoring is 'mathematically impossible' because we've never had a suit that was an absolutely perfect fit, it would be unwise to deny the possibility of translating form just because we've not yet done so in a way that is utterly impeccable in every respect.

13. *What* Can't *be* Said *Can't* be *Translated*: The Axiom of Effability

When the baggage carrousel comes to a halt and your suitcase isn't there, the weary traveller goes to the airline service desk and complains that your suitcase has been lost. The desk clerk quite reasonably asks for evidence – a baggage stub, for instance – and a detailed description of what has gone missing, so that it may more easily be found.

People who claim that poetry is what gets lost in translation could be asked to follow a like routine. Granted, there's no check-in desk for poetic effects, so the missing ticket stub can be excused. But it's not unreasonable to request a description of the missing goods. If you can't provide one, claiming that something called 'poetry' has been lost is like telling an airline it has mislaid an item that has no identifiable characteristics at all. It doesn't cut a lot of ice.

A reader who says that poetry is what has been lost in translation is also claiming to be simultaneously in full possession of the original (which is poetry) and of the translation (which is not). Otherwise there would be no knowing if anything has been lost, let alone knowing that it was poetry.

A good knowledge of the two languages involved isn't sufficient to justify the claim that what has been lost in translation is poetry. You could only make a convincing case if you knew both languages and their poetic traditions sufficiently well to be able to experience the full scope of poetic effects in both of them. Not many people meet the standard, but there's nothing unreasonable about the test.

You would have to meet this entrance requirement to declare a loss of poetry in either direction – in a translation from a foreign language into your own (say, on reading Chapman's version of Homer), or from your own language into a foreign one, if for example you wanted to say that the French or Spanish or Japanese version of John Ashbery's poem 'Rivers and Mountains' just doesn't move you as the English one does. Only if you have these skills in language and poetry can you make a credible claim that something has been lost; but even if you do have them, you will find it hard to tell the desk clerk just what it is.

It would not be relevant to your complaint to say that the relationship between sound and meaning is not the same in the translation as in the original. With the sounds changed because the language is different and the meaning preserved broadly if never precisely, the relationship between the two – a relationship all linguists since Saussure insist is an arbitrary one – must perforce be other.

The belief that the poeticalness of poetry is just that relationship between sound and sense is widespread in the teaching of English and other modern languages. However, it doesn't follow from this at all that once a poem is translated it has lost its poeticalness. The new poem in the new language representing and re-creating the poem in the old also possesses a relationship between its sound and its meaning. It is not the same as the original, but that is no reason – no reason at all – to claim that it is devoid of poetry. Of course, the new poem may be awful when the original was sublime. Few poets write sublime verse every time. But it stands to reason that the quality of a poem in translation has no relation to its having been translated. It is the sole fruit of the poet's skill as a poet, irrespective of whether he is also writing as a translator.

You may not like the poem by Douglas Hofstadter quoted at the start of this book on p. 6. You may like the poem by Clément Marot much more. But all that you could reasonably say about the difference is that Hofstadter is (in this instance) a less charming writer of poetry than Marot. If you didn't know that Hofstadter's trisyllabic verse transposes sentiments first expressed by someone else in a form that has a quite strict relationship to it, you might still not like it – but you wouldn't think of justifying your disappointment by saying that poetry is what has been lost in translation. And since that is the case – as it is the case with many lines of poetry you undoubtedly know in your own language without knowing they have semantic and formal correspondences to lines or stanzas written in another language before them – you can't justify your dislike of Hofstadter's translation by saying that its less-than-perfect quality is related to the way that poetry gets lost in translation. Exactly the same argument applies if you like Hofstadter's poem much more than you like Marot's. Or if you had been led to believe that Marot's French, far from being prior to it, had been inspired by 'Gentle gem . . .' In fact, for the vast majority of poems, the ordinary reader has few reliable ways of establishing whether or not and to what degree it can be counted as a translation. Poets have been imitators, plagiarists, surreptitious importers and translators since the beginning of time.

Dante, Du Bellay, Alexander Pope, Ludwig Tieck, August Wilhelm von Schlegel, Boris Pasternak, Rainer-Maria Rilke, Ezra Pound, Jacques Roubaud, Robert Lowell, C. K. Williams – think of a great poet, and you've almost certainly thought of a translator too. In the Western tradition there is no cut-off point between writing poems, writing translations and writing poems in translation. Poetic forms – the sonnet, the ballad, the rondeau, the pantoum, the ghazal – have migrated between languages as diverse as French, Italian, Russian, Farsi, English and Malay over the last 800 years. Poetic styles – romantic, symbolist, futurist, acmeist, surrealist – are common European properties, as typical of German as of Polish poetry. Every so-called poetic tradition is made of other traditions. Against the dubious adage that poetry is what is lost in translation we have to set the more easily demonstrable fact that, from many points of view, the history of Western poetry *is* the history of poetry in translation.

Despite this, towards the end of 2007 there were 666 web pages in English that quoted the adage that 'poetry is what is lost in translation';[1] and by April 2010, when I ran the search again, the tally had risen to 15,100. Even more stunning is that in all but a handful of cases this adage was attributed to the American poet Robert Frost. But nobody has ever been able to find Frost saying anything like it in his works, letters, interviews or reported sayings.[2] Like so many other received ideas about translation, this one turns out to have no foundation in fact.

All the same it is true that poetry provides translators with a task that is not only difficult, but in some senses beyond translation altogether. Like many people I have a great fondness for poems that I learned in my youth. I'm attached to them in a special way and treasure the very sound as well as the sense that they have. As I was a student at the time, I read poetry in foreign languages – mostly, in order to learn the language they were in. I struggled to understand them and probably for that reason they have stuck in my mind ever since.

Wer, wenn ich schrie, hörte mich denn
aus der Engel Ordnungen?
und gesetzt selbst es nähme
einer mich plötzlich ans Herz:
ich verginge von seinem
stärkeren Dasein.

For me, no English translation can have the same weight or familiarity or perfection or mystery – nor can any paraphrase in German. I cherish these sounds and words of a language I wanted to master and which I learned in part through the unscrambling and memorization of just these lines. The emotion that for me and me alone is wrapped up in the opening of Rilke's *Duino Elegies* derives from my past, and although I can tell you about it in this roundabout way, you can't share it directly with me. What can't be shared can't be translated, obviously enough. But that doesn't make the poem untranslatable for anyone else:

Who, if I cried, would hear me among the angels' hierarchies?
And even if one would take me suddenly to his heart
I would die of his stronger existence.

I might have translated the lines that way when I was learning German by learning Rilke. The English says pretty much what the German says. Is it poetry? That's a judgement everyone makes independently, by criteria which have absolutely nothing to do with the quality of the translation. This one, in fact, wasn't done by a poet or by a translator. It was done (with a little help from a friend) by a machine translation service available for free on the Internet.

Personal, quasi-biographical reasons for valuing poems are

probably very common. We may say that we treasure a line or a rhyme or a lyric 'in and for itself', but it's easier to demonstrate that poems often get attached to us, or we get attached to poems, in contexts that endow the attachment with personal emotion. It does not matter whether the focus of such affective investment and aesthetic appreciation was first written in another language and then translated, or written in the language in which we read it. In any case, you can't tell. A Russian reader may know that Pasternak's *быть или не быть – вот вопрос* is a translation, but if she hasn't been told, she has no way of assessing – and no reason to ask – whether it is more or less poetical than Shakespeare's 'To be or not to be, that is the question'.

We can grant that emotional relationships to things, including poems and forms of language, may be ultimately incommunicable. However, beliefs about the uniqueness and ineffability of emotional attachments have no relevance to the question of whether or not poetry is translatable. That is a much less abstruse matter.

Some people doubt that there are any affects or experiences that cannot be expressed, on the commonsensical grounds that we could say nothing about them and would therefore have no way of knowing if they existed for other people. The philosopher Ludwig Wittgenstein presumably meant to adopt an agnostic position on this issue in the famous last line of his *Tractatu*s when he wrote that 'what one cannot talk about must be left in silence'.[3] The infinite flexibility of language and our experience of shared emotion in reading novels and poems and at the cinema must also cast doubt on whether there are any human experiences that cannot in principle be shared. On the other side of this thorny tangle is the intuitive knowledge that what we feel is unique to us and can never be fully identified with anything felt by anyone else. That inexpressible residue of the individual is ineffable – and the ineffable is precisely what cannot be translated.

Should translation studies pay any attention to the ineffable, or to notions, intuitions, feelings and relations that are held to be unspeakable? Oddly enough, anguished engagement with the problem of ineffable essences is not at all characteristic of Bible translation, where you might expect to find mystical and religious issues taken seriously. Instead, it has preoccupied secular scholars of the twentieth century, from Walter Benjamin to George Steiner and Antoine Berman. I would rather approach this boundary of translation from the opposite direction, for it seems to me more important to realize not that the ineffable is a problem for translation, but that translation is one big problem for the ineffable.

Let's imagine a crew returning from a space flight at some future point in time. They've visited a faraway earth-like planet and are holding a press conference at NASA headquarters. They have something spectacular to announce. Yes, KRX29[1] is inhabited, they say, and what's more, the little green men that live on it have a language.

'How do you know that?' a journalist asks.

'Well, we learned to communicate with them,' the captain responds.

'And what did they say?'

'We can't tell you that,' the captain answers coolly. 'Their language is entirely untranslatable.'

It's not hard to predict how our descendants would treat the captain and his crew. They would have the astronauts treated for flight-induced insanity, and, if that proved to be unjustified, treat them as liars, or as laughing-stocks. Why so? Because if the inhabitants of the distant planet did have a language, and if the space crew had learned it, then it must be possible for them to say what the aliens had said. Must, not should: radically untranslatable sounds do not make a language simply because we could not know it was a language unless we could translate it, even if only roughly.

There are intermediate and problematic positions, of course. Not all utterances can be translated even when we are quite sure they are in a language. Egyptian hieroglyphs were indecipherable until two brilliant linguists, Thomas Young and Jean-François Champollion, worked out how to do it with the help of the Rosetta Stone. More generally still, we can't translate from languages we don't know. But to claim that something is in a language is to posit that, with the appropriate knowledge, it can be translated.[4]

Translation presupposes not the loss of the ineffable in any given act of interlingual mediation such as the translation of poetry, but the irrelevance of the ineffable to acts of communication. Any thought a person can have, the philosopher Jerrold Katz argued, can be expressed by some sentence in any natural language; and anything which can be expressed in one language can also be expressed in another. What cannot be expressed in any human language (opinions vary as to whether such things are delusional, or foundational) lies outside the boundaries of translation and, for Katz, outside the field of language too. This is his *axiom of effability*. One of the truths of translation – one of the truths that translation teaches – is that everything is effable.

Especially poetry. America and Britain are awash with poetry magazines, and every year small publishers put out hundreds of slim volumes containing poems in translation. Our present army of amateur poetry translators are keeping poetry alive. Poetry is not what is lost, but what is gained from their work.

An individual poem may have a quality that, for any one of

us, is so personal and unique that it might as well be ineffable, but the issue of unspeakable ideas arises much more obviously in a quite different domain. It is in our interactions not with works of genius but with other species that the ineffable looms before us like a brick wall.

On a short trip to South America Romain Gary picked up a 25-foot-long python, whom he called Pete the Strangler and then donated to a private zoo in California. When he was Consul General in Los Angeles, Gary used to go and see Pete in his cage.

> We would stare at each other in absolute astonishment, often for hours, deeply intrigued and wondering, awed and yet incapable of giving each other any kind of explanation about what had happened to us, and how and why it had happened, unable to help each other with some small flash of understanding drawn from our respective experiences. To find yourself in the skin of a python or in that of a man is such a mysterious and astonishing adventure that the bewilderment we shared had become a kind of fraternity, a brotherhood beyond and above our respective species.[5]

Maybe Romain Gary was right to feel that a python can no more imagine what it is like to be one of us than we can imagine what the mental world of a reptile is like – and it's typically generous of him to allow a fearful and pea-brained monster like Pete the Strangler a reciprocating intuition of the ineffability of human life. On the other hand, many non-human species – and perhaps all living things – do communicate with each other, and some most definitely communicate with us. Dog-owners, to take the most obvious example, easily distinguish between the meanings of different kinds of bark. But the dog-language we can access is a fairly limited thing. It consists of a small set of individual signals. Signals are generally treated as the isolated vehicles of specific pieces of information – 'There's an intruder in the house', 'Hello and welcome' or 'Take me for a walk.' They can't be combined with each other to produce more complex meanings – as far as we know, dog-language has no grammar. In addition, the set of signals possessed by domesticated dogs – like the signals used by monkeys or bees – is inherited and fixed. There's no new word formation going on in dogs, just as the signalling system of traffic lights is incapable of producing more than 'slow down', 'stop', 'get ready' and 'go'. (The green and orange 'get ready' combination is only used in the UK, as a politeness to drivers of ancient sports cars with gear-shift sticks.) Those are the main criteria by which human language is distinguished from all other kinds of communication by most modern theorists of language. Monkeys can only say what they have to say, and nothing else; whereas human signalling systems are forever changing, and always capable of adapting themselves to new circumstances and needs. These are fairly persuasive reasons for keeping animal language outside the field of 'language proper', and far away from the concerns of translation. But we could try to be as generous and as imaginative as Romain Gary. From such a perspective, human language may well seem to a dog to be just such a limited and inflexible signalling system as linguists imperiously declare dog-language to be.

From infancy to the onset of puberty, children of every culture have always known that animals have things to say to them. There's no folklore in the world that doesn't similarly break the alleged barrier between human and other.[6] But in our Western, script-based cultures, growing up (which is so heavily entwined with formal education that it might as well be treated as the same thing) involves unlearning the instinctive childhood assumption of communicative capacity in non-human species. No wonder our philosophers and priests have long insisted that language is the exclusive attribute of humans. That self-confirming axiom makes children not yet fully human, and in real need of the education they are given.

However, the traditional reasons for making a radical separation between 'signalling' and 'speaking' are not quite as hard-edged as they are often made to seem. Some animal signalling systems that have been studied (among ants and bees, for instance, where the channels are not by voice but by physical and chemical means) communicate what for us would be extremely elaborate geographic and social information. Whales emit long streams of haunting sounds when they gather in a school in waters off the coast of Canada. The tonal and rhythmic patterns of whale song are of such complexity as to make it quite impossible to believe that what we can hear (and pick up on instruments more sensitive than human ears) is just random noise. Even more striking is the recent behaviour of a group of monkeys in a Colchester zoo. They have added two new gesture-signals to their prior repertoire of communicative behaviour. Even if the 'monkey-sense' of these gestures is not absolutely certain, they are indisputably meaningful signs within the community, and indisputable inventions of the monkeys themselves.[7]

But what makes the communicative behaviour of ants, bees, whales, monkeys, dogs and parrots mysterious to us, what takes cross-species communication into the realm of the ineffable, is the fact that, save for a very limited range of noises from a limited range of long-domesticated pets, nobody knows how to translate 'animal signals' into human speech or vice versa. When and if we ever can translate non-human noises into human speech, species-related ineffabilities will evaporate like the morning haze.

Translation is the enemy of the ineffable. It causes it to cease to exist.

14. *How* Many *Words* Do *We* Have *for* Coffee?

The number of Londoners who can say 'good morning' in any of the languages spoken by the Inuit peoples of the Arctic can probably be counted on the fingers of one hand. But in any small crowd of folk in the capital or elsewhere you will surely find someone to tell you that 'Eskimo has one hundred words for snow.' The Great Eskimo Vocabulary Hoax was demolished many years ago,[1] but its place in popular wisdom about language and translation remains untouched. What are interesting for the study of translation are not so much the reasons why this blooper is wrong, but why people cling to it nonetheless.[2]

People who proffer the factoid seem to think it shows that the lexical resources of a language reflect the environment in which its native speakers live. As an observation about language in general, it's a fair point to make – languages tend to have the words their users need, and not to have words for things never used or encountered. But the Eskimo story actually says more than that. It tells us that a language and a culture are so closely bound together as to be one and the same thing. 'Eskimo language' and 'the [snow-bound] world of the Eskimos' are mutually dependent things. That's a very different proposition, and it lies at the heart of arguments about the translatability of different tongues.

The discovery and understanding of what makes different languages different and also the same has a curious modern history. In a lecture on the culture of the Hindus given in London to the Asiatic Society in 1786, an English judge in post in Bengal made a claim that overturned long-held beliefs in the superiority of the languages of the 'civilized' West and the lesser jargons of the rest of the world:

> The *Sanscrit* language, whatever be its antiquity, is of a wonderful structure; more perfect than the *Greek*, more copious than the *Latin*, and more exquisitely refined than either, yet bearing to both of them a stronger affinity, both in the roots of verbs and the forms of grammar, than could possibly have been produced by accident; so strong indeed, that no philologer could examine them all three, without believing them to have sprung from some common source, which, perhaps, no longer exists; there is a similar reason, though not quite so forcible, for supposing that both the *Gothic* and the *Celtic*, though blended with a very different idiom, had the same origin with the *Sanscrit*; and the old *Persian* might be added to the same family.[3]

This is generally reckoned to be the starter's gun in a fascinating race that lasted for much of the nineteenth century to map all the world's languages and to work out how they were related to each other, in 'family trees' each springing from a single progenitor. But even on the Old Continent some languages – Albanian, for example – didn't seem to have any close relatives at all, and one of them stuck out like a sore thumb. Basque, spoken in parts of northern Spain and south-western France, was just so different as to resist any kind of 'family' treatment. Wilhelm von Humboldt, elder brother of the great explorer Alexander, learned this strange idiom and wrote a grammar of it,[4] and in so doing developed the intellectual tools that in watered-down form ultimately led to the great Eskimo hoax.

Humboldt was struck not so much by the list of words that Basque has for different things as by the radically different structure of the language. It seemed to him that the grammar of Basque was the core and also the mirror of Basque culture. The observation was generalized into a theory: insofar as the formal properties of different languages are different from each other, each of the world's languages gives access to a different mental world.[5] Basque cannot be 'reduced' to French, German or anything else. It is just itself – the embodiment and the root cause of 'Basqueness'. Different languages, Humboldt saw, were different worlds, and the great diversity of natural languages on the planet should be seen as a treasure-house of tools for thinking in other ways.

The observation that 'other people just don't think the way we do' was made long before Humboldt's essays appeared, but for most of human history it was dealt with quite easily. In Greek eyes, 'barbarians' who couldn't speak Greek were obviously not capable of saying anything interesting. Similarly, for the grammarians of seventeenth-century France other languages could barely allow their speakers to engage in approximations to real thought, which was only truly possible in Latin and French. It must have taken great courage to express Humboldt's insight in the colonial era, when the otherness of other languages was generally thought to confirm the intellectual inferiority of people less fortunate than the French (or the Greeks, or the Romans, and so forth). Like Sir William Jones, the Bengal lawyer, Humboldt dared to assert that other languages offered speakers of 'West European' a wonderful mental resource.

Colonial expansion and conquest brought Europeans into contact with languages that were even more different than Basque. Some of them, dotted here and there around the globe in no obvious pattern, are very different indeed. Imagine a language in which there is no term for 'left' and right', but only expressions for laterality cast in terms of cardinal orientation. 'There's a fly on your south-west leg' might mean 'left' or 'right', depending on which way the speaker and his interlocutor are facing. (This is less unfamiliar than it first sounds: in contemporary Manhattanese we use cardinal orientation whenever we say 'go uptown from here'. To the dismay of many a lost tourist, that can't be translated into *tournez à gauche* or *à droite* unless you also know which of the four cardinal points you are facing.) Speakers of Kuuk Thaayorre (Cape York, Australia), for example, lay out ordered sets (say, numbers from 1 to 10, or photographs of faces aged from babyhood to maturity) not from 'left' to 'right' or the other way round, but starting from east – wherever east happens to be with respect to the table at which their anthropological linguist interrogator is seated.[6]

But languages can be even weirder than that. In Nootka, a language spoken on the Pacific coast of Canada, speakers characteristically mark some physical feature of the person addressed or spoken of either by means of suffixes, or by inserting meaningless consonants in the body of a word. You can get a very faint idea of how this works from vulgar infixes like 'fan-bloody-tastic' in colloquial English. In Nootka, however, the physical classes indicated by these methods are children, unusually fat or heavy people, unusually short adults, those suffering from some defect of the eye, hunchbacks, those that are lame, left-handed persons and circumcised males.[7]

One example of the radical difference of human languages was made famous by the American linguist Benjamin Lee Whorf, who had learned and studied many Native American languages. In the language of the Hopi (but also in quite a few others, distributed with no obvious pattern around the globe), there is a grammatical category called evidentials. For each noun-phrase, the grammar of Hopi marks not so much the categories of definiteness or indefiniteness ('a farmer', 'the farmer') but whether or not the thing or person referred to is within the field of vision of the speaker. 'The farmer I can see' has a different form from 'the farmer I saw yesterday', which is different again from the form of 'the farmer you told me about'. As a result, the English sentence 'The farmer killed the duck' is quite untranslatable into Hopi without a heap of information the English sentence doesn't give you – notably, whether or not the farmer in question is present to the speaker as he speaks and whether or not the duck is still lying around. If you speak Hopi, of course, and are speaking it to other Hopi-speakers in an environment where the duck and the farmer are either with you or not, you know the answers to these questions and can express your meaning grammatically. What you can't translate in a meaningful way is the sentence 'The farmer killed the duck' out of context. But as we have seen in earlier chapters, this kind of untranslatability holds for any decontextualized sentence in any language. The use of Hopi-type grammars as evidence of the untranslatability of tongues is really a red herring. Isolated, unsituated, written example-sentences are often more hindrance than help when it comes to thinking about translation.

However, the rapid exploration of the diversity of human languages in the nineteenth century also led people to wonder in what ways the languages of less developed peoples were different from 'civilized' tongues. Greek had 'produced' a Plato, but Hopi had not. Was this because so-called primitive languages were not suited to higher thought? Or was it the lack of civilization itself that had kept primitive languages in their irrational and alien states? Humboldt's hypothesis of an indissoluble bond between language and mentality could be used to argue either way round. Were there any general features of the languages of 'natives' that marked them off as a class from those few languages that were spoken by the civilized nations of the world? And if so, what were they?

Explorer-linguists observed quite correctly that the languages of peoples living in what were for them exotic locales had lots of words for exotic things, and supplied subtle distinctions between many different kinds of animals, plants, tools and ritual objects. The evidence piled up at a disproportionate rate simply because the explorers wanted to know first of all what all these strange objects in their new environment were called. Accounts of so-called primitive languages generally consisted of word-lists elicited from interpreters, or from sessions of pointing and asking for names.[8] But the languages of these remote cultures seemed deficient in words for 'time', 'past', 'future', 'language', 'law', 'state', 'government', 'navy' or 'God'. Trique, a language spoken in Mexico, has no word for 'miracle', for example, only specific words for 'heal the sick', 'part the waters' and so forth.[9] Consequently, it was difficult to translate into such languages most of the things that colonial administrators and missionaries needed to say. How could these strange folk be granted the benefits of civilization if the languages they spoke did not allow for the expression of civilized things? More particularly, the difficulty of expressing 'abstract thought' of the Western kind in many Native American and African languages suggested that the capacity for abstraction was the key to the progress of the human mind.

Savages will have twenty independent words each expressing the act of cutting some particular thing, without having any name for cutting in general; they will have as many to describe birds, fish and trees of different kinds, but no general equivalents for the terms 'bird', 'fish' or tree'.[10]

The 'concrete languages' of the non-Western world were not just the reflection of the lower degree of civilization of the peoples who spoke them, but the root cause of their backward state. By the dawn of the twentieth century, 'too many concrete nouns' and 'not enough abstractions' became the conventional qualities of 'primitive' tongues.

That's what people actually mean when they repeat the story about Eskimo words for snow. The multiplicity of concrete terms 'in Eskimo' displays its speakers' lack of the key feature of the civilized mind – the capacity to see things not as unique items, but as tokens of a more general class. *We* can see that all kinds of snow – soft snow, wet snow, dry snow, *poudreuse*, melting snow, molten snow, slush, sleet, dirty grey snow, brown muddy snow, banks of snow heaped up by wind and snowbanks made by human hand, avalanches and ski-runs, to name but fourteen – are all instances of the same phenomenon, which we call 'snow'; 'Eskimos' see the varieties, not the class. (This isn't true of real Inuit people, only of the Eskimos who figure in the Great Eskimo Vocabulary Hoax.

Translation between 'civilized' and 'primitive' languages distinguished in this way was clearly impossible. The solution was to teach colonial subjects a form of language that would enable them to acquire civilization, and the obvious tool to carry out the *mission civilisatrice* was the language of the imperial administrators themselves. In some cases, as in the Spanish conquest of the Americas, the impoverished resources of native languages were seen as such a threat to the spread of civilization that the languages and their written records had to be eradicated. But the destruction of the Maya codices wasn't solely an expression of naked power, religious fervour and racism.[11] The suppression of lesser tongues was not a policy reserved by the Spanish for other continents – it was already the European norm. France had already begun its long campaign to stop people speaking anything that was not French within its own borders. Breton, Basque, Provençal, Alsatian, Picard, Gascon and many other rural *patois* were almost hounded out of existence by laws and institutions over a period of several hundred years. The long pan-European drive towards 'standard languages' was powered not only by political will, economic integration, urbanization and other forces at play in the real world. It also expressed a deeply held belief that only some languages were suited to civilized thought.

What then can it mean to 'think in Hopi'? If it means anything, can it be called 'thought'? The linguist Edward Sapir came up with a revolutionary answer in the early part of the last century. Breaking with millennial practice and prejudice, he declared that all languages were equal. There is no hierarchy of tongues. Every variety of human language constitutes a system that is complete and entire, fully adequate to performing all the tasks that its users wish to make of it.

Sapir didn't argue this case out of political correctness. He made his claims on the basis of long study of languages of many different kinds. The evidence itself brought him to see that any attempt to match the grammar of a language with the culture of its speakers or their ethnic origins was completely impossible. 'Language', 'culture' and 'race' were independent variables. He turned the main part of Humboldt's legacy – European linguistic nationalism – upside down.

Sapir showed that there is nothing 'simple' about the languages of 'simple' societies – and nothing especially 'complex' about the languages of economically advanced ones. In his writings on language he showed like no one before him just how immensely varied the forms of language are, and how their distribution among societies of very different kinds corresponds to no overarching pattern. But he did not reject every part of the inheritance of Humboldt's study of Basque. Different languages, because they are structured in different ways, make their speakers pay attention to different aspects of the world. Having to mark presence or absence in languages that have evidentials (see p. 164) or being obliged to mark time in languages of the Western European type lays down what he called 'mind grooves' – habitual patterns of thought. The question for translation (and for anthropology) is this: can we jump the grooves and move more or less satisfactorily from one 'habitual pattern' to another?

The view that you can't ever really do this has become known as 'the Sapir–Whorf hypothesis', despite the fact that Edward Sapir never subscribed to the idea. The trouble with the simple form of this misnamed prejudice – that translation is impossible between any two languages because each language constructs a radically different mental world – is that if it were true you would not be able to know it. The parable of the NASA captain's report of an alien language, given on p. 155, is one way to show how flawed the 'Sapir–Whorf hypothesis' really is. A more sophisticated version of the same line of thinking runs up against equally powerful blocks. If we grant that different languages provide different kinds of tools for thinking but allow for substantial overlaps – without which there could be no translation – we are left with the idea that there are just some things in, let us say, French, which can never be expressed in English, and vice versa. There would then be an area of 'thinking in French' that was 'ineffable' in any other tongue. That contradicts the axiom of effability, which, as we argued on p. 156, is the sine qua non for translation to exist. It makes no difference to the argument against it whether the ineffable is held to be an attribute of God or of poetry, or a property of French.

Sapir actually had much more interesting things to tell us about languages and the way they relate to social and especially intellectual life. Greek and Latin have served as the vehicles of sophisticated thinking that deals in abstract entities. Both have grammatical features that make it easy to create abstract nouns from verbs, adjectives and other nouns. A strong trace of the grammatical facility for creating abstract entities in classical languages can be seen in those large parts of the English vocabulary that have Latin and Greek roots: human⇨humanity, just⇨justice, civil⇨civility, translate⇨translation, calculus⇨calculate⇨calculation, and so forth. Sapir's point was that instead of saying that Latin and Greek are well suited to abstract thought, we should rather say that abstract thought is well suited to Greek and Latin, and view the particular kinds of philosophical discourse that were developed by their speakers as a consequence of the grammar they used. The mind-grooves laid down by the forms of a language are not prison walls, but the hills and valleys of a mental landscape where some paths are easier to follow than others. If Plato had had Hopi to think with, he would not have come up with Platonic philosophy, that's for sure – and that's probably not a merely retrospective illusion based on the observable fact that there's no Hopi-speaker who thinks he is Plato. Hopi thinkers think something else. That does not make Hopi a primitive language unsuited to true thought. It means that speakers of what Sapir called 'Average West European' are poorly equipped to engage in

Hopi thought. To expand our minds and to become more fully civilized members of the human race, we should learn as many different languages as we can. The diversity of tongues is a treasure and a resource for thinking new thoughts.

If you go into a Starbuck's and ask for 'coffee' the barista most likely will give you a blank stare. To him the word means absolutely nothing. There are at least thirty-seven words for coffee in my local dialect of Coffeeshop Talk (or *tok-kofi*, as it would be called if I lived in Papua-New Guinea). Unless you use one of these individuated terms, your utterance will seem baffling, or produce an unwanted result. You should point this out next time anyone tells you that Eskimo has a hundred words for snow. If a Martian explorer should visit your local bar and deduce from the lingo that Average West Europeans lack a single word to designate the type that covers all tokens of small quantities of a hot or cold black or brown liquid in a foam cup, and consequently pour scorn on your language as inappropriate to higher forms of interplanetary thought – well, now you can tell him where to get off.

15. *Bibles* and *Bananas*: The Vertical Axis of Translation Relations

Let's start with the maths. For any three languages there are 3 x 2 = 6 different translation relations. Check it out: French⇨Russian, Russian⇨French; French⇨German, German⇨French; Russian⇨German and German⇨Russian. Between any four there are 4 x 3 = 12; for n languages there are $n*(n-1)$ directions of translation possible. So since there are approximately 7,000 known languages in the world, there are 24,496,500 pairs of languages between which translation could in principle take place in either direction, giving rise to nearly 49 million potentially separate translation practices, each with its own tools and conventions. Translation is a universal capacity of human societies, and a level playing field of that size cannot be ruled out on purely theoretical grounds. In reality, however, the number of language pairs with established practices of translation is infinitesimal compared to all those that could exist.

Translation does not happen every which way nowadays and never has. But in which ways does it happen? The fundamental answer, though a very broad one, is that it happens either UP or DOWN. As these are technical terms of my own invention, I've put them in small capitals.

Every human language serves as a full means of communication for some community, and in that sense there is no hierarchy between them. But acts of translation, which are rarely isolated events, typically exploit and support an asymmetrical relationship between source and target tongues.

Translation UP is towards a language of greater prestige than the source. The prestige may be the fruit of ancient tradition – as it was when Akkadian was translated into Sumerian in the Assyrian era, for example, or when translation into Latin was used to spread news of Marco Polo's adventures far and wide (see p. 204). At other times UP may be towards a language with a larger readership – typically, when the target tongue is used, like French in nineteenth-century Russia, as a vehicle of intercultural communication. It may also simply be the language of the conquerors, or of a people with greater economic power, such as Russian in the Central Asian lands in the period of the USSR. Prestige can also be located in a language because it is the preferred vehicle of religious truths. Arabic, Latin and Sanskrit among others have played this role at different times.

Translation DOWN is towards a vernacular with a smaller audience than the source, or towards one with less cultural, economic or religious prestige, or one not used as a vehicular tongue. Translation from German into Hungarian during the dual kingdom of the Austro-Hungarian Empire, for example, was DOWN, as is translation from English nowadays into any other tongue.

The rank order of languages when seen as pairs is extremely hard for any individual act of translation to shift, but it is not stable over long periods of time. Sumerian, Greek, Syriac, Latin, English and French, to take obvious examples, have seen their places in the pecking order change dramatically over the centuries. In addition, the ranking is often not all-encompassing. In specific fields, the relationship can be reversed or substantially modified. The standing of German as the language of a prestigious philosophical tradition means that shifting Kant, Hegel or Heidegger into English (or

French) is usually handled by translators as if they were translating DOWN; the translations of French novels into English in the nineteenth century exhibited the most obvious signs of that same direction of travel.

What distinguishes translating UP from translating DOWN is this. Translations towards the more general and more prestigious tongue are characteristically highly adaptive, erasing most of the traces of the text's foreign origin; whereas translations DOWN tend to leave a visible residue of the source, because in those circumstances foreignness itself carries prestige. When Marcel Duhamel launched the *Série noire* crime fiction series in Paris just after the Second World War, for example, he ensured that the translations of the American novels he aimed to make popular in France used plenty of Americanisms in French. He went further: he insisted that his French-language authors (who provided more than half the texts) adopt American-sounding pseudonyms to deceive readers into thinking they were getting the real thing.

However, the complexity and contradictions of language hierarchies are most richly illustrated by the history of Bible translation – in the West, to begin with, but subsequently worldwide.

Bible translation got off to a slow start. The first foreign-language version of the Jewish Torah was the Septuagint, written in *koiné* Greek around 240 BCE (see p. 107). Other Greek-language versions followed, but it was not until shortly before the start of the Christian era that it came into Latin, around the same time that the Jews themselves began writing down the oral translations they had long practised to make their holy texts accessible in Aramaic. Five centuries later there were still only 11 languages possessing versions of the Old and New Testaments (Greek, Latin, Aramaic, Syriac,

Coptic, Armenian, Georgian, Old Gothic, Ge'ez and Persian); and five more centuries were needed for the total to grow to 19, around the end of the first millennium. By the time printing was invented in the late fifteenth century, there were maybe 50; by 1600 CE there were 61, by 1700 there were 74, and by 1800 there were 81. A remarkable number, admittedly, but small change compared to what happened thereafter. In the course of the nineteenth century, more than five new languages were added every year, bringing the total to 620 by the turn of the twentieth century. Then things really began to shift. On average, one new Bible translation was completed *every month* between 1900 and 1999, and so, by the year 2000, the number of languages possessing all or part of the Old and New Testaments in translation shot up to 2,403.[1]

Despite its roots in ancient and medieval times, in quantitative terms Bible translation is a preponderantly twentieth-century affair. Throughout many decades of that era, much of it was overseen by one man, Eugene Nida, was treated as the most respected authority on Bible translation in the world.

Nida never translated the Bible himself. He worked as linguistic consultant to the United Bible Societies, helping to exercise quality control over a great number of Bible translation projects that arose after the Second World War. In that capacity, he lectured all over the world, and sought to explain in layman's terms some of the contentious issues of language and culture that have been tackled from a different perspective in chapters of this book.

Nida made a distinction between two kinds of equivalence in translation: formal equivalence, where the order of words and their standard or common meanings correspond closely to the syntax and vocabulary of the source; and dynamic equivalence (later renamed functional equivalence), where the translator substitutes for source-text expressions other ways of saying things with roughly the same force in the culture of the receiving society. He was an unashamed proponent of the view that, as far as the Bible was concerned, only dynamic equivalence would do. In that sense he was renewing the translator's defence of the right to be free and not 'literal'. Nida's overriding concern, which is also that of the United Bible Societies, was that the holy scriptures be brought to all people – and that what is brought to them be the scriptures, as nearly as can be managed. A Bible that makes no immediate sense in the target language, or Bibles that can only be read or understood by trained theologians or priests, are not well suited to missionaries' aims. Nida's preference for dynamic equivalence was in the first place an encouragement to translators to sacrifice whatever was necessary to 'get the message across'. As he titled one of the chapters of the handbook he co-authored with Jan de Waard: 'Translating Means Translating Meaning'.[2]

As explained on p. 172, this approach is characteristic of translating up. Yet the source languages of the scriptures – Hebrew, Greek and Latin – are still, without doubt, and especially for adherents to the faith, much nearer the essence of the texts' religious meaning than any of the vernacular translations they could turn out. Seen in this light, twentieth-century Bible translation ought to be the largest case-study we have of translating DOWN – translating from a language of prestige to a local idiom, from a 'general language of truth' to a specific vernacular. However, the majority of Bible translations that Nida oversaw were not from Greek or Latin (and Hebrew even less), but from the American versions of the Bible in English, and from two influential Spanish versions, the Reina-Valera of 1909, and a simplified text called *Dios*

Habla Hoy ('God Speaks Today').[3] These are of course the 'general languages' or 'dominant idioms' in many parts of the world nowadays.

Retranslation (translating a text that is already a translation) is not a modern departure for the Bible. Only the Aramaic *targums* and the Greek Septuagint were translated directly from Biblical Hebrew. The Armenian, Coptic, Old Latin, Syriac, Ge'ez, Persian and Arabic translations of the Old Testament were done from the Greek; the Georgian Bible was probably first translated from Armenian (though it may have also used the Syriac and the Greek); the Old Gothic likewise, probably with some reference to Latin versions. Jerome used Hebrew and Aramaic texts to complement the Septuagint for his long-influential version of the Old Testament in Latin, and the original Greek for the New Testament. Early German translations of the Bible in the fifteenth century were done from Jerome's Latin, as were the first Bibles in Swedish. Martin Luther was the first among European translators to use Greek and Hebrew as source texts; his German formulations were, however, copied by many translators into other European languages, who sometimes used Luther's version as their sole source (the Icelandic Bible is a case in point). The Bible was not translated into French until the sixteenth century – from Latin and Italian, not from Hebrew or Greek. The first complete English Bible, by Miles Coverdale, also had no contact with the original languages, but drew on Jerome's Latin, a later Latin translation by Erasmus and Luther's German. The use of modern European translations to retranslate the scriptures into nearly 2,000 mostly non-European tongues in the last hundred years is therefore no innovation in the long history of these texts, but it raises issues of great magnitude. It confirms and drives the perception of

English and Spanish, not of Hebrew or Greek, as 'languages of truth'; their status as the source for Bible translation is hard to separate from the political, economic and cultural status of the speakers of these two vehicular tongues.

Translating DOWN from a dominant to a vernacular language is typically accompanied by substantial imports of vocabulary and syntactic constructions from the source. Such was the process that enriched and expanded Syriac when it was used as a vehicle for the preservation of Greek medicine and astronomy. Such was the process that altered and enhanced French when it became the target language for mass translation from Italian in the sixteenth century. Such was the process that Schleiermacher strongly recommended for German as the recipient of the treasures of Greek philosophy in the early nineteenth century. Target-language modification was also, in fact, the fate of English at the hands of the translation committee established by King James I. 'The Lord Our God', for instance, is less a Jacobean way of expressing the first-person plural possessive in English than it is a calque of Hebrew grammar: the corresponding expression in the Torah, יי אלהינו, pronounced 'adonai ilehenu', can be worded out as 'God, the Lord-Our'.

The spread of English-language terms in the field of electronic communications into almost all the vehicular languages of the world (*computer, internet, to surf, hardware, USB* and so forth) is a contemporary reminder of what a language hierarchy is. The French would rather not be so reminded, and their government set up the *Commission générale de terminologie et de néologie* in 1996 to push back the tide of foreign words. It may have more success than King Canute, but I wouldn't bet on it.

Target-language modification through translations of

prestigious works from a language of higher status may in some instances be imposed on the receiving cultures, but in most cases it is not. More characteristically, it arises from the wishes and needs of the translating community itself. (It hardly needs pointing out that there were no 'Hebrews' around to spur King James's translators to bend English into shapes more typical of Hebrew grammar.) But Bible translation in the twentieth century is a different kettle of fish. The agents of modern Bible translation into indigenous languages are closely involved in the missionizing project itself, and many of them are American as well.

They work into languages they have learned long after the critical age of language acquisition – they are what we called L2 translators in earlier chapters of this book. They therefore run the same kind of risk of creating unintentionally comical or offensive effects as do the creators of international signage in Croatian seaside hotels. Eugene Nida's main concern was to try to ensure they did not.

Bible translation into non-European languages, which began with European colonial expansion as early as the seventeenth century, was highly inventive from the start. Albert Cornelius Ruyl, a junior trader in the Dutch East India Company with unusual linguistic skills, first taught himself Malay – a regional contact language – when he began his service in Sumatra. He wrote a grammar, then translated the Gospel of Matthew from Dutch. Ruyl altered and adapted Malay as he went along, using words from Arabic, Portuguese and Sanskrit when he knew no corresponding term in Malay. But he also did something more.

Where the Dutch version of Matthew talks of a fig tree, Ruyl's version has *pisang* – which means a banana tree in Malay. The substitution was justified by the fact that there were no figs on Sumatra. But what really marks it as special is that it signals a new ideology in the age-old business of translating DOWN. Ruyl initiated the principle of cultural substitution which Nida would theorize and promote three centuries later.

From Hebrew into Greek, from Greek into Latin, from Syriac into Arabic and so forth, when the receiving language didn't have a word for some item, it got a new one – the word of the source language, adapted to its new linguistic home. Not so from Dutch into Malay. The receiving language did not get a new word for a new thing. It got a substitute thing, with its existing word.

Douglas Hofstadter once asked: 'How do you say "jazz-ercise" in Aramaic?' He meant it as a mind game, not as a question about what the small group of Aramaic-speakers in contemporary Jerusalem would say if they joined a gym club and found themselves doing aerobics to a Dave Brubeck track. There is no reason why speakers in the ancient world should have had a word for a thing they did not have, but speakers of Aramaic or any other language today would have to choose between one of three ways of making up a word for 'jazz-ercise'. They might import the word as it stands, making whatever modifications in form that are needed to allow it to function in a sentence. Or they might take two Aramaic words with meanings analogous to 'syncopated music' and 'exercise' and run them together to make a new compound in imitation of the English. Finally, they might take an existing Aramaic word and expand its use to include musical stretch-and-jump. Those are the three ways in which new things can be represented in any receiving language – by a foreignism (the first option), a calque (second option) or semantic expansion. Each of them changes the target language by one item, with possible repercussions over time on the use and form of other words. But cultural substitution would simply put some other, more or less analogous activity current in the world of Aramaic-speakers in the place of 'jazzercising'.

That's what Ruyl did to Malay: he didn't invent a new word for a new thing ('fig'), he used an existing word to say something else ('banana'). It worked only because there are no figs on Sumatra. When the referent of a term is available, such as a musical gym in an Aramaic-speaking quarter of Tel Aviv, cultural substitution can't work as a way of translating an exotic term.

Imagine: Sir Walter Raleigh presents Queen Elizabeth I with an amazing root vegetable he's brought back from the New World, and beseeches Her Majesty to reward him for the discovery of . . . the turnip. It wouldn't have worked because it was not a turnip. When you have a potato in your hand, you can't call it by the name of anything that you could be holding in your other hand. 'Cultural substitution' is a naming and translation device that is suited exclusively to things that aren't there. You can't just expand the meaning of 'turnip' by using it to name things that aren't turnips. Similarly, when Ruyl wrote *pisang* for 'fig', he did not expand the meaning of the Malay term. No new class of tree suddenly arose that included both bananas and figs. What this kind of cultural substitution really says is: you can't really understand, and we're not going to try to explain. Have a banana instead.

Analogy-based substitutions are frequent in non-European Bible translations. 'White as snow' in the Bible text may become 'white as a cockatoo's feathers' in languages spoken in areas where snow has never been seen, or 'white as a cotton boll' in some languages of South America. In Asmat, a language spoken in a swampy area of Indonesian Papua where houses are all built on stilts, the parable of the wise builder who builds on stone and the foolish builder who builds on sand turns into a story about a wise builder 'who builds a house on stilts made of iron wood . . . while the foolish builder is the one who builds a house on stilts made of white wood' (white wood being used only for temporary hunting shacks, because it rots quickly).[4]

Nida reports examples of even more extensive cultural transpositions he encountered and approved. In many parts of Africa, he says, casting branches in the path of a chief expresses contempt, whereas in the Gospels it is done to mark Jesus's return to Jerusalem as a triumph. Similarly, fasting is not easily seen as a form of devotion in many parts of the world – it is more likely to be understood as an insult to God.[5] Revision of the Gospel's account of Palm Sunday and of the role of fasting in the Old Testament is both absolutely necessary to avoid giving the wrong message to African readers and at the same time impossible without profoundly altering the story being told. Nida's job was to help produce texts that were functionally equivalent to the Bible considered not as sacred script, but as the repository of a sacred story.

Nida also promoted the use of native speakers of indigenous languages as full partners and wherever possible as prime movers in Bible translation projects. That's because reliable judgements about the appropriateness of cultural substitutes are not easily made by L2 speakers. If acceptability is the paramount aim, then L1 speakers are in a much better position to invent and adapt. Their intuitions about acceptability are the ones that count.

Nida's insistence on adaptive translation can be understood in two ways. First, it follows from the beliefs he shares with other Christians that a religious truth must be accessible to all humans, whatever their culture and language. Equally important, however, is Nida's wish to respect the cultures that Bible translators inevitably affect and alter by their work. Adaptive translation is a compromise between these two contradictory aspirations. It helps the receiving culture accept and integrate something completely new by using terms that are already familiar.

Nida's position is not popular among translation studies scholars, particularly those mainly concerned with the translation of literary works. They might point out how preposterous it would be in the translation of an oral epic from an African language into English to replace 'banyan' by 'chestnut' on the grounds that banyan trees are nowhere to be seen in England's green and pleasant land. Such attacks miss the main point, which is this: translating UP doesn't normally use the same techniques as translating DOWN. There's no good reason to think that a single undifferentiated set of practices or principles should or ever will hold sway over the whole vast field of translation. The hierarchical relationship between source and target isn't the sole determinant of the methods that translators may use, but it affects what they do and how they do it quite fundamentally.

Cultural substitution, for example, can at times be used in translating UP, but to different effect. Arthur Waley's influential translations of Chinese and Japanese poetry and prose give us English-sounding 'Lords' and 'Ladies' in place of altogether different social ranks in the ancient societies of the Far East. Waley's reasons for making these substitutions are as complicated as Nida's approval of 'cockatoo' in place of 'snow'. On the one hand, 'Lords and Ladies' protects English-language readers from having to acquire too much arcane information about a culture they don't especially wish to learn about. On the other hand, the use of domestic markers of high status reinvests the foreign society represented with recognizable signals of prestige, and thus makes it worth learning about. Translators' strategic decisions are always two-edged swords.

The technique that seems furthest removed from cultural substitution is the intentional alteration of the target language. Bible translation once again provides us with some extreme examples. In the twentieth century, several scholarly Bible retranslation projects have sought to restore the foreignness of the scriptures for readers already familiar with them in more adaptive forms. The Context Group of the Society of Biblical Literature, for example, argues that 'the Bible is not a Western Book' and that it was 'not written for us'.[6] Members of the group point out that because language cannot be isolated from the social context in which it is embedded, and because the ancient Middle East is a completely alien land, the Hebrew Bible cannot be fully represented in a translation that makes ordinary sense today.[7] Their programme of defamiliarizing biblical texts follows in the footsteps of Martin Buber and Franz Rosenzweig, Jewish theologians who retranslated the Old Testament into German in the 1920s so as to restore what they saw as the poetic, religious and communal characteristics of their faith as it was in the beginning.[8] To achieve this, they reproduce the word-repetitions and patterns of sound found in the Hebrew at the expense of easy legibility. Thus where Exodus 3:14–15 in a barely updated version of the King James translation of 1611 is fairly accessible:

> And God said unto Moses, I AM THAT I AM; and he said, Thus shalt thou say unto the children of Israel, I AM hath sent me unto you. And God said moreover unto Moses, Thus shalt thou say unto the children of Israel, The Lord God of your fathers, God of Abraham, the God of Isaac, and the God

of Jacob, hath sent me unto you: this is my name for ever, and
this is my memorial unto all generations.

The Buber–Rosenzweig translation, which respects the line
breaks of the Hebrew as well as many other features of that
ancient tongue, would sound something like this if it were put
into English in like manner:

> God said to Moshe:
> I will be-there howsoever I will be-there.
> And he said:
> Thus shall you say to the Children of Israel:
> I AM THERE sends me to you.
> And God said further to Moshe:
> This shall you say to the Children of Israel:
> HE,
> the God of your fathers
> the God of Avraham, the God
> of Yitzhak, and the God of Yaakov,
> sends me to you.
> That is my name for the ages,
> that is my title
> generation unto generation.[9]

Both Nida and Buber were concerned with translating from
a 'language of truth' into a vernacular – both were translating
DOWN, as were Luther, Ruyl and King James's translators.
One major difference between them lies not in the direction
of travel but in the broader location of their particular language pairs in the world hierarchy of tongues: Hebrew,
German, Dutch and Malay occupy places that are not interchangeable with each other. But the main difference is what
the translators thought their respective audiences needed and

desired. For Ruyl, seventeenth-century Sumatrans needed to learn the story and its overall meaning; but in Buber's mind what German Jews in the Weimar Republic needed to learn was what the authentic, original community of Jews had believed. These differences produce curious flips and loops in translation history, whose course has been more sinuous than any theory can easily accommodate.

Buber's 'foreignizing' approach is characteristic of those major programmes of translations DOWN – from Greek into Syriac, Italian into French, and Latin into most Western languages – that have left lasting imprints on the receiving language. Ruyl's and Nida's strongly adaptive approach, on the other hand, is obviously more often found in translations UP – from vernaculars, be they regional or exotic, into central languages that don't want to know too much about the source. Modern Bible translation has thus produced a reversal of age-old trends.

By insisting on as much respect for the (foreign) target culture as possible, Nida's recommended style of translating scriptures DOWN applies procedures more commonly found in translations UP; whereas the exoticizing style of Buber (and, after him, of Henri Meschonnic in France), which has been more typically applied to translation DOWN in the last few thousand years, is motivated by scrupulous respect for the radical difference of a now almost inaccessible culture and form of speech.

Both methodologies seek to pay respect where respect is due: there is no conflict in overall motivation. But where Buber has little respect for the linguistic norms of contemporary German, Nida doesn't think that the specific qualities of snow matter very much when set beside the overriding aim of getting the message across.

The degree to which either of these ideas of translation can affect the receiving language and culture doesn't really depend on their intrinsic merits as translation methodologies or on the brilliance of their users. It depends on volume. Leaving the special features of Bible translation to the side, we can say that the reciprocal flow of translations between any two languages is never equal and in most cases utterly unbalanced. The direction of flow is the key to understanding which way is UP, and what happens down below.

16. *Translation* Impacts

Some Bible translations have had profound and lasting effects on the receiving language. Luther's Bible is considered the first monument of modern German, and the King James Bible remains an inescapable reference point in the history of English. However, such impacts are not typical of translation in general. Individual translators do not often produce the smallest ripple in the target culture. However, continuing waves of translated works in particular fields always leave the receiving language in a significantly different shape.

That was clear to Friedrich Schleiermacher when he set out to explain how the Greek classics should best be translated into German. It wasn't any one book that would make the difference, he insisted, but only large-scale translation of Greek philosophy and drama that could help the German language 'to flourish and develop its own perfect power through the most varied contacts with what is foreign'.[1] But depending on the relation between the original and the receiving society, the target may get hit in radically different ways.

English-language translations of French critical theory from the 1960s to the 1990s, for example, have made abstract discourse about literature in English sound much more like French than it ever did before. In the reverse direction, the language of celebrity journalism in French has been quite transformed by the mass import of English-language styles: *la presse people* (pronounced *pi-pol*) exhibits unmistakable signs of what is now denounced as the homogenization of tongues.

It's not just a matter of vocabulary. A small but quite pro-found change in the way dialogue is introduced in Swedish narrative can be traced back to its source in translations of English-language novels.[2] Constructions of the following type are ten a penny in modern English fiction of all kinds:

1. 'Don't try,' she said with disdain.
2. 'It doesn't matter,' he said calmly.
3. 'And now you must go to sleep,' he said in a tone that was friendly but authoritative.
4. 'Get out,' said Frank abruptly.

The grammar of Swedish does not make this kind of construc-tion impossible. However, placing a verb of saying together with a modifier ('with disdain', 'calmly', 'abruptly') after direct speech is fairly unusual in Swedish novel-writing style. In a repre-sentative corpus of thirty novels written originally in Swedish, the construction occurs 64 times, but in a parallel corpus of about the same size consisting of novels translated into Swed-ish from English, it occurs 484 times. This 'fingerprint' of English – of one of the English novel's habitual 'dialogue props' – has now been integrated into original writing in Swedish, where it is characteristic not of literary fiction in general, but of detective fiction in particular. It's one of those small yet sig-nificant mergings of language and style that are often attacked as unintended results of globalization. But Swedish detective fiction has had sweet revenge. Its language may have been infil-trated by an English-language device for the presentation of dialogue, but hard-boiled Swedish crime fiction by Henning Mankel and Stieg Larsson has now conquered the world's best-seller lists.

Merging of another kind has been vigorously proposed by

the American lawyer Preston Torbert. In his work for US companies doing business in China he has had to deal with hundreds of contracts which have to be written in two languages – English and Chinese – and have equal validity and force in two jurisdictions. It's a tall order because the legal traditions of the two countries have grown up in isolation over many centuries and don't have many matching terms.[3]

One difficulty arises from what is called 'the class presumption' in American law. If a contract says that one of its clauses applies to 'any house, flat, cottage or other building' on some piece of land, for example, that 'other building' means, by the force of the class presumption, only another building of the class constituted by 'house, flat, cottage' – that's to say, a residential building. This construction of the sentence is contrary to English usage in a non-legal context, where the words 'other building' may plausibly refer to a factory, a space station or a folly.

Chinese does not have a term for 'class presumption' and its legal culture does not allow for it either. If the restriction expressed in English is translated without additional modification, the Chinese characters for 'other building' refer equally plausibly to a factory or a workshop as to a residential building, a meaning that the 'class presumption' of American legal English specifically excludes. You could of course insert additional Chinese characters to say 'or any other *similar* building', 'or any other building *of the same class*', 'or any other *residential* construction'. But if it came to a dispute in court, a smart lawyer might be able to claim that the two versions of the contract were not exactly equivalent, since the English contains no words that correspond to the added characters.

The solution proposed by Preston Torbert is to draft the English in such a way that its Chinese translation is not a problem – that is to say, to modify the source language text to make it better suited to translation into the target. Moreover, such a change would make American legalese less arcane, which is of benefit to everybody. The solution is so simple that it makes you wonder why American contracts have not always said 'house, flat, cottage, or other *similar* building'. Torbert's answer is: because legal drafters have not had Chinese to help them until now. Chinese can teach English lawyers how to say what they mean.

Translation impacts such as these are obviously tiny. French, English, Swedish and Chinese have not been altered by them, just lightly massaged at the edge – at least, so far. But the translation of the gospels into Bosavi, a language spoken by small communities of rain-forest dwellers on the Great Papuan Plateau, has had much more far-reaching effects.[4]

Before the Bosavi were converted to Christianity in the 1970s, their culture (somewhat like that of Ancient Rome) did not recognize sincerity as a concept. It was what people said in public that was taken seriously; private thoughts and the conformity of outward behaviour to inner states was not a concern. But sincerity – the correspondence between saying something and meaning it – is integral to the message that Christian missionaries brought. The Asia Pacific Christian Mission regarded vernacular languages as 'the shrine of a people's soul', and was therefore committed to teaching the gospels in Bosavi. However, none of the missionaries was a field linguist, and none became fluent in the language. In addition, Bosavi people in general spoke no other tongue: for trade contacts, they had always relied on speakers in bordering villages who could translate through a neighbouring language, and, in more recent times, on the regional contact language, Tok Pisin.

The missionaries used the *Nupela Testamen*, the New Testament translated into Tok Pisin – not from Latin or Greek, but from the simplified English text called the American Good News Bible, first published in 1966, aimed at children and uneducated adults. Use of the intermediary language limited the mission's initial contact to a small group of young Bosavi men who had worked outside the area and acquired some Tok Pisin. The missionaries taught them basic literacy, and then set them on the road as missionizers themselves. At the rudimentary services these new converts organized in the small villages, they read aloud from the *Nupela Testamen*, then improvised an oral translation into Bosavi, either in small sections, or after a whole passage. Given the translation method, it's not surprising that they introduced many Tok Pisin words and ways of saying into Bosavi as they went along. But the true impact of these 'language turners' lies at a deeper level than that.

Bosavi is one of the many languages that possess evidentials, grammatical forms that indicate how something is known – by sight, by hearsay or by deduction (see p. 164). Tok Pisin, by contrast, does not. So when it came to improvising a Bosavi version of the Tok Pisin version of the Good News version of a Bible story focused on the difference between what people thought and what they said, the newly minted Papuan missionaries had a huge problem, exemplified by the phrases in italics below:

> Jesus said to the paralyzed man, 'My son, your sins are forgiven'. Some teachers of the law who were sitting there *thought to themselves*, 'How does he dare talk like this? This is blasphemy! God is the only one who can forgive sins. At once Jesus *knew what they were thinking*, so he said to them, '*Why do you think such things*? Is it easier to say this to a paralyzed man, 'Your sins are forgiven', or to say 'Get up, pick up your mat, and walk?' I will prove to you then, that the Son of Man has authority on

earth to forgive sins.' So he said to the paralyzed man, 'I tell you, get up, pick up your mat, and go home!'[5]

Tok Pisin uses *na long bel belong*, literally 'in belly of them', to express 'in their hearts' or 'in their minds', and in the *Nupela Testamen* this phrase stands together with *tingting*, 'think', to express the fact that the teachers of the law 'thought' something without saying so. The Bosavi oral translators couldn't say anything quite so ungrounded in evidence. One recorded version has Jesus knowing what the men of law were thinking by direct visual evidence – the evidential suffix *-lo:b* is added to the verb 'think'. Also, it adds a tag, *a: la : sa: lab*, to the whole line, meaning something like 'it says', or at any rate grounding the source of the knowledge not in the actual speaker but in some external authority. But versions varied between different preachers and occasions quite considerably, until a formal borrowing (a syntactic calque) from Tok Pisin became accepted as a new way of referring to 'inner thought', thought not evidenced by words spoken aloud: *kufa*, literally, 'of belly', prefixed to the verb 'think'. The effort of translation has altered the language of Bosavi, and with it, a whole mental world. 'Private thoughts' are now 'belly-think' in Bosavi, or, to put it the other way round, thanks to frontline and improvised language mediation, what a speaker of Bosavi can now do with his belly has undergone a huge change.

Changes brought about in the life of the Bosavi by the missionary effort obviously go far beyond the grammar and vocabulary of their language. However, the change in the way speakers of Bosavi can now conceptualize and refer to 'inner life' is not only an effect of conversion to Christianity, but also a direct impact of translation – the translation of the gospels from Tok Pisin into the Bosavi tongue.

Most commentaries on the effects of translation on receiving cultures of the remote or recent past use words like 'enrich', 'extend' and 'improve' to describe how the target was hit. But when we can see and hear it happening in our own present time, quite other metaphors crop up: 'distort', 'mangle' and 'homogenize' come to mind. The role of evidentials in Bosavi grammar has been irreparably diminished by the improvised calques from Tok Pisin that provide a way of talking about things that have no evidential status at all. From some points of view that has mangled a unique and irreplaceable mental world. Similarly, we could say that the mass import of English-style celebrity gossip into French media has produced a stylistic monstrosity that cheapens the language itself. However, in other times and places much greater lexical and stylistic changes of the same nature have given rise not to lamentation but to feelings of the opposite kind. For example, Japanese translators imported many scientific terms from European languages in the late nineteenth century, and most users of those new terms considered their language had been enriched by them. Similarly, in the fourth to eighth centuries CE, Syriac (a Semitic language closely related to Aramaic) is said to have flowered in the hands of Severus Sebokht, a bishop, scholar and translator who imported quantities of Greek words and expressions together with the mathematical, medical and astronomical knowledge of the ancient Greeks that the Latin West had ignored (and would not rediscover for centuries, until Arabic translations of those Syriac translations of Greek science were translated once again in the middle of the twelfth century CE, in Toledo (Spain), by Gerard of Cremona, into Latin, for wider distribution throughout Europe).[6]

The Christian fundamentalists who converted the Bosavi people may indeed believe they enriched the language of the souls they have saved; and I suppose there may have been Syrian naysayers all those years ago who thought the mass import of Greek terms had wrecked their own ancient tongue. But the fact is that attitudes towards language change induced or accelerated by translation are not motivated exclusively by feelings about language or about translation. They arise from deeply seated and far less tractable ideas.

The first of these is the place you think your language *ought* to occupy in the hierarchy of translation tongues. For many people, especially those caught in the mind-set of a monolingual European nation-state, this is a sensitive topic; because the imagined rank of a language often conflicts with reality, this can give rise to collective hypocrisy and spite. French people who look down on the use of English words that they nonetheless import by the bucket-load are in this kind of plight. They are not alone.

The second major constituent of attitudes towards language change propelled by translations is the value you place on what it is that the new vocabulary brings. Translation impacts on a receiving language can't really be separated from the impact that the translated material has. At different times, translations may flood receiving cultures with Hollywood glitz, shipbuilding techniques, religious salvation, saucy stories about Marie-Antoinette – just about anything that's ever been thought worth writing down. The value you attach to the linguistic traces of such flows is subordinate to your need or desire for the material that the translations in question make available for the first time.

The damage done to other cultures by lop-sided translation flows is no different from the benefits brought to receiving languages by lop-sided translation flows. The real damage and the real benefits lie not in translation as such or in its impacts on receiving languages, but in the nature of the works that translation spreads.

17. *The* Third *Code*: Translation as a Dialect

What language do you speak? That sounds like a merely factual inquiry with an uncomplicated answer, whatever it is. But as I was reading an American newspaper during the financial crisis of 2008, I learned that the US Treasury Secretary was about to unveil the big megillah to put an end to the tsunami that was rocking Wall Street at the time. What language was that? Well, English – but only sort of. It was also, marginally, in Hebrew (mediated by Yiddish) and in Japanese too. I can translate it into French – *M. Paulson s'apprête à dévoiler la bonne méthode pour calmer la tourmente des marchés* – but that doesn't prove the sentence was in English, only that I understood it. I can back-translate the French sentence in any number of ways – but that would only show that 'English' is a far from determinate thing.

Translators working into English are confronted on every page with decisions about the nature, scope, identity and audience of the language they are writing. I write in a personal idiom that bears traces of my upbringing in England, my long stay in Scotland, and my present life on the East Coast of the United States. When I write a translation, however, I have to make choices in every paragraph about what variety of written English to use. As is well known, spellings, numbering systems, greetings and curses as well as several hundred common vocabulary items have different forms in different parts of the English-speaking world. It drives me mad. How do I know what is 'English' and what is something else?

The practical solution is this: I write the way I like, and then a skilful copy-editor amends my prose to make it conform to the style appropriate to the output and the target audience of a particular publishing house. But that is only the outward form of the solution. The target audience of most English-language publishing houses, for most of the books they put out, is indeterminately large, and includes American, Australian, Indian, Canadian and South African readers – each large grouping feeling most at home in significantly different varieties of the spoken and written tongue. So what gets edited out in any of my translations – and in any translated literary or non-fiction work of more than local interest – are those quirks of language which mark it as belonging to any geographical variety of English. In other words, I get de-Britted if I am being edited for US publication, and de-Yanked (a less difficult job, since my Americanisms are few and far between) when a London publisher takes the lead. What you get at the end of the process is 'English-*minus*' – ideally, a common centre-ground of the English language, stripped of vocabulary and turns of phrase that are not understood or understood in different ways in any part of the messy spread of what is still called, for want of a better word, the English tongue.

The language of translations-in-English is therefore not a representation of a language spoken or written anywhere at all. Because its principal feature is to be without regional features it's hard to see from outside – and that's precisely the point of this sophisticated stylistic trick. 'Tranglish' is quite different in nature from the clumsy International English of social science and global journalism. It's smooth and invisible, and it has some important advantages. Detached with skill and craft by professional language doctors from any regional variety of the tongue, it is much easier to translate than anything actually written in 'English' by a novelist from, say, Queensland, Ireland, Wessex or Wales. But as it is already translated (from French, in my case, but this would be just as true if I were working from Russian or Hindi), any remaining strangeness in the prose, in the ears of a speaker of any of the myriad varieties of English the world over, is automatically construed as a trace of the foreign tongue, not of the translator's identity. The 'translator's invisibility', eloquently denounced by Lawrence Venuti as a symptom of the anti-intellectual, anti-foreign bias of Britain and America,[1] is also the unintended result of the unbounded nature of the English language itself.

The suspicion that the language of translated works is not quite the same as the language the translations purport to be in has given rise to scholarly work based not on anecdotes and intuition, but on the automated analysis of quite large bodies of translated texts in machine-readable form. These techniques allow insights into what is now called 'the third code' – the language of translations seen as a dialect that can be distinguished from the regular features of the target language.[2] In one such investigation, it's been found that English novels in French translation have at least one language feature that seems quite at variance with novels originally written in French.

When you want to add emphasis to one part of a French sentence, you take it out of its normal grammatical place and put it right at the start, replacing it in its ordinary location with a pronoun, or dummy word. For example, if you want to disagree with what your children ask for as a treat at the fair, you can say – in English – 'But *I* want ice cream', using the tone of your voice to stress that ice cream is what *you* want when the kids are clamouring for candy-floss. The regular way to do this in French is to put 'I' in a special form at the head and then to repeat it: *Moi, je veux une glace.* Left dislocation, as this feature of French is most often called, is pretty common in all sorts of circumstances in speech and writing, not just in arguments with kids. In a corpus of extracts from recent prize-winning novels written in French, it occurred 130 times in an expanse of around 45,000 words. But in a parallel corpus extracted from similarly well-seen novels translated around the same time into French, it occurred only 58 times. The difference is quite marked and can't be explained by any individual translator's style. A 'third code' does seem to exist.[3]

What's even more interesting and especially relevant to understanding translation is that the use of left dislocation in the corpus of translations into French is highly concentrated in one kind of context – in dialogue. In the corpus of texts originally written in French, however, more than half of the occurrences crop up in third-person narrative. None of the occurrences of left dislocation in the entire double corpus is grammatically wrong or stylistically inappropriate, but it seems clear that the language norm to which translators of English novels in French adhere (whether they know it or not) is not identical to the language use of novel-writers in French.

The reason for this particular feature of the 'third code' in French is not difficult to find. French grammar books and the teaching of French in schools have traditionally categorized left dislocation as typical of oral speech. Translators seem to have internalized that lesson, even though it runs counter to the observable practice of native writers of French. Translators therefore tend to write in a normalized language and are more attentive to what is broadly understood to be the correct or standard form. In fact, anyone who has personal experience of translation work knows this truth. Translation tends towards the centre – to whatever linguistic regularities are conceptualized as belonging to the standard language, irrespective of what native speakers typically say. The plight of the English translator edited into 'English-*minus*' is therefore not exceptional in the world of translation. French translators seem to get to the same place even before copy-editors go over their work.

The movement of translation towards the standard form of the receiving language can be highlighted by the fate of regional and social dialects. Bournisien, one of the minor characters of Flaubert's *Madame Bovary*, speaks with turns of phrase and vocabulary items that are comically typical of the region where the action is set – rural Normandy in the 1830s. English obviously does not have a conventional way of representing the speech of nineteenth-century countryfolk from Normandy. In principle, a translator could make Bournisien speak in English like a Wessex farmer out of Thomas Hardy or a Scottish preacher invented by Walter Scott. But representing one regional dialect of the source by some regional dialect of the target is rarely attempted in translation.[4] Most people currently think it is just silly to make a Bavarian dairy farmer use Texas cowboy slang, or to have a woman on the St Petersburg tram express herself in Mancunian in order to suggest her geographic and linguistic distance both from the capital and the standard language. The culture of translation as it presently exists in English as well as in French and many other languages eradicates regional variation in the source. It drives written representations of dialectal speech towards the centre.

An obvious case of movement towards the centre occurs in Charles Baudelaire's translation of Edgar Allan Poe's *The Gold*

Bug. The African-American slave in the story, Jupiter, is represented as speaking in this manner: 'Dar! dat's it! – him never plain of notin – but him berry sick for all dat.' Baudelaire doesn't try to find a dialect of French to fit, he just says what Jupiter means to say in standard French: *Ah! Voilà la question! – il ne se plaint jamais de rien, mais il est tout de même malade.*

What else could Baudelaire have done? No resources were available in nineteenth-century French to match an English convention for the representation of African-American Vernacular. [5]

Strange to say, the same treatment is not generally accorded to variations in form and style that correspond not to region, but to social class. High-flown, pompous, elegant or regal forms of language in the source are generally represented by forms of corresponding social rank in the target. Real difficulties only arise when the class register is low, and especially when the language of the source represents the speech forms of uneducated folk. This difficulty runs through all kinds of translating, not just literary prose. No consecutive interpreter, for example, would think of adopting lower-class diction to reproduce for the benefit of a visiting foreign dignitary the kind of language spoken to him by a factory hand or collective farm worker: it would surely seem disrespectful, and cause a mighty scandal. In written prose, too, translators shy away from giving the uncouth, truly uncouth, forms of language in the target text. The reason is obvious – grammatical mistakes, malapropisms and other kinds of 'substandard' language must not be seen to be the translator's fault. It's actually easier to translate the ravings of a certified lunatic than the intentionally rude and vulgar language of many modern novels. The outright sanitization of bawdy classics carried out in seventeenth-century France (see p. 130) is quite out of fashion – but something of the same sort goes on in almost any translation project. The 'third code' effects that have been revealed in translations (in French, but also in Norwegian, Swedish and English) and the strong prejudice against regional variation are, even so, mere sidelights on the less easily pinpointed but far more general tendency of all translations to adhere more strongly than any original to a normalized idea of what the target language should be. To put that a different way: translation always takes the register and level of naturally written prose up a notch or two. Some degree of raising is and always has been characteristic of translated texts – simply because translators are instinctively averse to the risk of being taken for less than fully cultivated writers of their target tongue. In important ways, translators are the guardians and, to a surprising degree, the creators of the standard form of the language they use.

18. *No* Language *is* an *Island*: The Awkward Issue of L3

The invention of printing, the rise of dictionaries, the spread of literacy and the establishment of nation-states are probably the main forces that have led us to accept without question that one language is not another, and that the boundaries between, say, English and Yiddish, French and Italian, are real, insuperable and firmly fixed. The idea that a translation always occurs between an L1 and an L2, between a 'source' and a 'target', is only one reflection of this specific culture of language, where different ways of speaking are conceptualized as distinct entities with clear lines between them. But it was not always thus.

On his return to Genoa in 1298 CE, Marco Polo was flung into jail. He wasn't put in solitary, and had the additional good fortune to find an old acquaintance inside. Marco Polo told the tale of his great adventures on the Old Silk Road to his cellmate, Rustichello da Pisa, who wrote it all down. Marco spoke in what we would call Italian and Rustichello wrote his words down in French. The 'original' *Divisament du Monde* (*The Travels of Marco Polo*) was in all probability an improvised translation, and it contains a tell-tale sign of the way it was composed: the first person pronoun 'we' sometimes designates Marco and Rustichello, sometimes Rustichello and his readers, sometimes Marco and his companions.[1] This kind of person-switching is typical of oral translation, and it makes it pretty certain that Marco spoke his account in one dialect and that Rustichello wrote it down in another. You can see the same phenomenon of 'unstable anchoring' in Claude Lanzmann's *Shoah*, a French-language film about the present traces of the extermination of European Jewry in the period 1941–4. *Shoah* is quite exceptional among movies because it does not edit out of the final cut the many acts of two-way translation between the French of the interviewer and the Polish, Yiddish, Hebrew, Czech and German spoken by survivors and informants. (That is partly why it lasts nine hours.) In many sequences, the translator switches between repeating the words of the speaker without changing the orientation of the speech (as in: 'I saw the trains being shunted . . .'), and giving the information provided by the interviewee in indirect report (as in: '*He said that he used to* see the trains being shunted . . .'). On occasions, when Lanzmann wants to pick up on an evasive answer and press the witness further, he falls into the same language-situational trap himself, and asks the interpreter, not the witness: 'What does that really mean?' Instead of transforming such a riposte into a question in Polish for the witness ('What did *you* really mean by that?'), the Polish interpreter answers Lanzmann directly in French in her own voice, giving him a personal explanation of what the witness had meant to say.[2] Such alternations are natural, almost unavoidable departures from the artificial interpreting norm, which overrides the fundamental equation of speaker and voice. In two-way human interaction using a linguistic intermediary who is physically present, it is uncommonly difficult to maintain the fiction of the translator's non-existence. Even at the UN, where professionals observe strict rules of non-interference and are put in sound-proof glass boxes just to make sure, interpreters still occasionally break off from reproducing the other's speech (using the same personal pronouns and tenses as the original speaker) and resort to a third-person report when something arises that lies outside the common run of diplomatic speech. Nikita Khrushchev, the Soviet leader in the 1950s and 1960s, was notorious for his impromptu use of impenetrable Russian proverbs and jokes, and his interpreters would often find themselves saying – in the third person – that 'the General Secretary of the CPSU just made a joke.'

Marco and his translator-scribe were using two related but different languages to tell the world about the fantastic diversity of human societies. They were living among a welter of partly intercomprehensible dialects of an originally common tongue, but only one of them was well suited to bringing news of Shangdu to the West – and that was French. In the lands bordering the Mediterranean in the late Middle Ages, French was roughly the equivalent of what English is today;[3] the hybrid features of the first manuscript of *The Travels* might best be likened to the 'Globish' written by non-native speakers the world over nowadays.

But as soon as the manuscript of *The Travels* got into circulation, other scribes did what any copy-editor would do in the modern world – they tidied it up, subjected it to what French publishers call the *toilette du manuscrit*, and put it into what was considered, respectively, 'proper French', 'proper Tuscan' and, for purposes of wider distribution and retranslation, 'proper Latin' too. By the end of the fourteenth century there were versions in Czech, Gaelic, German, Tuscan and Venetian as well as French, all of them retranslated from the Latin translation which had itself been done from an early version in the Italian dialect of Venice, based on a source that was either the text of the first known manuscript or something very close to it.[4] These progressive emendations of Marco Polo's narrative mostly suppressed the voice-switches of the original translation and turned it into a more situationally consistent narrative. That's because those later scribes were not translating the traveller's speech, but a story that already was a written text. You could say that something very important was lost; you could also say that *The Travels* became a classic of exploration literature precisely because, like many modern novels, it was rewritten by professionals. Then as now, the borderline between translating and improving a text – between 'helping the reader' and 'trashing the source' – is not at all clear-cut.

The borderline between translating and rewriting is in fact no more wiggly than the one between source and target language in the case of many extended texts. Tolstoy's *War and Peace* is an oft-quoted example of this. In the Russian original, parts of the novel are in French. This reflects the language practice of its characters – Russian aristocrats of the early nineteenth century used French for much of their social and intellectual lives. Indeed, when challenged by a Freemason to speak of his hopes and desires, Pierre Bezukhov found himself unsure of how to answer, 'being unaccustomed to speak of abstract matters in Russian'.[5]

Translating *War and Peace* into French is both impossible and easy. Reproduced without alteration in French, the French speech of Russian aristocrats loses all its meaning as a marker of class, and there is no way of indicating by linguistic means alone that a sentence spoken in French is different from the other sentences that are (by force of translation) in French as well. The title page of the French translation may well say *Traduit du russe* but that is only partly true. It is 'translated' from French as well.

Identical translation problems arise in a vast array of European fiction. The first page of Balzac's *Le Père Goriot* contains a sentence in English (*All is true!*) that has an entirely different environment and force when reproduced in an English translation of the text. But what can you do? Translate 'All is true!' back into French? Or alter the spelling to *Oll eez troo* to indicate it having been thought by a Frenchman with an atrocious accent? Balzac had no qualms about altering the orthography of French to represent the regional accent of Nucingen, a Jewish banker from Alsace, who also appears in *Le Père Goriot*. Current conventions don't allow translators to do that to the diction of narrators – but there's no strictly logical reason for withholding a lousy accent from Balzac's narrator too.

In fact, the more you read in any language, the harder it gets to find an extended text written in that language alone. Two novels I read last year with much pleasure illustrate this point. Michael Chabon's *The Yiddish Policemen's Union* is an entertaining fantasy of a Yiddish-speaking colony in modern-day Alaska. The English dialogue of the characters is understood to represent a translation from Yiddish – or rather, from an imaginary state of Yiddish enriched by fifty years of further existence as a living, growing language on American soil. Chabon's text is a wonderful hybrid of real and imaginary languages that play with each other – and a translation of it into any other tongue could hardly be considered a translation 'from English' alone. Similarly, *English, August* by Upumanyu Chatterjee mixes Hindi and Bengali with standard literary English to create a language-picture of its central character, Agastya, nicknamed August in his English-language boarding school. A keen reader who speaks only English could use it to learn a number of Bengali and Hindi words, just as a reader of the short stories of Junot Díaz can pick up a good amount of Spanish from his hybrid, 'Spanglish' texts. But Tolstoy, Balzac, Chabon, Chatterjee and Díaz don't switch around between tongues just to provide language lessons. They do so because language alternation (called 'code-switching' in some kinds of language study) is endemic to *all* kinds of language use.

I used to have a friend who ran a bank branch in a rural backwater of south-western France. We always spoke to each other in French, but whenever he came across me in the street or a field, he would begin by saying 'Peace and love', which he pronounced *pissanlerv*. In the same period I knew a Scottish doctor who used to hurry his children along by saying 'the tooter the sweeter', blending *tout de suite* with something like 'the sooner the better'. Both those acquaintances were speaking in a language (respectively, French and English) but they were also speaking another at the same time (respectively, English and French).

Translation is usually thought of as a process involving only L1 and L2, or source and target tongues. But, as we've seen, sources typically include smaller or larger amounts of L3, a language that is not either of translation's traditional twins. When L3 is L2 (as in the case of *War and Peace* translated into French), it is inevitably rubbed out, but when it is not (in a Swedish translation of Michael Chabon's novel, for example) it's not at all obvious how it should be handled. Mind-boggling though they may seem, these problems are not marginal to the way language is commonly used, and therefore not irrelevant to translation either. However convinced we may be that different languages are different things and not to be confused with each other, in practice we never stop muddling them up. The borderline between, say, English and French is more ragged and foggy than grammars and dictionaries would have us believe. 'Sayonara, amigo!' may not be an officially English way of saying farewell, but few English-speakers have any trouble in knowing what it means.

19. *Global* Flows: Centre and Periphery in the Translation of Books

The Harvill Press was founded in London in 1948 to publish literary works of high quality from other languages, initially from Eastern Europe. By the time of its fiftieth anniversary it was proud to announce that it had published English translations of works originally written in forty-three different tongues. In Paris, Ismail Kadare's French publisher regularly informs readers of back-panel blurbs that the Albanian novelist's works have been translated into 'more than forty languages'. Are these the same ones? With only a few exceptions, the answer is yes. Nowadays there are only about fifty languages between which imports and exports of translated books occur with any regularity.[1] That represents a minute fragment of global linguistic diversity, yet it covers a large proportion of the population of the world. That's because translation languages are, by necessity, vehicular ones, read (if not also spoken) by vastly more people than those who have them as their native tongues.

But what of the rest? All or part of the Jewish and Christian scriptures exist in nearly 2,500 languages. Some of these also have translations of legal and administrative texts and a few possess news or gossip magazines and a small quantity of popular fiction. But what's obvious from these numbers is that more than half the world's languages probably receive no translations at all, and all but fifty or so export almost nothing either. Print translation only happens in special places. That's not to minimize its importance, but to point to the peculiarly asymmetric relations that have always obtained between the different forms of speech on this planet.

UNESCO, the cultural arm of the United Nations Organization, has attempted since its foundation to keep track of the global flow of translations through the *Index Translationum*, which is now available as a searchable database on the web. It can be used as a rough measure of the huge imbalances in translation in the world today.

Chinese is spoken by about a quarter of the world's population and in a well-balanced and reciprocating global society you would expect it to be the receiver of about a quarter of the translations done in the world. The truth is nothing like that at all.

Taking seven world languages of different kinds for the ten years from 2000 to 2009, Chinese is the receiving language of barely 5 per cent of all the translations done in all directions among these tongues – about the same as Swedish, whose speakers number less than 1 per cent of the speakers of Chinese. But the picture in the reverse direction is even worse. Only 863 books were translated from Chinese into Hindi, Arabic, English, French, German and Swedish combined, whereas more than twice that number of books written in Swedish were published in Chinese, Arabic, Hindi, English, French and German combined.

BOOKS TRANSLATED BETWEEN SEVEN LANGUAGES, 2000–2009 INCLUSIVE

From	Into Swedish	Chinese	Hindi	Arabic	French	German	English	Totals from
Swedish		18	0	12	297	1116	359	**1802**
Chinese	22		1	14	492	200	134	**863**
Hindi	0	1		1	38	18	67	**125**
Arabic	20	18	4		712	232	127	**1113**
French	330	554	11	556		5945	5463	**12,884**
German	330	477	11	153	5890		5238	**12,069**
English	6,092	5,974	181	2,130	47,512	42,231		**104,120**
Totals into	**6,794**	**7,012**	**208**	**2,866**	**54,941**	**49,742**	**11,388**	**132,951**

Nearly 80 per cent of all translations done in all directions between these seven languages over a decade – 103,000 out of 132,000 – are translations from English. Conversely, barely more than 8 per cent of all translations done in the same set are translations into English – whereas French and German between them are the receiving languages of 78 per cent of all translations.

The asymmetry is striking, and in some senses quite alarming. Granted, published books do not provide the only channel of intercultural communication; in addition, the data stored by UNESCO may not be complete and its search engine may have its own quirks. But the overall picture – which is confirmed by what any traveller can see in any airport bookstall in the world today – must be broadly true. Translations from English are all over the place; translations into English are as rare as hen's teeth.

It is neither accurate nor even interesting to pin the responsibility for our lop-sided translation world on the Almighty Dollar alone.[2] Translation flows measured in this way also fail to give a particularly convincing map of military power in our own or recent centuries. The initial spread of British English around the globe was certainly the fruit of colonial expansion – but the huge scope and increasing pace of its dominance followed the dismantling of empire that began in 1947. The imperial hypothesis fails to explain why French, Spanish, Portuguese and Dutch, the languages of equally far-flung and densely populated empires between the sixteenth and twentieth centuries, are nowhere near the top of today's global translation tree. For every work in Spanish translated into English in the first decade of the twenty-first century, fifteen were translated from English into Spanish. Yet there are almost as many native speakers of Spanish (around 350 million) as of English (400 million) on the planet today.

Translation DOWN often takes place for mostly practical reasons from the language of dominance to the languages used by peoples living within the field of domination. In the Habsburg empire, for example, laws, regulations, official announcements and daily news were translated from German, the language of the court and imperial administration, into the seventeen official languages of that ramshackle state. But books didn't follow behind to any great extent. No lively culture of literary translation sprang up into Slovene, Slovak, Serbo-Croat, Ruthenian, Czech and so forth. That's because there was a much more straightforward way of becoming a cultivated citizen of the Austro-Hungarian Empire: by learning German. In like manner, many serious books in English about history, science, literature and the arts cannot be commercially translated into Swedish, Danish, Norwegian or Dutch because interested readers in these communities read them in English already. Economic, military and cultural domination obviously affects translation flows, but typically not in direct or straightforward ways. A truly dominant language that has a great army and a well-filled treasury behind it – say, Latin throughout the period of the Romans' domination of Europe and the Mediterranean – is the one tongue from which you do not ever need to translate. People just learn it, because without it their prospects are blocked. English does not dominate the world in the way that Latin did, because it is massively translated into vernaculars. Translation is the *opposite* of empire.

When speakers of Spanish, Portuguese and English spread into the New World between the fifteenth century and the eighteenth, they did not initiate translations into any of the languages of the native inhabitants of the Americas. They created empires. But when Soviet Russia consolidated its hold on the many peoples of Siberia, the Caucasus and Central Asia in the 1920s, it did so with firm political convictions that were explicitly anti-imperial. To demonstrate and implement those self-directed beliefs, the Soviet Union launched a huge programme of translation from and into the indigenous languages of what were called 'the nationalities' – Kazakh, Turkmen, Georgian, Azerbaijani and so on. There was a good deal of hypocrisy in the Soviet stance, but the important thing to realize is that only translation could serve as a public alibi for what was in most other ways a classic instance of imperial expansion. Russian literary classics were made available in Kazakh, Ingush, Daghestani and so on, but translation UP was a necessary complement. Two-way trade was needed to demonstrate the truly anti-imperial nature of the Union.

The problem Soviet language-planners faced was that it takes a long time to establish functioning translation relations

between two languages. Schools have to be established to educate a generation of bilinguals, who then have to develop their
own translation tools and conventions. It can't be done overnight, however great the need. But Soviet Russia was a
revolutionary enterprise in a great hurry to usher in a new
world. That's why it began to cheat. Native poets in the main
non-Russian languages were hard to find, and it was even
harder to find Russian poets able to translate them. The Soviet
solution was to invent them. Dzhambul Dzhabayev is the
most famous example of Soviet pseudo-translation, partly
because the deception was so long-drawn-out. A well-known
Kazakh folk singer at the time of the Revolution, Dzhabayev
was compelled to lend his name to patriotic poems written in
Russian by a whole factory of hacks, who presented them as
having been translated from Kazakh. Dzhabayev was translated into many other languages – from Russian, in fact, but
always officially from Kazakh. Because 'Kazakhstan's national
poet' lived on to the age of ninety-nine, the Moscow song
factory was able to maintain the illusion for many decades.[3]

However, not all empires treat the language of the conquerors as the conquering language. In many known instances, a
culture of translation sprang up that gave prestige and authority to the language of the conquered. When the Akkadians
overran Sumer around 2250 BCE, they did not sweep away the
much older culture and language of their new subjects. They
adopted Sumerian script – the wedge-shaped letters made by
incising wet clay with the sharpened tip of a reed – and treated
the (linguistically unrelated) Sumerian language as a cultural
asset. Laws and legends, rules and chronicles, were translated
from Sumerian into Akkadian, and knowledge of Sumerian
became the mark of an educated man throughout the many
centuries of Akkadian and Assyrian civilization. Despite having

ceased to be associated with any political, military or economic authority, and progressively disconnected from any identifiable ethnicity as well, Sumerian went on being used as a sacred, ceremonial, literary and scientific language in Mesopotamia until the first century CE – giving it a lifespan as a source of translations DOWN of approximately 3,000 years. English has a long way to go to equal that.

Between the fifth and third centuries BCE, Greek-speaking seafarers spread their language far and wide in small pockets stretched out along coastlines from Marseilles to Odessa, and Alexander the Great took it overland as far as Egypt and Afghanistan. But the role of Greek as a source language for translation has nothing to do with Macedonian military might. Even before it conquered and occupied the Greek peninsula at the start of the second century BCE, Rome became eager to take possession of Greece's culture and thought. In due course the language of the conquered was recognized as a repository of cultural and intellectual prestige. The learning of Greek became the main content of a proper education in ancient Rome, and translation into Latin the main skill associated with high rank.

The stories of Sumerian and Greek oblige us to be more than doubtful about economic, military and political explanations of the translation map of the world today. In one sense, of course, these ancient examples of the languages of subject peoples being invested with cultural prestige through translation are exceptional, because there don't seem to be any good examples in medieval or modern times. When the Normans conquered England they did not adopt Anglo-Saxon as their language of culture – they carried on using French, and let the common folk speak a Franco-Saxon mishmash that eventually turned into English. When the French seized the throne of Sweden in the Napoleonic wars, they didn't start translating from Swedish. In fact, the new Swedish royal family and its court carried on speaking French for over a hundred years – and their descendants still maintain a palace in Nice.

But we could just as easily take the opposite view. The general history of translation in the European sphere in the last few hundred years may itself be an exception to a longer-running norm. And even within that domain there are examples of languages of culture and translation being retained against political or military logic. Latin remained dominant, both as the source language of translations DOWN and as the target language of many vernacular texts principally for the purpose of retranslation into other vernaculars that had no translation relations between them for more than a thousand years after the fall of Rome. Jews have continued to use Hebrew for more than three millennia despite having had a thousand practical reasons for dropping it like a hot brick.

What makes a language culturally dominant, today as at all other times, has no relationship to the number of centurions, tanks or missiles it has to back it up or the quantity of gold in its treasury. A culturally dominant language is one that maintains significant volumes of translation activity between itself and a significant number of languages which have smaller bilateral translation relations between them. The dominance of Latin in fourteenth-century Europe, for example, is not just exemplified by the way in which *The Travels of Marco Polo* were spread: it was created and maintained by just that kind of use, as the interlanguage which enabled the same (or a similar) text to be made available in languages like Czech and Gaelic between which bilateral translation skills were practically non-existent. It had nothing to do with the economic or military power of 'native Latin-speakers', of whom there were precisely none.

The position of English as source and target for the vast

bulk of translation done in the world to date is brought out by ranking the most popular source languages for translations into any selection of languages you care to choose. This table shows the main source languages for translations of books into thirteen widely spoken languages since UNESCO first started keeping records:

TOP FOUR SOURCE LANGUAGES

Most popular source language, into:	1	2	3	4
Arabic	English	French	Russian	German
Chinese	English	Japanese	French	German
Dutch	English	German	French	Italian
English	German	French	Russian	Spanish
French	English	German	Italian	Spanish
German	English	French	Russian	Italian
Hindi	English	Russian	Sanskrit	Bengali
Italian	English	French	German	Spanish
Japanese	English	French	German	Russian
Spanish	English	French	German	Italian
Swahili	Russian	English	German	Arabic
Swedish	English	Finnish	German	French
Tamil	English	Russian	Sanskrit	Malayalam

What's clear is that English, French and German dominate translation worldwide. Russian has a perhaps surprising role in fourth place, but the eight others that appear on this ranking – Spanish and Italian three times each, Sanskrit twice, Japanese, Finnish, Bengali, Malayalam and Arabic only once, and Chinese not at all – are peripheral to the global business of translating books.

The raw numbers of translated books on which this ranking is based produces an even more startling picture of the pyramidal structure of global translation today. Of the nearly one million translations used to compile the ranking, more than 650,000 are translations from English and a further one tenth of the total number consist of translations into English. English is the medium as source or target of 75.12 per cent of all translation acts.

What these figures also show is that around 42 per cent of all the translations recorded in the UNESCO database between the thirteen languages listed above have taken place in closed circuit between just three of them – English, German and French. This is not an ineluctable consequence of the fact that of the million books we are dealing with, over 47 per cent were published in one of those three languages too. Culture is not the prerogative of any part or place in the world, but book culture – and, within it, the culture of translation – is heavily concentrated in France, Germany, Britain and the USA.

As a result, at any truly representative gathering of translators from across the globe, between 70 and 90 per cent of delegates must be L1 speakers of a language other than English. To put it another way: if you would really like your children to earn their living as translators, you'll give them a much better chance if you don't raise them in Britain or

America. This also explains why translation is much less easy to see and understand when you are based in the English-speaking world. You don't meet many translators in the normal course of life in London, Sydney or Cork – but they're all over the place in Geneva and Berlin.

The flow of translations has always had a hierarchical structure: the present situation reproduces a pattern that can be observed many times in the historical past. Translation typically takes place not between languages felt by their speakers to be on an equal footing, but between those that in some respect have a vertical relationship between them. Laws, commands, instructions and treaties are translated DOWN – from Sumerian, Greek and Latin in ancient times, from German in the Habsburg empire, from Ottoman Turkish in the long period of Ottoman sway in the Mediterranean Basin – into vernaculars spoken by people who needed to grasp what the rules and agreements that affected them were. Novels, plays, philosophical and mathematical treatises, and religious texts may accompany them, but not always. Out of these kinds of situations the world over have grown ideas among the speakers of culturally dominant tongues that their language is inherently superior, and the only true vehicle of thought. In the Muslim world, for example, there was little doubt in past centuries about which language was top:

> The perfect language is the language of the Arabs and the perfection of eloquence is the speech of the Arabs, all others being deficient. The Arabic language among languages is like the human form among beasts. Just as humanity emerged as the final form among animals, so is the Arabic language the final perfection of human language and of the art of writing, after which there is no more.[4]

Seventeenth-century French grammarians made much the same assertion about French, and similar expressions of confidence in the superiority of Greek, Persian, Latin, Chinese and who knows how many others among the world's temporarily dominant tongues could easily be lined up.

Obviously, there are no rational grounds for such kinds of linguistic preference: all languages can be made to serve whatever ends their speakers wish to achieve. But the feeling that a difficult foreign text only makes real and proper sense when it's been put into the language we prefer to use for thinking hard thoughts can easily ambush an otherwise sensible mind. Years ago I sat in a library in Konstanz trying to make sense of Hegel by reading him very slowly in German, with a pencil in my hand. It was hard going, and I never really got the hang of it. I sneaked a look at what the German student in the next carrel was reading. It was Hegel, too – but in English translation! Well, I thought to myself with relief, if even native speakers use the English translation as a guide to Hegel's thought . . . Such experiences can easily lead you into a barely conscious, self-comforting persuasion that your language alone is the one in which real meaning is to be found. But however great the service that a clarifying, explanatory translation of a foreign text may provide, we should always resist the false conclusion that the target language – whatever language it is – is 'better' at expressing this or that kind of thought.

Despite their numerical insignificance, translators into English play an important role in the international trade in books. Because it is the most translated language in the world, it is far easier to get a book into any other language if it exists in English already – whatever language its original language was. But English is by no means the only 'pivot tongue' in the world.

French continues to play a significant role as a conduit for global translation from less widely spoken languages. France's proud tradition of openness to other cultures is one of the reasons why this is so. In the twentieth century, many of its leading writers – Romain Gary, Samuel Beckett, Eugène Ionesco, Andreï Makine and Jorge Semprún, for example – were immigrants who had chosen to write in French. However, a more important reason for the continuing role of French in the circulation of cultural goods is not one that the defenders of French culture really like very much. French has long been the most widely taught foreign language in the English-speaking world, which makes it the main inter-language for English and American publishers and literary scouts.

German also remains a crossroads for literature from little-studied languages. Jaan Kross, the Estonian author of *The Czar's Madman, Professor Maarten's Departure* and many other wonderful novels, was first translated into German, and that was what brought him to the attention of international literary scouts. The role of German as medium for exophonic writers has actually been growing strongly in recent years. Alongside several Japanese, Bulgarian and Turkish novelists who have chosen to write in German, a Mongolian shaman called Galsan Tschinag is translated from his German translations into many other European tongues.[5]

In the Middle Ages, Arabic was the pivot language which allowed Greek philosophy to be translated into European tongues – in some cases, written in Hebrew script. In the period 1880–1930, Japanese was the relay language for translations of Russian literature into Chinese.[6] Even in the last fifty years, a handful of international literary careers have emerged from translation into languages outside the top three. They include the works of Bernardo Atxaga, first written in Basque, which reached a wider readership initially through their translation into Spanish, and from Spanish into French; and the Chuvash poetry of Aigui, translated independently into English and French from its Russian translations. But the use of pivot languages can be a risky affair. The Belarusian novelist Vasil Bykau, for example, was translated into Russian, which provided first entry to the world concert of books. However, Soviet translators did not dare reproduce his meaning too closely. In *Alpijskaja Balada* (Alpine Ballad, 1963), the hero tries to explain to a naïve foreigner about his country, saying 'It will get better some day. Things cannot go on being lousy for ever.' In Russian translation, the sentence reads: 'The collective farm is good.' After such distortions, Bykau started to translate his own works into Russian soon after they had been published and also Russianized his name to Vasil Bykov. This allowed the Soviet authorities to present him as a Russian novelist, concealing the fact that his works were originally written in another (related) tongue. In Bykov's case, translation UP simply absorbed a writer in a 'minor' language into the regionally dominant one.[7]

However, even in places not afflicted by political appropriation of that kind, the drift away from small languages towards a dominant tongue has been felt again and again. In the late nineteenth century, an editorialist for the Japanese daily newspaper *Yomiuri Shimbun* opined that his country had much to give to the world beyond Mount Fuji and Lake Biwa – it had magnificent literary works like *Genji Monogatari* or Bakin's *Hakkenden*. But the distance between Japanese and the European languages was too great to make translation feasible, in his view:

However great our future writers may be, their fame will never succeed in crossing beyond our borders ... And so I would like to suggest to the public spirited men of the world that they engage themselves in the writing of English ... In this day and age, it is self-evident that a man with great ambitions should study English writing. Study it, and strive, by using the language, to make his glory shine abroad. There is nothing great about a fame solely garnered in the context of this pathetic string of islands.[8]

Typical in this respect of a culture that feels peripheral to the conversation of the world, the Japanese journalist jumped to a conclusion that many have followed in the last hundred years. Maryse Condé, the distinguished French writer from Guadeloupe, has admitted that were she fifty years younger she would probably have chosen English instead of French as her language of expression. Edwidge Danticat, a French-speaking writer from Haiti who *is* fifty years younger, has done just that.

If you do write in a minor language – and all languages, even French, are minor ones now – getting translated into English is the summit of your ambition. If you write in Italian, you're quite likely to get translated into Spanish, and if you write in Finnish, you're almost certain to get translated into Swedish for the significant minority of Finnish citizens for whom Swedish is L1. But getting translated into Spanish or Swedish is unlikely to get your work out into the wider world. Whatever language you write in, the translation that counts is the English one.

English-speakers are obviously not directly responsible for the use of English as a pivot, because the only folk for whom English is never a pivot language are the speakers of English themselves. Like all interlanguages of the past, English is made into a pivot by speakers of other tongues. China's Confucius Institute, for instance, has commissioned an international team of scholars to make the philosophical and literary treasures of Classical Chinese accessible to the rest of the planet. The Wu Jing Project aims to translate *The Five Classics* (a conventional term referring to a large number of separate texts, about 2,500 pages in all) into 'the major languages of the world'. However, these difficult works will not be translated into French, German, Spanish, Russian, Arabic, Hebrew, Hindi and Malay from the original Chinese. The dissemination of *The Five Classics* into the eight languages selected will be done 'on the basis of the English translation', which will be treated, once it has been done, as the reference text.[9]

The position of English-language translators of literary texts from languages that have not been widely taught in the rest of the world is therefore unique. They control their source text's access not just to their target audience, but through the international trade in books and sometimes through double translation as well, they may open or shut the door to the rest of the world.

The solar structure of the global book world wasn't designed by anyone. With its all-powerful English sun, major planets called French and German, outer elliptical rings where Russian occasionally crosses the path of Spanish and Italian, and its myriad distant satellites no weightier than stardust, the system is all the more remarkable for being in stark contradiction to the web-like network of cross-cultural relations that most people would like to see. But the orbital image of translation flows is only a metaphor. The structure of global translation is not a natural phenomenon, but a cultural one. If enough people really want it to change – it will.

20. *A* Question *of* Human *Rights*: Translation and the Spread of International Law

Translation Studies as currently practised in the academy concentrates heavily on the circulation of books, especially books of literary merit. But despite the six-figure numbers bandied about in our survey of global translation, literary works make up only a small part of translation in the world today.

Legal texts are translated in vaster quantities than books and in more varied directions. Dreary as it may seem to all but legal eagles, the translation of law is a prerequisite for the construction and maintenance of a global society. Without it, business and diplomacy would come to a stop. But there's something quite important to learn from it. Law is the very model of an untranslatable text, because the language of law is self-enclosed, and refers to nothing outside of itself. In practice, however, laws do get translated, because they must.

In France you can say *impossible n'est pas français* when you want to assert that something hard can nonetheless be done. 'Impossible' doesn't exist in other languages either when it comes to translation. Translation is a voluntary act.

Lay folk the world over know why the law is untranslatable. It's written in a language of its own that is almost impossible to understand, and what can't be understood can't be translated. We pay our lawyers good money just to reassure us that *they* understand the small print on the contract we've just signed without reading it through to the end.

The words of law often look like words of the language you speak, but when they are legal terms, they are not. They don't refer to anything outside of the social institution and intellectual system that the law constructs. You may have a pretty good idea what 'murder' means when you use it in an English sentence, but what looks like murder to you may be *first degree*, *second degree*, *manslaughter*, *homicide* or even *collateral damage* in a legal description of the event. The offence committed is determined by the legal system in force in the place where the killing occurred, and within that system it is determined only by the definitions of the offences that the system distinguishes – by the words of the law as it has come to be written down.

In the first years of the twentieth century a professor of linguistics at the University of Geneva gave a course of lectures about the nature of human languages. Ferdinand de Saussure never wrote the lectures down, but after his early death in 1913 students put their notes together and produced a *Course in General Linguistics* that has served as a breviary for much of the thinking about language that has gone on since then. Whether or not Saussure's teaching should be regarded as the last word on what language is overall, it's an excellent tool for getting at the reasons why the language of law is such a tricky thing to translate.[1]

Saussure was already very learned in the history of languages, but in his lectures on general linguistics he sought to explain what a language is as a whole and systematic thing at any given point in time. His account was grounded in what was then a revolutionary new definition of the linguistic sign. A sign possesses both a material existence as a string of sounds or written marks, which he called the signifier (in French, *signifiant*); but it necessarily also has a power to mean – a significandum, or *signifié*. The sign is neither a signifier nor a significandum, but their combination, in a pairing so tight that the one can no more be separated from the other than the two sides of a single sheet. However, unlike a piece of paper, the two sides of the sign are attached to each other for no necessary reason – they just are attached that way. A sign in Saussure's teaching has five special qualities. It has to be inherited, because the signs of a language can never be invented on the spot. It has to be shared, because signs mean what we agree they should mean, not just what some individual thinks they mean. It has to be unchangeable, because nobody can turn *table* into *cable* just for fun and still be using the same sign. It has to be free to be combined with other signs in an act of speech or writing. Finally, the inner relationship between signifier and signified that makes the two together coalesce as a sign has to be arbitrary: you can't explain why the letters TABLE as distinct from any others can be used to refer to a 'table' except by saying they just do.

What, then, allows us to know that *this* sign is not *that* sign? That 'cable' and 'table' represent two different signs? Because they differ in respect of something that is a structural part not of 'language' in any abstract sense, but of the language called English. That is to say, the difference between the sounds represented by 'c' and 't' is a basic element of the structure of the English language – and the entire structure that is the English language consists exclusively of sets of differences or oppositions of this fundamental kind. A language is then nothing other than a system of differences, because a sign in any language is exhaustively defined by all the things that it is not. What makes English not French or Chinese, for example, is the specific set of differences on which it is built. Rising and falling tones, for example, exist in any act of speech, but they are not parts of English. On the other hand, tones are signs in Chinese. Similarly, the difference between the sounds usually written as *l* and *r* is part of English, but not of Japanese. To map the differences that are made use of in a language is to map the structure of the language itself.

Saussure's approach to language makes each actual language *sui generis*, 'of its own kind', that's to say, an internally coherent system that can never be satisfactorily mapped on to any other. The automatic consequence is that no sign in any one language is fully identifiable with any sign in any other equally unique system of signs. Throughout the twentieth century, the Saussurean doctrine of the sign provided a reason for disregarding translation and ignoring the resources it gives for understanding how languages are used.

Saussure certainly didn't have law in mind when he pursued this rich train of thought, but his doctrine of the sign is directly applicable to it. Law is a systematic use of language that relies for its coherence on the precise distinctions it makes between its own constituent terms. In any given legal language, 'murder' is what the book of statutes and the records of cases judged have said it is – not what the ordinary language sign 'murder' might be taken to mean among lay folk. Law is a system of signs.

Legal systems have different histories, different norms, different distinctions and ways of doing things. Even when the languages of different legal systems look the same – as in English and Scottish law, for example – the terms they use are not interchangeable. Each one is truly *sui generis*, constituted exclusively by the particular distinctions it makes. That's the reason why you can't translate legal language – except that you must.

Defendants in many parts of the world are entitled to

understand their own trial, and courts are obliged to find translators and interpreters for whatever languages are involved. They often have to scour far and wide. A request for an English-Hungarian interpreter for a murder trial in rural Scotland landed on my doorstep thirty years ago. The brave person who took on this awesome responsibility in the end had never seen a courtroom before, and was barely more aware of the meaning of what was going on than the defendant herself. In the state of New Jersey today, the courts service employs many hundreds of mostly part-time interpreters, predominantly in Spanish, at low rates of pay and with little supervision. In New York City, where no less than 140 languages are represented, finding language intermediaries for court cases is a huge administrative task. In South Africa, too, where eleven languages now have official status, court interpreting is often a lamentable mess.[2] The language rights of linguistic minorities are important achievements, but their implementation often leaves a lot to be desired.

Court interpreting of this kind is internal to a single system of law: where the minority language does not have a strictly equivalent term – for 'prosecutor', 'attorney' or 'QC', for example – the source language term is mostly used, as it is indeed the proper term for the individual or instance that matters at that point. But the interpreter may also have to add explanations or rephrase what is said in altogether different terms, to make sure that what are understood are not just the words, but the force and real-world consequences of the expression used. It is an extremely difficult and responsible job. It is rarely recognized as such.

Legal translation between the official languages of countries that have more than one – Canada, Belgium or Finland, for example – is not exactly easy, but it is usually better rewarded and less stressful, partly because the translators often have legal training themselves. The issue of the incommensurability of legal systems does not really affect this kind of work, since it is the same language of law that is being expressed in both tongues. All the same, it is crucial that the two versions be construed in exactly the same way. Given the natural anisomorphism of languages, that is often very difficult to achieve. Law translation in such circumstances tends towards a homogenization of tongues – creating similar-sounding formal equivalents in the two versions of the law – to reduce the risk of a clever lawyer exploiting an apparent verbal discrepancy between two versions of the same text.

The trend towards making legal languages look the same when put into a different tongue seems to be driven on the one hand by a rather naive idea of how languages work and on the other by an overriding concern that laws be seen as the same by all who fall under their sway. An illustration of the seemingly irresistible drift towards homogenized transnational legalese is provided by the history of the words used to express the broadest and least national juridical principle of all – the notion of fundamental human rights.

In 1789, the new revolutionary regime in France drew up its famous declaration of the rights of man and called it the *Déclaration des droits de l'homme et du citoyen*. Its purpose was to sweep away the religious and feudal underpinnings of the legal system inherited from the monarchy and to establish, under the authority of a Supreme Being who could not be called God lest that be seen as a sop to the Catholic Church, the basic rights of the citizen in his relationship to the new French state.

There was no question of these rights being accorded to any who were not fully emancipated citizens. As no one had yet thought of enfranchising women, the use of a masculine term, *homme*, was not only a convenience of language: it was what the declaration meant to say. It established and made explicit the rights of male subjects who were also citizens.

Unlike French or English, German has a noun for 'human being' that covers men and women without distinction – *ein Mensch* is just any member of the human race. The other word for 'man', *Mann* refers exclusively to a male, and in many contexts it also means 'husband' or 'married man'. That's why *Männerrechte* can't serve as a translation of *droits de l'homme* – it could too easily be taken to cover conjugal and domestic affairs, which 'human rights' obviously do not. So French *droits de l'homme* was quite naturally represented by *Menschenrechte* in German translation. In fact, the Declaration needed translating into German within a few years of its drafting because large parts of what is now Germany were conquered by France and incorporated into the republic and then the empire, where they stayed until 1814.

Because *Mensch* cannot be translated directly into English without saying either more or less than the original, it became customary to refer to *Menschenrechte* in English as *Human Rights*, even though the phrase 'Rights of Man' had been made famous by Tom Paine's pamphlet of 1791. The English formula of a generalizing adjective plus a plural noun (*human+rights*) is the third alternative form of a concept that began as a plural noun plus a singular noun phrase linked by a genitive (*droits+de+l'homme*) that had transited by way of a noun plus noun compound of which both parts are plural (*Menschenrechte*). These changes in grammatical form engendered subtle shifts in implication that only became apparent in later times. 'Human rights' was intended as a 'translation' of *les droits de l'homme et du citoyen*, but it was something more, and something less. It went on to acquire a life – and a power – all its own.

From the inception of the United Nations Organization in 1945, Eleanor Roosevelt, the widow of the US president, devoted her energies to promoting the declaration of a World Charter of Human Rights, which was duly adopted in 1948. In its official French version it is called *Déclaration Universelle des Droits de l'Homme*. But one major thing had changed since the phrase *droits de l'homme* had first been monumentalized in 1789: in 1946, French women became entitled to vote, and were now citizens in the same sense (or almost the same sense) as men. The traditional use of masculine *homme* to mean *Mensch* began to seem discriminatory. By the 1970s, French feminist campaigners were clamouring for a parallel declaration of *les droits de la femme*, even though such a thing, if it had ever been made, would most likely have excluded women from the provisions of the Universal Declaration of Human Rights – which would have been counterproductive, to say the least.

German *Menschenrechte* would have solved the problem for everybody, but German is not an official UN language.[3] So it was the English adjectival formulation that was transported back into nearly all other European languages of the Germanic and Romance families – Italian *diritti umani*, Spanish *derechos humanos*, Swedish *mänskliga rättigheter* and so on.

In French, however, the expression *droits humains* has a real problem: *humain* means, indistinctly, what we mean by human and what we mean by humane. Consequently, to call human rights *droits humains* in standard French puts them closer to humanitarian concerns, which are not the principal objects of laws on human rights.

These areas of ambiguity have led to the exclusion of the

term 'human rights' from many international instruments that deal with them: the International Covenant on Civil and Political Rights (1966), the International Covenant on Economic, Social and Cultural Rights (1966), the Convention on the Elimination of Discrimination against Women (1979) and the Convention Against Torture (1984) all avoid the term, and even Europe, home of the original formulation, felt the need to complement it in the title of its European Convention of Human Rights and Fundamental Freedoms (1953). With the passage of time and because of the spread of the ideas which it conveyed, 'human rights' slowly ceased to be a term of law. As it percolated into general use it found itself expelled from juridical language. Which is precisely what the systematic nature of legal language would require.

This has created an awkward issue for French. The historical priority of the revolutionary decree of 1789 has made France unwilling to dispense with what it still regards as the classical, transparent formulation of the idea.

The solution found was to change the language to make the old formulation still fit for use. The word *Homme* written with an upper case letter now refers to men and women indistinctly and is the declared exact written equivalent of German *Mensch*; whereas *homme* with a lower case initial refers only to males. Although legally enforceable, the distinction is hard for people to remember. I've read many newspaper articles where upper- and lower-case *homme* are used in alternation, as substitutes for each other.

Russian, on the other hand, retains even in its current constitution a form of words copied directly and somewhat unnaturally from eighteenth-century French: права и свободы человека и гражданина, 'rights and freedoms of man and citizen', with the masculine serving for the general, and the word for 'human being' being used in place of the more plausible человечество, 'humanity'.

Despite this French-style solution to the problematic status of a phrase that began life in French but has come back to plague it, the adjective + noun version of 'human rights' has continued to spread across all European languages – even in German, where it is hardly needed. In journalism and general usage, *menschliche Rechte*, patterned directly on 'human rights', is now used as an uncontentious alternative to *Menschenrechte*, which remains the proper term. Despite French language laws, moreover, *droits humains* is heard more and more often as the functional equivalent of *droits de l'Homme*: Rama Yade, French secretary of state 'chargée des droits de l'Homme' from 2007 to 2009, was frequently called (and also called herself) the minister for *droits humains*.

It's quite likely that this new use of *humain* in French will shunt its parallel sense of 'humane' into the cognate word *humanitaire*, and cause a minor reorganization of the lexical and semantic environment.

With the assistance of San Marino, the smallest member state of the UN, the Commission for Human Rights (UNCHR) encourages and disseminates translations of the Universal Declaration into all languages. The set currently exceeds 300, from Abkhaz to Zulu, and what is obvious from the effort so far is that, with only a few possible exceptions to add to Russian, the source language for translation is not French, but English.

The intellectual, political, moral and other consequences of the homogenization of languages into a single structure for the semantic field of 'the human' is beyond the scope of this book. What we can say, however is that the history and present state of the translation of 'human rights' provides clear evidence that international law tends to create a language of its own. In this instance, which is undoubtedly typical, the language of international law – whatever language it seems to be in – is increasingly calibrated to English-language norms.

It could be seen as historical revenge, for England was under the thumb of Law French for many centuries. French was the language of Law imposed by the Norman Conquest in 1066, but it was understood only by the ruling class. It continued to be used for centuries in the courts, in spite of or probably because of the fact that the majority of the population didn't have a clue as to what was being said. But Law French underwent its own process of contamination from below over a period of 600 years, adopting phrases, words and grammatical structures from the actually dominant tongue. By the seventeenth century, the official language of English justice sounded like something out of Miles Kington's comic column for *The Times*:

> Richardson, ch. Just. de C. Banc al Assises at Salisbury in Summer 1631. fuit assault per prisoner la condemne pur felony que puis son condemnation ject un Brickbat a le dit Justice que narrowly mist, & pur ceo immediately fuit Indictment drawn per Noy envers le Prisoner, & son dexter manus ampute & fix al Gibbet sur que luy mesme immediatement hange in presence de Court.[4]

Quite different problems arise when a court of law seeks not only to prosecute defendants speaking a different tongue, but to do so in a jurisdiction that has authority in a transnational sphere. The idea of there being an international law – universal norms of legitimate behaviour not determined by any one sovereign state – is very recent. It first dawned in horrified reaction to the sufferings of troops in the Crimean

War in 1857–8, then took its initial form in the various Geneva conventions about the rules of combat. The first major institution resting on an idea of international law was the League of Nations, set up in the aftermath of the First World War. But it was only the Second World War and awareness of the unspeakable persecutions carried out by the Nazi state that finally prompted sovereign nations to abandon their historical prerogatives and to establish a jurisdiction that sat above them all.

Translation was at the heart of the International Military Tribunal that opened in Nuremberg, Germany, in November 1945. What had to be established first was the overall legal procedure to be used, and that was no straightforward task. Two of the victorious Allies used a common-law system, and the other two, France and the USSR, like defeated Germany, had different but related versions of what is called civil law. In civil law systems, defendants make opening and closing statements, but do not participate in any other part of their own trial. They sit in a special place, and cannot be subject to further examination, since that is supposed to have been conducted exhaustively by the examining magistrates, who brief the prosecuting team. In the common law tradition, on the contrary, a defendant is held to be innocent until found guilty, and is therefore treated formally as just another witness to the crime. That's the reason why American courtroom dramas are so much more exciting than French versions of the same genre. The Nuremberg court adopted a mixed system: it was not a jury trial, as it would have been had it been conducted entirely within British or American systems, but a tribunal judged by an international panel of judges. But it did impose cross-examination on the defendants, who were called to the witness box in German. However, in German, 'witness' is *Zeuge*, and a *Zeuge* cannot give testimony at his own trial. The arguments about how to proceed at the Nuremberg trials were not only about language, but about the incommensurable differences between the languages, institutions and customs of different languages of law. Law translation in international affairs always runs up against huge obstacles of that kind: law words do not mean the same thing when translated, and the institutions they serve are not the same.

Over the last sixty years the scope and implementation of international law has expanded at a prodigious rate. The sought-after effect – sought after by political will, but implemented by legal translation teams – is to bring the different meanings of words belonging to incommensurable systems of law into greater harmony, or, as critics of this process protest, to homogenize and standardize the idea of what the law is. Karen MacAuliffe reports that lawyer linguists working at the European Court of Justice are aware that EU law is a legal system 'built from approximations of law and language from different legal cultures and different legal languages, which come together to form a new supranational legal system *with its own language*'.[5]

This is exactly what the Saussurean theory of the sign would entail. What language scholars rarely take into account is that, given sufficient effort and political will, new systems can be made.

21. *Ceci n'est pas une traduction*: Language Parity in the European Union

> This Treaty, drawn up in a single original in the Danish, Dutch, English, French, German, Greek, Irish, Italian, Portuguese and Spanish languages, the texts in each of these languages being equally authentic, shall be deposited in the archives of the Government of the Italian Republic, which will transmit a certified copy to each of the governments of the other signatory States. Pursuant to the Accession Treaty of 1994, the Finnish and Swedish versions of this Treaty shall also be authentic. Pursuant to the Accession Treaty of 2003, the Czech, Estonian, Hungarian, Latvian, Lithuanian, Maltese, Polish, Slovak and Slovene versions of this Treaty shall also be authentic.

So reads a recent version of the basic language rule of the European Union. It was originally laid down in article 248 of the Treaty of Rome that first set up the European Economic Community in 1957: that body, and any offices under its authority, was to communicate with the governments of each of the member states in the language of the member state in question. It sounds a modest requirement, but it was actually a revolution. Unlike all previous empires, communities, treaties and international organizations, the European Union has no one language and no finite set of languages either. It speaks in all the languages that it needs, whatever they may be. An act of political will made the previously ungrammatical expression

– 'a single original in Danish, Dutch, English . . .' – an authoritative rule.

To begin with there were six states – Belgium, France, Holland, Luxembourg, Italy and Germany – and four languages involved – French, Dutch, German and Italian. The Union has grown meanwhile and now has twenty-seven states using twenty-four different languages. But whether we are dealing with four or twenty-four languages, the revolutionary meaning of the basic rule, ill understood when adopted and not widely acknowledged even now, is that in the whole huge mass of paper put out by the EU, there are no translations. Everything is the original, already.

Each language version of a law, regulation, directive or letter emanating from the Commission or any of its institutions has the same force, the same authority, the same validity as any other. Nothing is a translation – except that everything is translated. This has been the unprecedented language rule under which increasingly large numbers of people have now lived and worked for more than fifty years.

You might think it would have made a difference to what people say about translation, but for the most part it has not. Since it is theoretically impossible to have more than one original of a text in the long-standing traditions of literary study and language teaching, people have tended to disregard the language reality of the EU, to denigrate it as a waste of a huge amount of money, or to utter dire warnings of the risks it incurs. However, I've yet to meet a translator who has turned down a well-paid job in Brussels or Strasbourg on language-theoretical grounds.

The language rule of the Treaty of Rome was obviously not thought up by philosophers, linguists or translators, let alone by theorists. It arose from the need to make all members of this daring new venture feel they had equal respect and equal rights – to abolish what I have dubbed translation UP and DOWN. It was invented by politicians for eminently political reasons. What's more, those politicians and several generations of their successors have been prepared to devote substantial sums of money to making the language parity rule work. DG Translation (the translation division of the European civil service) currently employs 1,750 linguists and 600 support staff, and spends vast amounts of money to produce millions of pages of administrative and legal prose every year – probably more than has ever been spent on translation by any community ever before.[1]

From the 1960s it became fashionable to think, in a manner attributed to Michel Foucault, that language is power and that all power is language. The EU language story, like Orwell's polemical invention of 'Newspeak' in *Nineteen Eighty-Four*, doesn't invalidate that entirely – but it does go to show that, in the last analysis, power is power. Language is no less a possible object of political will than any other human activity.

The language parity rule has many interesting consequences. It means that no official EU text can be faulted or dismissed or even queried on grounds of it having been incorrectly translated from the original, since every language version *is* in the original. Faced with a single original in twenty-four different languages, none of the inherited and traditional issues of translation commentary has much purchase. You could call this a political fiction. But it is not theoretical. It exists.

Paired texts in different languages each having equal force are nothing new, in fact. The Rosetta Stone bears a decree written in 196 BCE in honorific legalese to record a tax amnesty granted to temple priests in Egypt. It was carved on a slab of basalt in *koiné* Greek, in demotic Egyptian and in hieroglyphics. The decree was clearly intended to have the same force for three different groups of people among its potential addressees. Commonly treasured as the source of the clues that led to the decipherment of hieroglyphic script, the Rosetta Stone should also be taken as proof that the founders of the EU were not seeking the impossible when they adopted the language parity rule.

The written history of the two main languages of the original EU also began with a bilingual edict. The Strasbourg Oath was sworn in 842 CE by two grandsons of Charlemagne who ganged up on a cousin they suspected of trying to elbow them out of their inheritance. Charles and Louis spoke different languages – the one having an early dialect of German, the other an early dialect of what would become French. Each swore allegiance to the other in the language of his ally. This was not just feudal politeness. The Oath was written down so it could be copied and taken around and read out to the armies of Charles and Louis. Louis did not need it to tell his own people not to fight Charles, nor did Charles need it to tell his own people not to fight Louis's men. Each needed to give assurance to the other side that he was no longer an enemy, but an ally in the common fight against cousin Lothaire. That is why they produced a bilingual screed, with the texts in the two languages in parallel columns, each intended not to say exactly the same thing, but to have exactly the same force when read out loud to bands of illiterate soldiers. The Strasbourg Oath, the founding document of two languages and also the key to the geographical shape that European nations have taken since then, is also the founding document of the EU's language norm.

But there is a catch. It's unlikely that the signatories of the Oath actually spoke to each other in either of the languages written down. They probably used Latin for face-to-face negotiation of the terms of the treaty, and then left their scribes to find a way of writing down the agreement in the (previously unrecorded) languages of their troops. So although there is no explicit original of the Strasbourg Oaths, it is very likely there was an implicit master-text which would have been the out-turn of a bargaining session in learned Latin that was probably translated by scribes or educated slaves into Old High German and Old French respectively.

It's an open secret that the EU also possesses an interlanguage for most practical uses in the corridors of the Berlaymont building, in the canteens and private meeting rooms – and it's English. However, it is definitely not the case that EU texts are first written in English and then translated. Things work in an altogether more interesting way. A panel or subcommittee meets to draft a regulation. It uses one of the four official working languages of the EU – German, French, English, Italian – but there are always other language drafters present. The first draft is argued over not only for content but also for how it is going to be expressed in the other working languages. The draft is then translated and the committee reconvenes with the drafters to smooth out difficulties and inconsistencies in the different versions. The drafters are indistinguishably language professionals and civil servants participating in the development of the substantive text of EU regulations. The back-and-forth movement of the draft between the committee and the drafting departments produces, in the end, a text all consider equal in all its versions, and in that sense the 'language fiction' of the EU's rule of parity is not fictional at all.

The European Court of Justice in Luxembourg (ECJ), which resolves questions of law that cannot be answered by any of the national appeals courts of the states that make up the Union, is run in a slightly different way. It has a single working language, which is French. All documents used at every level by the court are either written in French or translated into French by members of the army of language professionals who work there. However, plaintiffs – who may be member states or authorities within a national jurisdiction – may bring cases in whichever language they wish, which is normally the language of that state. The language of the state becomes 'the language of the case' and all documents in the file, whatever their source, must be translated into that language. More work for (different members) of the law-and-language team. But that is only half the story. The legal decisions of the court are made by all or some of the twenty-seven European Advocates General, one appointed by each of the member states. The ultimate authority consists of a set of distinguished judges collectively speaking and writing all twenty-four languages of the Union. They use French for lunchtime conversation, informal consultations and committee discussion, but they give their all-important opinions on the cases before them in their home tongues. For example, a case brought by the Portuguese government against a Bavarian dairy farming consortium that is judged by the Estonian Advocate General involves translations in five directions – POR⇨FRE, FRE⇨POR, FRE⇨GER, GER⇨FRE, and EST⇨FRE, allowing four additional transmissions by relay from French POR⇨[FRE]⇨GER, GER⇨[FRE]⇨POR, EST⇨[FRE]⇨POR, and EST⇨[FRE]⇨GER. The three remaining directions (see p. 171 for the maths), from French, Portuguese and German into Estonian, are not needed because, except when giving his opinion, the Advocate General operates in the language of the court, which is French.

However, since the rulings of the ECJ have force in the entire Union, legal opinions are not released and do not come into effect until they have been translated into all twenty-four of the Union's official tongues. Every section of the 750-strong corps of lawyer-linguists at the ECJ becomes involved at some stage in every decision that is made.

Eurosceptics treat this lavish provision of multidirectional translation at the ECJ as a scandal of waste – a mere job creation scheme. It's true things didn't happen that way in the appeal courts of the multilingual Ottoman and Habsburg states, and the ECJ does cost a lot to run. It's also true that the law of unintended consequences means that language parity as implemented in the steel-and-glass palace on the Kirchberg plateau creates very awkward disparities of its own. If you are a trained lawyer from Malta, Estonia or Hungary with excellent French and a good knowledge of one other European language, the job opportunities in Luxembourg are very attractive indeed. The effect is that Malta, Estonia and Hungary have difficulty recruiting such individuals for their own national civil services, where their skills are very much in need. But if you are a British lawyer with excellent French and one other European language under your belt, you have far more lucrative careers waiting for you in London and New York, and the ECJ thus has a chronic shortage of translators into precisely those languages it most frequently needs.

But the Union cannot exist without the ECJ. If the ECJ were to abandon its own version of the language parity rule, it's not obvious how European law could have force in any of its twenty-seven member states. That's why for the last fifty years all supposedly commonsensical or budgetary objections to its translation regime have been overruled. The political will to make Europe work is too strong and too grand to let translation issues stand in its way. Europe really has built a radically new kind of translation world.

What's quite specific to the ECJ, however, is that it does not employ translators as such. Language professionals in the Kirchberg complex are all also lawyers, and they are involved in the work of the court at many levels beyond strict language transfer.

Lawyer-linguists have access to confidential material and work under the same procedural rules as lawyers; they also advise on drafting, down to the small details that might produce ambiguities when expressed in other languages. The work of a lawyer-linguist is much more than translation – it is the manipulation of the law as language and language as law.[2]

Many of the cases brought before the ECJ arise from conflicting interpretations in different member states of regulations made by the European authorities – in effect, clashes between different interpretations of different language versions of what is held to be the same text. Given that all language versions have force of law, how does the court deliver the judgement of Solomon that *this* version is to be preferred over *that*?

They can't call either version a translation since all versions are originals; because the court's working language is French, moreover, there are almost always three texts or formulations involved. On rare occasions the taboo word 'translation mistake' has been used – for example, when the German version of a regulation about the import of sour cherries used the term *Süßkirschen*, 'sweet cherries', instead.[3] Such an easy judgment is untypical of the court's work. More frequently the court has to decide what the law was intended to achieve, over and above any one of its linguistic expressions. In monolingual national cultures of law, the best evidence of the legislator's intention lies in the words of the law, and much traditional legal argument is about the meanings of words. In European law, you have to go one further than that. Questions of legal interpretation in the appeal court of the EU are also always questions about language in twenty-four different forms.

Let's suppose in some practical circumstance not foreseen by the drafters of an EU directive there is a substantive difference in the force of the French and the German texts, and that this has given rise to a complaint by France that Germany is not applying EU law correctly. The ECJ has to decide whether France is right or not. But since there is no master-text (in Latin, for instance) to provide a higher authority or a standard of judgment, the court has basically only two ways of working out what it thinks. Using the skills of its divisions of lawyer-linguists it can list all the language versions that support the French interpretation, and all those whose sense in the context of the case leans more towards the German interpretation – and grant victory to the larger group, whichever it is. But the ECJ does not have to proceed by this kind of 'majority verdict'. It may identify one language version that it considers to have expressed the legislative intention of the directive more clearly, or more precisely, than any of the others.

Both these procedures hark back to the tools developed by the Church Fathers for establishing the 'word of God' through comparisons of the different translations of the Bible (principally, the Greek and Latin ones). What has been called the 'Augustinian approach' to the interpretation of European law effectively seeks to establish a meaning that transcends any one of its language versions but which animates them all. It runs into some fairly obvious problems.

In *Peterson* v. *Weddel & Co. Ltd*, the issue was a criminal prosecution within the UK for violation of a regulation setting limits on the operations of lorries. An EU regulation exists that allows member states to make exemptions from the general rule for the 'transport of animal carcasses or waste not intended for human consumption'. The firm that had been fined in the UK had been transporting animal carcasses *to butcher's shops*, which clearly intended to sell them for human consumption. But the lorry firm claimed it was exempted from the rule by the EU clause just quoted, and was appealing against a British court's refusal to allow it to get away with its behaviour. The lorry firm's lawyers claimed that waste not intended for human consumption and animal carcasses in general (whether intended for human consumption or not) were exempted, whereas the UK courts had considered that the exemption only applied to waste and animal carcasses NOT intended for human consumption. It may sound arcane, but the issue was clear enough: was the lorry firm cheating on the rules or was it not?

The issue at the heart of this case is a familiar problem in the language of law and in language in general: when you have a list of nouns followed by a qualifying or restricting phrase, where do you put the brackets? Does the restricting phrase restrict every member of the list, or only the last one? Does the expression 'children and women with babes in arms' include children with babes in arms or does it not?

In daily usage we leave disambiguation of this kind to common sense and context. In law, it's fertile ground for pernickety legalese. When this issue came before the ECJ, however, the lawyers, the linguists and especially the lawyer-linguists began by reviewing and comparing all twenty-four language versions of the exemption. They found one among them – the Dutch text – where the restriction to goods 'not intended for human consumption' precedes both 'animals' and 'waste'. It does so for almost exclusively grammatical reasons.

The court treated it as a godsend, however, not as a grammatical variant of the same ambiguous text. It chose to regard the Dutch order of words as a clearer and more precise expression than all the others of the true intention of the law – and turned down the appeal. The lorry firm had to pay the fine.[4]

Let's assume that the EU body which first thought of exempting certain classes of trucks from general rules was thinking about trucks full of potentially rotting and smelly flesh. What's of interest here is not the ECJ's final judgment, with which we can easily agree, but the reasoning it used to justify itself. The reasoning is of a very simple grammatical kind: it says that qualifications preceding a list of nouns apply to all nouns in the list. This semantic principle is made manifest in the Dutch version, but all the others, which for grammatical or stylistic rules put the qualification at the end of the list, must be taken as expressing the same thought.

The reasoning does not make sense in most of the languages of the EU and especially not in the court's working language, French, where all kinds of qualifiers, including simple adjectives attached to single nouns, follow and do not precede the noun. Where does the ECJ's insight into the clarity of Dutch come from? The most likely answer is the grammar of English. It is English, not French, Spanish or Hungarian, that lends intuitive support to the view that 'not-intended-for-human-consumption animal carcasses and waste' is a less ambiguous expression than 'animal carcasses and waste not intended for human consumption'. Despite the huge and conscious efforts it makes in precisely the opposite direction, the ECJ cannot resist the slow but steady homogenization of the languages it uses to uphold European law.

I don't mean to snipe at this particular judgment or to undermine the important work that the legal-cum-linguistic contortionists of Luxembourg do. However, the comparative method used to establish the ultimate intention of a law – a method that can be likened to St Augustine's practice of biblical exegesis – must itself be conducted in a language. Suppositions and assumptions about the meanings of words, grammatical structures and rhetorical turns are necessarily rooted *in one language*, not suspended on a hook from a supra-linguistic legal sky. In the polyglot corridors and canteens at Kirchberg, however, where you may start a conversation with a Spanish judge in French and switch to German to say hello to a nice person from Prague, it's a truth that is easy to forget. As one lawyer working there said to me when I visited, he never really thinks about which of his four languages he is speaking or writing at any given time – he switches without conscious effort, as if he was just shifting the weight of his shoulder bag from the left to the right side. The outcome of such unconscious linguistic determinations of legal finagling is that the meaning and grammar of twenty-four languages have begun to merge into an ECJ language culture that is all its own – *sui generis*, in Saussure's terms, or 'Eurospeak' in common language. As one of the few scholars to have studied the language maze of Luxembourg closely puts it, 'the unique situational factors in the production of European jurisprudence have led to a hybridization of law and language.' It seems to me – admittedly an outsider and an amateur in this field – that the underlying structure of this new hybrid, even though it is formally expressed through the medium of French, is provided by the English tongue.

Some people from both 'Europhile' and 'Eurosceptic' factions think that it would be better if European institutions were run in English anyway. This is because the language parity rule of the EU is a constant cause for delay, and also tends to make official decisions and opinions more contorted and obscure than they really need to be. As stated earlier, the rulings of the ECJ come into force when they are published, simultaneously, in all the official languages of the Union. Judges are therefore under constant if discreet pressure from their permanently overworked lawyer-linguists to keep it short. European jurisprudence is therefore typically tight-lipped and does not provide the many pages of argument and justification that normally accompany a ruling from the House of Lords or the US Supreme Court. The laudable political aim of treating all the languages of Europe as equal produces the unwanted but perhaps inevitable result that ECJ rulings are sometimes so pithy as to defy comprehension in any of them.

22. *Translating* News

In 1838, when travelling on a slow boat to Trieste, the poet Robert Browning imagined how in times past news was brought from Ghent in Belgium to Aix in Germany:

> I sprang to the stirrup, and Joris, and he;
> I gallop'd, Dirck gallop'd, we gallop'd all three ...

What he doesn't say, however, is how the mounted couriers turned the information they bore from Flemish into German, which is what people understand in Aix. In ages past, news rushed from any European A to B would most likely have been issued and received in French. But nowadays we are accustomed to receiving topical information in print and on radio, television and the web in our home languages, with minimal lag between event and report. But how do good and bad tidings now get from Shenzen to Chicago, from Marseilles to Melbourne, from Rio to Ryazan? Electronic media account for the speed, but do not explain how political and human events deemed to be news happen in a language which is rarely our own but reach us almost instantaneously in the language that is.

The quantity of information flowing round the globe in uncountable languages might be taken to suggest that in some hidden anthill a busy troop of language insects lives on permanent standby, ready to turn news from any of the world's languages into all the others at the drop of a hat. But it can't be so, because that would require almost 49 million separate teams of language ants (see p. 171) – and a human anthill of that size would be difficult to hide. Even if a hypothetical global news translation HQ served only eighty vehicular languages, it would still require 6,320 different language desks. Given a forty-hour work week for each translator and allowing for sudden peaks in demand when great events happen in Paris or Peoria, you couldn't house the enterprise in anything less than the Empire State Building. But no skyscraper in New York, London or Rio houses a world news translation centre. In fact, news bureaus the world over have hardly any translators on their staff at all. Like the lawyer-linguists at the European Court of Justice, language mediators in the news business are almost always something else as well.

Most of the world's languages are spoken by quite small groups, and news media do not exist in many of these tongues. Even so, there are hundreds of languages – perhaps more than a thousand – which have some modest level of news service in print or on the air. Latin, for example, has daily thirty-minute news bulletins broadcast from Helsinki; Gaelic has seven hours of programming per day, part of which is news, on BBC Alba TV. But most consumer news media don't make the news, save on rare occasions. Most of them are themselves consumers of worldwide agency services, called wires, which process and put out news in no more than half a dozen tongues. The main hubs are Reuters (the first news agency in the world, founded in 1851), Associated Press (AP), Agence France-Press (AFP), and Inter Press Service (IPS), massively supplemented in recent years by CNN, Al Jazeera, the BBC on the web and, for financial news especially, the Bloomberg wire.[1]

News of flooding in Bangladesh or a coup d'état in Rwanda

or Kyrgyzstan does not come to you, wherever you are, from Dhaka, Kigali or Bishkek. It comes to your local news source from the agencies, in English, French, Spanish, German (all agencies), Portuguese (Reuters, AFP), Dutch (AP only) or Arabic (Reuters since 1954 and AFP since 1969). It is rewritten almost instantaneously by journalists working for your local paper or radio station from whichever language version they receive from one or more of the wires. The global transmission languages are those of the colonial empires of the nineteenth century, plus Arabic. Chinese, Japanese, Hindi, Indonesian and all other languages are not in the game.

Journalists who compose the articles and stories you actually read often have language skills, but they do not think of themselves as translators. They would be offended if you said that's what they are – even if some news stories you can read in the London press, for example, are very close indeed to what you read in yesterday's *Le Monde*. Journalists think of their jobs as turning plain information into arresting, entertaining or readable prose suited to the culture, interests and knowledge of the people who read them – and that's more than what most people think translation is. The pecking order is reflected in pay and conditions of service the world over: *journalist* outranks *translator* everywhere.

The language operations performed in news agency work are of particular interest because they are predicated not only on the total invisibility of translation, but also on anonymity and impersonality. A note originating in language A reaching an agency desk is transformed into a wire in language B in a way that fits it for reuse in the culture of language B without respect for any of the discursive, stylistic or cultural features of the original. Agency work does not seek to respect the text or its origin, only the facts that lie behind the narrative. The resulting wire is a collective composition and also a reduction or expansion attributable to no one individual, only to the service provider. The wire text is then reformulated in the other languages in which that particular agency operates, again with additions and subtractions, all designed to achieve maximum clarity and usefulness in languages C through N, and made available worldwide so as to be rewritten a fourth time in any of the languages used by subscribers to the service. In its fourth redaction the story may be completely re-contextualized in a news article attributed to a local journalist. That is to say, before you read a speech in English originally made in Teheran and in Farsi about an hour after it has been uttered, it may have been reformulated in Arabic by Al Jazeera's man in Iran, then rewritten as an English wire by the AP bureau in Kuwait before being rephrased by a journalist in London; similarly, the news of an earthquake in Thailand may have been first reported in French by AFP's Bangkok bureau and then issued on AFP's English-language service from Paris before being rewritten into Farsi for the Iranian TV news a few minutes later. The structure of this elaborate network of skilled professionals producing international news ensures that the different language versions of a given note do not ever say exactly the same thing. They are held to communicate the same *information*, but the ways in which it is communicated are calibrated to well-founded assumptions about the political, social, religious, intellectual, moral and other sensitivities that are prevalent in the receiving language and culture.

In these circumstances, how can you possibly know that the news is true? Well, you can't. You just trust the news, which means that even if you don't realize it and often claim the opposite in dinner party talk, you trust journalist-translators, completely. How else could you believe that you know the first thing about what's going on in the world?

Paradoxically, but not unreasonably, global news is a local product. This is not because of any *linguistic* obstacles to the circulation of information. Rather, it is because communication tasks in this field are subordinated to the real or perceived constraints imposed by the receiver. To get the nugget of new news from Ghent to Aix, contemporary postillions adjust, adapt, excise or add almost anything to the source save that part of the reference deemed to be 'news'. In a relatively short rhetorical leap, you could use this to reassert the radical position that all facts about the world are linguistic constructions and nothing else. But news agencies and the people who work in them are not interested in deconstruction. They pursue their trade with the firm conviction that the information they disseminate in different linguistic and rhetorical versions lies beyond language, in the domain of the real.

The way that translating is integrated into other kinds of language work in global news distribution is far from unique. In transnational law (at the ECJ, for instance), in diplomacy and in the work of many international organizations, no precise boundary can be drawn between translation, on the one hand, and drafting, editing, correcting, reformulating and adapting a text, whether written in the same or in some other tongue. In these many important domains, translating is just one element in the progressive refinement and wider circulation of texts.

Two side-effects of the manner in which news is transmitted between different languages and communities of users are worth noting. The first is that it makes the 'translatedness' of news completely invisible. However, even if the occlusion of translation is the express intention of the EU's language parity rule, it is not a fatality in the circulation of news, and could easily be countered. A report of the latest speech by the Iranian president, for example, could perfectly well be attributed to a named journalist's adaptation of a Reuters English-language wire originating in Kuwait based on a report in Arabic from Al Jazeera which had provided the information from listening to a radio broadcast in Farsi from Teheran. The second consequence of our collective unwillingness to track the language history of the things we are told by the media is to make us believe that the provision of international news is a straightforward matter, dependent only on the marvels of satellite telephones and data transmission. It is not. It is a burdensome business carried out by talented linguist-journalists working under tight constraints of time.

23. *The* Adventure *of* Automated *Language* Translation *Machines*

The reluctance of European peoples to retain Latin or to adopt some other transmission language – such as Esperanto – for the dissemination of important information has created a costly and difficult set of translation tasks, carried out under time pressures unimaginable in earlier ages. Now that nearly all other aspects of news transmission are carried out not by couriers but by electronic devices, it seems natural to ask why the core activity itself cannot be handled likewise, by automatic translation machines.

Although it is still in its infancy, machine translation has had an eventful and uneven history. It first arose in dramatic historical circumstances and in response to an overriding political need. It wasn't initiated by an explicit act of political will, like the language rules of the European Union, but its launching ground was the climate of terror at the start of the Cold War. The United States had developed and used the atomic bomb. For the time being it had a monopoly on this terrible weapon. How long would the monopoly last? When would the Soviet Union catch up? One way of guessing the answer was to comb through all the research journals being published in the USSR, looking for clues as to the state of knowledge in the relevant disciplines.[1] The journals were in Russian. The US needed either to train up a veritable army of Russian–English scientific translators – or to invent a machine that would do the job for them.

But it takes a long time to constitute a large group of translators from a language not widely known. There was no obvious source of English-educated, scientifically literate Russian translators in 1945, and so the authorities began to look towards machines. There were good reasons to think they could help with the urgent task of tracking the Soviets' ability to design an atomic bomb.

The Second World War had fostered great advances in cryptography, the making and breaking of secret codes. Statistical techniques had been developed for decoding messages even when the language that had been encoded was not known. The astounding successes of the code-breakers at the Bletchley Park site in England prompted some thinkers to wonder whether language itself could not be treated as a code. In a famous memorandum written in July 1949, Warren Weaver, then a senior official with the Rockefeller Foundation, found it

> very tempting to say that a book written in Chinese is simply a book in English which was coded into the 'Chinese code'. If we have useful methods for solving almost any cryptographic problem, may it not be that with proper interpretation we already have useful methods for translation?[2]

Weaver was aware of the pioneering work of Claude Shannon and others in the nascent disciplines of information theory and cybernetics, and could see that if language could be treated as a code, then there would be huge development contracts available for mathematicians, logicians and engineers working on the new and exciting number-crunching devices that had only just acquired their modern name of computers. But the temptation to see 'language as code' comes from much deeper sources than just an intuition that it would create interesting jobs for very smart boys.

A code or cipher is a way of representing a piece of information in a way that is only receivable if the (secret) key to the code is available. However sophisticated the key, however complicated the algorithm that turns the 'source' into 'code', there is always a discoverable relationship between the expression in code, and the encoded expression. If a language itself is a code of that kind, what does it encode? There's only one possible answer in the long Western tradition of thinking about language since the time of the Greeks, and that answer is: meaning (sometimes called 'thought'). A translation machine would need to strip away from the actual expression in language A all that is 'code', so as to access the real thing that it encodes, namely, the actual, irreducible, plain and basic meaning of the expression. It's really no more than a rehearsal of the ancient idea that language is the dress of thought. Weaver himself proposed the following analogy:

> Think of individuals living in a series of tall closed towers, all erected on a common foundation. When they try to communicate with one another, they shout back and forth, each from his own closed tower. It is difficult to make the sounds penetrate even the nearest towers, and communication proceeds very poorly indeed. But when an individual goes down his tower, he finds himself in a great open basement, common to all the towers. Here he establishes easy and useful communication with the persons who have also descended from their towers.[3]

That dream of 'easy and useful communication' with all our fellow humans in the 'great basement' that is the common foundation of human life expresses an ancient and primarily religious view of language and meaning that has proved very hard to escape, despite its manifestly hypothetical nature. For what language would humans use to communicate with each other in the 'great basement'? The language of pure meaning. At later stages in the adventure of machine translation and modern linguistics, it came to be called 'interlingua' or 'the invariant core' of meaning and thought that a communication in any language encodes.

The task that machine translation pioneers set themselves was therefore almost identical to the task of the translator as expressed by many modern theorists and philosophers: to discover and implement the purely hypothetical language which all people really speak in the great basement of their souls.

How was that to be done by machines? Plenty of intellectual machinery already existed that seemed designed for the purpose. Ever since the Romans started teaching their young to read and write Greek, language learners in Western tongues have always been told they have two basic tasks: to acquire vocabulary in the foreign tongue; and to learn its grammar. That's why we have bilingual dictionaries separate from our grammar books, which give the set of rules by which the 'words' in the vocabulary may be combined into acceptable strings. That's what a language is, in our ancient but undimmed language theology: a Meccano set, made up for one part of nuts, bolts, girders, beams, cogwheels and perforated bars (let's say, prepositions, verbs, nouns, adjectives, particles and determiners) and, for the other part, rules about how to fix them together. A nut goes on to a bolt but not on to a cogwheel, just as a verb clicks on to a subject before and an object after ...

It was theoretically possible at the start of the machine translation adventure (and it soon became practically possible as well) to store a set of words on a computer, divided into the grammatical classes the Greeks and Romans devised. It was equally possible to store two sets of words, one for Russian, one for English, and to tell the computer which English word matched which Russian one. More dubious was the proposition implicit in Weaver's fable that you could bring people down from their separate towers to the common basement – that's to say, tell a computer what to do to unwrap the meaning of a sentence from the form of the sentence itself. To do that, the computer would first need to know the entire grammar of a language. It would have to be told what that consists of. But who knows the entire grammar of English? Every language learner quickly realizes that systematic regularities are frequently overruled by exceptions of arbitrary kinds. Every speaker of a native language knows that she can (and frequently does) break the 'rules' of grammar. A complete linguistic description of any language remains an aspiration, not a reality. That is one of the two reasons why the first great phase of machine translation hit the buffers. The second is that even humans, who can be assumed to be in full possession of the grammar of their language, still need a heap of knowledge about the world in order to fix the meaning of any expression – and nobody has figured out how to get a computer to know what a sentence is *about*. A classic conundrum that computers could not solve is to attribute the correct meanings to the words in the following two sentences: 'The pen is in the box' and 'The box is in the pen'. Understanding them calls on knowledge of the relative sizes of things in the real world (of a pen-sized box, and a sheep-pen, respectively) that can't be resolved by dictionary-meanings and syntactic rules. In 1960, the eminent logician Yehoshua Bar-Hillel, who had been hired by MIT specifically to develop 'fully automated high-quality translation', or FAHQT, sounded a testy retreat:

> I have repeatedly tried to point out the illusory character of the FAHQT ideal even in respect to mechanical determination of

the syntactical structure of a given source-language sentence . . . There exist extremely simple sentences in English – and the same holds, I am sure, for any other natural language – which, within certain linguistic contexts, would be . . . unambiguously translated into any other language by anyone with a sufficient knowledge of the two languages involved, though I know of no program that would enable a machine to come up with this unique rendering unless by a completely arbitrary and *ad hoc* procedure . . . [4]

That pretty much put an end to easy money from the grant-giving foundations. But the establishment of the European Union in 1957 provided a new political impetus – and a new funding source – for the development of the tools that Bar-Hillel thought impossible. Ambitions were scaled down from FAHQT to more feasible tasks. As computers grew in power and shrank in size, they could more easily be relied upon for tasks that humans find tiresome, such as checking that a given term has been translated the same way each time it occurs in a long document. They could be used for compiling and storing dictionaries not just of technical terms, but whole phrases and expressions. The era not of fully automatic translation, but of CAT – computer-aided translation – began. Private companies started developing proprietary systems, for although the big demand came from transnational entities like the EU, there was a real need for such tools among major companies producing aircraft, automobiles and other goods to be sold all over the world.

It is easier to achieve good results from CAT when the input conforms not to a natural language in its raw and living state, but to a restricted code, a delimited sub-species of a language. In an aircraft maintenance manual you find only a subset of the full range of expressions possible in English. To produce the hundred or so language versions of the manual that are needed through an automatic translation device, you do not need to make the device capable of handling restaurant menus, song lyrics or party chit-chat – just aircraft maintenance language. One way of doing this is to pre-edit the input text into a regularized form that the computer program can handle, and to have proficient translators post-edit the output, to make sure it makes sense (and the right sense) in the target tongue. Another way of doing it is to teach the drafters of the maintenance manuals a special, restricted language – Boeinglish, so to speak – designed to eliminate ambiguities and pitfalls within the field of aircraft maintenance. This is now a worldwide practice. Most companies that have global sales have house styles designed to help computers translate their material. From computers helping humans to translate we have advanced to having humans help computers out. It is just one of the truths about translation that shows that a language is really not like a Meccano set at all. Languages can always be squeezed and shaped to fit the needs that humans have, even when that means squeezing them into computer-friendly shapes.

Computer-aided human translation and human-aided computer translation are both substantial achievements, and without them the global flows of trade and information of the past few decades would not have been nearly so smooth. Until recently, they remained the preserve of language professionals. What they also did, of course, was to put huge quantities of translation products (translated texts paired with their source texts) in machine-readable form. The invention and the explosive growth of the Internet since the 1990s has made this huge corpus available for free to everyone with a terminal. And then Google stepped in.

Using software built on mathematical frameworks originally developed in the 1980s by researchers at IBM, Google has created an automatic translation tool that is unlike all others. It is not based on the intellectual presuppositions of Warren Weaver and it has no truck with interlingua or invariant cores. It doesn't deal with meaning at all. Instead of taking a linguistic expression as something that requires decoding, Google Translate takes it as something that has probably been said before. It uses vast computing power to scour the Internet in the blink of an eye looking for the expression in some text that exists alongside its paired translation. The corpus it can scan includes all the paper put out since 1957 by the EU in two dozen languages, everything the UN and its agencies have ever done in writing in six official languages, and huge amounts of other material, from the records of international tribunals to company reports and all the articles and books in bilingual form that have been put up on the web by individuals, libraries, booksellers, authors and academic departments. Drawing on the already established patterns of matches between these millions of paired documents, Google Translate uses statistical methods to pick out the most probable acceptable version of what's been submitted to it. Much of the time, it works. It's quite stunning. And it is largely responsible for the new mood of optimism about the prospects for FAHQT, Warren Weaver's original pie-in-the-sky.

GT could not work without a very large pre-existing corpus of translations. It is built upon the millions of hours of labour of human translators who produced the texts that GT scours. Google's own promotional video doesn't dwell on this at all. At present it offers two-way translation between fifty-eight languages, that is to say 3,306 separate translation services, more than have ever existed in all human history to date. Most of these translation relations – Icelandic⇨Farsi, Yiddish⇨ Vietnamese, and dozens more – are the newborn offspring of Google Translate: there is no history of translation between them, and therefore no paired texts, on the web or anywhere else. Google's presentation of its service points out that given the huge variations between languages in the amount of material its program can scan to find solutions, translation quality varies according to the language pair involved.[5] What it does not highlight is that GT is as much the prisoner of global flows in translation as we all are. Its admirably smart probabilistic computational system can only offer 3,306 translation directions by using the same device as has always assisted intercultural communication: pivots, or intermediary languages. It's not because Google is based in California that English is the main pivot. If you use statistical methods to compute the most likely match between languages that have never been matched directly before, you must use the pivot that can provide matches with both target and source.

The service that Google provides appears to flatten and diversify interlanguage relations beyond the wildest dreams of even the EU's most enthusiastic language parity proponents. But it is able to do so only by exploiting, confirming and increasing the central role played by the most widely translated language in the world's electronic databank of translated texts, which can only be the most consistently translated language in all other media too.

A good number of English-language detective novels, for example, have probably been translated into both Icelandic and Farsi. They thus provide ample material for finding matches between sentences in the two foreign languages; whereas Persian classics translated into Icelandic are surely far fewer, even including those works that have themselves made the journey by way of a pivot such as French or German. This means that John Grisham makes a bigger contribution to the quality of GT's Icelandic–Farsi translation device than Rumi or Haldor Laxness ever will. And the real wizardry of Harry Potter may well lie in his hidden power to support translation from Hebrew into Chinese.

GT-generated translations themselves go up on the web and become part of the corpus that GT scans, producing a feedback loop that reinforces the probability that the original GT translation was acceptable. But it also feeds on human translators, since it always asks users to suggest a better translation than the one it provides – a loop pulling in the opposite direction, towards greater refinement. It's an extraordinarily clever device. I've used it myself to check I had understood a Swedish sentence more or less correctly, for example, and it is used automatically as a web-page translator whenever you use a search engine. Of course, it may also produce nonsense. However, the kind of nonsense a translation machine produces is usually less dangerous than human-sourced bloopers. You can usually see instantly when GT has failed to get it right, because the output makes no sense, and so you disregard it. (This is why you should never use GT to translate into a language you do not know very well. Use it only to translate into a language in which you are sure you can recognize nonsense.) Human translators, on the other hand, produce characteristically fluent and meaningful output, and you really can't tell if they are wrong unless you also understand the source – in which case you don't need the translation at all.

If you remain attached to the idea that a language really does consist of words and rules and that meaning has a computable relationship to them (a fantasy that many philosophers still cling to), then GT is not a translation device. It's just a trick performed by an electronic bulldozer allowed to steal other people's work. But if you have a more open mind, GT suggests something else.

Conference interpreters can often guess ahead of what a speaker is saying because speakers at international conferences repeatedly use the same formulaic expressions. Similarly, an experienced translator working in a familiar domain knows without thinking that certain chunks of text have standard translations that he or she can slot in. At an even more basic level, any translator knows that there are some regular transpositions between the two languages she is working with – the French impersonal pronoun *on*, for example, will almost always require the English sentence to be in the passive, adjectives following a noun in French will need to be put in front of the equivalent English noun, and so on. These automatisms come from practice and experience. Translators don't reinvent hot water every day and they don't recalculate the transformation 'French *on* ⇨ English passive construction' each time it occurs. They behave more like GT – scanning their own memories in double-quick time for the most probable solution to the issue at hand. GT's basic mode of operation is much more like professional translation than is the slow descent into the 'great basement' of pure meaning that early machine translation developers imagined.

GT is also a splendidly cheeky response to one of the great myths of modern language studies. It was claimed, and for decades it was barely disputed, that what was so special about a natural language was that its underlying structure allowed an infinite number of different sentences to be generated by a finite set of words and rules. A few wits pointed out that this was no different from a British motor car plant, capable of producing an infinite number of vehicles each one of which had something different wrong with it – but the objection didn't make much impact outside Oxford. GT deals with translation on the basis not that every sentence is different, but that anything submitted to it has probably been said before. Whatever a language may be in principle, in practice it is used most commonly to say the same things over and over again. There is a good reason for that. In the great basement that is the foundation of all human activities, including language behaviour, we find not anything as abstract as 'pure meaning', but common human needs and desires. All languages serve those same needs, and serve them equally well. If we do say the same things over and over again, it is because we encounter the same needs, feel the same fears, desires and sensations at every turn. The skills of translators and the basic design of GT are, in their different ways, parallel reflections of our common humanity.

In September 2009 the new administration in the White House issued a science policy roadmap, entitled *Strategy for American Innovation*. The last section of this document calls for science and technology to be harnessed to address the 'Grand Challenges of the 21st Century', of which it gives half a dozen examples, such as solar cells as cheap as paint and intelligent prosthetics. The last line of the whole strategy puts among these long-range targets for national science policy the development of 'automatic, highly accurate and real-time translation between the major languages of the world – greatly lowering the barriers to international commerce and collaboration'.[5] Not every science policy target is achieved, but, with serious backing from the US administration now in place for the first time since 1960, machine translation is likely to advance far beyond the state in which we currently know it.

24. *A* Fish *in* Your *Ear*: The Short History of Simultaneous Interpreting

Speech predates writing by eons, and oral translation is far, far older than the written kind. Because speech is such an ephemeral thing – it's gone in a puff of warm air, which is all it is in the material sense – nothing can be known directly about speech translation for almost the entire duration of its history. Two things caused a huge change in the twentieth century: the invention of the telephone by Alexander Graham Bell in 1876; and a political need of the most pressing kind.

The Nuremberg trial of Nazi war criminals in 1945 was one of the most important courts of law in modern history and also an unprecedented event in the history of translation. The panel of judges and the prosecuting teams came from the four Allied Powers – the United States, Great Britain, France and the Soviet Union – speaking three different languages, and the defendants spoke a fourth language, German. Nothing like this had ever happened before. In courts located in a national jurisdiction, interpreters work consecutively, repeating in the language of the court what the foreign defendant has just said, and then repeating what the court says to the defendant (when the client is not being addressed directly, it may be done at low volume in a 'whisper translation' or *chuchotage*). Two-way oral translation of this normal kind obviously slows down the proceedings. But four-way translation? In twelve directions? Consecutive interpreting would have so lengthened the International Military Tribunal's case that everyone might lose the thread. For the Nuremberg trial, something new was needed.

Technology for speeding up multilingual interaction already existed. The Filene–Finlay Speech Translator had been tried out a few times in the 1920s by the International Labour Organization in Geneva. Users of the system had a telephone in front of them, and when a delegate could not understand what was being said she picked up the handset, dialled in to the exchange, and heard the speech in a different language (only two – French and English – were involved at that time). The translators sat at the back listening to the speech and speaking their translation of it into a sound-proofed awning called a Hushaphone, connected directly to the telephone exchange. The original Speech Translator was also used in 1934 for Adolf Hitler's address to a Nazi Party rally in Nuremberg for live broadcast on French radio.[1]

The Speech Translator was designed and promoted not for rapid two-way interaction in multiple languages, but for speeches read aloud from prepared written text – what Germans call *gesprochene Sprechsprache*, 'spoken speech language', the standard genre of politicians and public figures the world over. The Filene–Finlay device was acquired by IBM in the 1930s, and the company offered a complete set of partly second-hand but much enhanced and extended equipment for free to the Nuremberg Military Tribunal. This act of generosity was to prove an epochal event in the way in which we now conceive the possibility of international communication.

Members of the court, including the defendants, were equipped with headphones and microphones, from which wires trailed over the courtroom floor to the exchange. Wires ran from the exchange to four separate translation teams in separated compartments. That made for a lot of complicated wiring, but the real magic was what happened in the interpreters' booths.

Members of the court had switch dials to select which language channel they wished to listen to. The output was produced by four teams of three interpreters each. The English team had a German interpreter, a Russian interpreter and a French interpreter sitting side by side, listening on headphones, and repeating in English what was said in the other languages; the set-up was the same in the three other booths. Altogether, thirty-six interpreters were recruited from among the 300 language professionals hired by the court and the prosecution and defence teams to work at this brand-new and not obviously manageable task of instantaneous oral translation. Each of the twelve-strong teams worked 85-minute shifts on two days out of three and was expected to rest in between. From the very start of the new profession, simultaneous interpreting was recognized as being one of the most exhausting things you can do with a human brain.

The difficulty is not only high-speed language transfer. The difficulty is that the sound of your own voice diminishes your ability to hear what the other person is saying. That's why we take turns in conversation, and only speak over someone else when we really do *not* want to hear what he has to say. A simultaneous interpreter must learn to overrule the natural tendency not to listen when talking, and not to talk when listening. Simultaneous interpreting only exists because some very adept people can train themselves to do such an unnatural thing. Try it yourself: switch on a TV news broadcast and repeat at your own normal speaking volume exactly what the newscaster says. If you can keep that up without losing a sentence for ten minutes or more, then maybe you too could be a simultaneous interpreter – provided you know another two languages extremely well. Millions of people know three languages well enough to be interpreters, but only a small proportion of them can manage the exhausting trick of dividing attention between what you are saying and what you are hearing – without missing a word.

The trickiest part of high-speed language transfer is that politicians and diplomats do not characteristically use short, simple sentences without subordinate clauses, or leave long gaps between them. They tend to drone on with sausage-like strings of evasive circumlocutions: 'I am instructed by my ambassador to inform this august assembly that contrary to rumours reported in one of the organs of the capitalist press no authorized agent of the state has knowingly exported to any other country any materials covered by the international convention on . . .' Unfortunately, there is no convention on the export of long-windedness, and so interpreters have to begin reformulating sentences of this kind without knowing for sure where they will go, what their real point is, or what alteration to the structure of the start-point the end of the sentence will bring. Extremely sophisticated mental skills are required to 'hold' features of meaning in provisional formulations until the real topic of the sentence is finally let out of the bag. An interpreter who has to repair a sentence after it has begun (as we all do in normal speech) loses valuable time. The ability to pick the right formulae in a flash and to keep the sentence loose enough to cope with what may crop up next is acquired by experience and practice – together with an uncommonly developed capacity for finding instant matches between sentence patterns that are grammatically and stylistically far apart.

Most of the people involved in preparing the Nuremberg trial doubted this new-fangled set-up would work. We owe the modern world of conference interpreting more to the can-do attitude of the victorious US Army than to the considered judgement of prosecutors, judges and language professionals. Chief doubter among them was Richard Sonnenfeldt, the head of the US prosecution team's translation service. He'd been picked from a motor repair pool in Salzburg by General 'Wild Bill' Donovan to serve as translator in the long interrogations of the defendants that preceded the trial. He'd interrogated the Nazi top brass on behalf of four-star generals, and was asked to take charge of the simultaneous-interpreting team in the trial itself. Sonnenfeldt turned the job down because he was intimidated by the speed requirement and by his own lack of familiarity with legal terminology. But the main reason he backed off from running the world's first simultaneous-interpreting service was his professional opinion that either the people, or the system, or both would break down.[2]

He was right about the glitches. Microphones and headsets went on the blink; lawyers and witnesses (including the chief US attorney, Robert H. Jackson) spoke too fast; on more than one occasion, an interpreter burst into tears on hearing testimony from Rudolf Höss, the ice-cold commandant of Auschwitz. But, despite the obstacles, the system worked. Hermann Göring is said to have remarked to Stefan Hörn, one of the court translators, 'Your system is very efficient, but it will also shorten my life!'[3]

The speech translation system inaugurated at the Nuremberg War Crimes Tribunal launched a new era in international communication. The interpreters' achievements not only created a new skill and a new profession, but had an immediate and far-reaching effect on world affairs. First of all, every new international agency wanted a simultaneous translation system straight away, and thought it could just be bought at the store. In February 1946, when the Nuremberg Speech Translation system was barely run in, the first General Assembly of the newborn United Nations adopted as its second resolution that 'speeches made in any of the six languages of the Security Council shall be interpreted into the other five languages.'[4] Thereafter all the dependent agencies – from the ILO to the FAO, from UNESCO to the World Bank – acquired the equipment and sought to recruit the personnel to produce the magical illusion that every delegate would always be able to understand what any other delegate was saying as he or she was in the process of saying it.

This led outsiders to take it for granted that the diversity of languages was no longer an impediment to collective international action and world harmony. Insiders – diplomats and negotiators in all the new bodies set up by the UN – were under no such illusion. As one student of international law points out, texts and speeches produced in multilingual form at high speed may be grammatically correct, but they are never quite coherent. The small deviations that arise, over which delegates argue for hours on end, 'intensify the collective awareness of the importance of translation'.[5] But the early years of simultaneous interpreting were also years of great hope for a new world order ruled by 'jaw-jaw' in place of the preceding decades of 'war-war'. In those circumstances, the general public easily forgot just what a fragile and mysterious feat was being accomplished by a very small group of language gymnasts in the glass boxes in the rear of the assembly hall.

It hardly needs explaining why simultaneity in translation is an illusion. You cannot translate anything until you have heard what it is: translation is always a 'speaking after'. The impression of simultaneity is created by a bag of impressive language tricks. First, many speeches are read out from a pre-pared text. Diplomats sometimes provide the translation teams with the text in advance of the meeting – often only just in advance, but even a few minutes' head start takes away a lot of stress. Second, international meetings are dominated by speeches of a fairly predictable kind. Once you acquire experience of the kind of business being conducted and of the formulaic language it uses, you can run ahead of what is actually said and give yourself a little brain-space to listen for the all-important variations that the speaker might intro-duce. Contraction and change of orientation are also used for non-formulaic digressions: 'The Soviet delegate has just made a joke' can replace the telling of a long Russian shaggy-dog tale. But, even so, the skill of the conference interpreter (the term that has come to replace 'oral translator', 'simultane-ous translator' and 'speech translator') calls for high levels of concentration and mental agility. There are few people who can do it at all, and even fewer who want to do it day in and day out.

Sixty years of experience have not made it any easier to predict whether an individual can be turned into a confer-ence interpreter or not. Even now, between one half and three quarters of all students admitted to interpreter training courses fail to enter the profession.[6] At the beginning, in the aftermath of the Second World War, the disastrous history of the twentieth century had produced many thousands of people with outstanding language skills in several of the six official international languages (Spanish, English, French, Chinese, Russian and Arabic) – children of refugees from the Russian Revolution brought up in Shanghai and edu-cated at the Lycée français, where they learned English, young refugees from German-occupied France who had spent months or years in Cuba or Mexico awaiting a US visa before going to college in New York, and so on. The first generation of the elite of the translating professions consisted mostly of young people from backgrounds of that kind, who remained in post for thirty years and more. These founding mothers and fathers of the conference interpreting community have now retired, and it has proved difficult to replace them. The lack of personnel is particularly acute for the two most needed languages in world affairs today – Arabic and Chinese. Even the Russian and French into English booths are getting harder to fill.

The structure of conference interpreting at the UN and its agencies and at most other international gatherings that can afford it is not now quite as it was at the Nuremberg trials. The rules invented for that first experiment were that all interpreters should work only into their 'native' language (now called their A language, 'A' standing for 'active'), and that all interpreting should be done from the 'original'. With six UN languages now in operation, that would require six teams of five translators, or thirty people in all, to service a single meeting. The job is now reckoned to be as stressful as the work of air traffic controllers; the 85-minute slots used at Nuremberg have been replaced with a routine of alternating thirty-minute shifts (the Chinese and Arabic booths change over every twenty minutes) through a three- or six-hour working day – so that in fact you would need sixty people, not thirty, to service an international meeting if the original rules were still applied. There just aren't sixty people with those high-level and variegated skills that can be gathered at any one time in any one place in the world, not even in New York City. The following schema allows the illusion of seamless language transfer to be achieved with a team of just fourteen members:

> *In the French booth*: two interpreters, one listening in
> Spanish and English, the other listening in Russian
> and English, and giving out in French
> *In the English booth*: two interpreters, one listening in
> French and Russian, the other listening in Spanish
> and French, and giving out in English
> *In the Spanish booth*: two interpreters, both listening in
> English and French, and giving out in Spanish
> *In the Russian booth*: two interpreters, both listening in
> either Spanish or French as well as English, and
> giving out in Russian
> *In the Chinese booth*: three interpreters working shifts,
> taking in English and Chinese and giving out in
> Chinese and English
> *In the Arabic booth*: three interpreters working shifts,
> taking in French or English and Arabic and giving
> out in Arabic and English or French

In other words, Chinese gets into Spanish, French and Russian by relay from the English channel, and Arabic gets into Spanish and Russian by relay either from English, or, most often, from French; Spanish and Russian get into Chinese by relay from the English channel, and into Arabic by relay from French. If the Russian interpreter in the English booth has gone to the bathroom, then the Russian channel also gets into English by relay from the French booth; similarly, if the Spanish interpreter in the French booth has a nose-bleed, Spanish gets into French by relay from English.

Relay, or double translation, is in principle a bad idea, as the possibility of error is increased, as is the time-lag between the delegate's speech and the output in listeners' headphones. Also, the fact that Chinese and Arabic interpreters work both

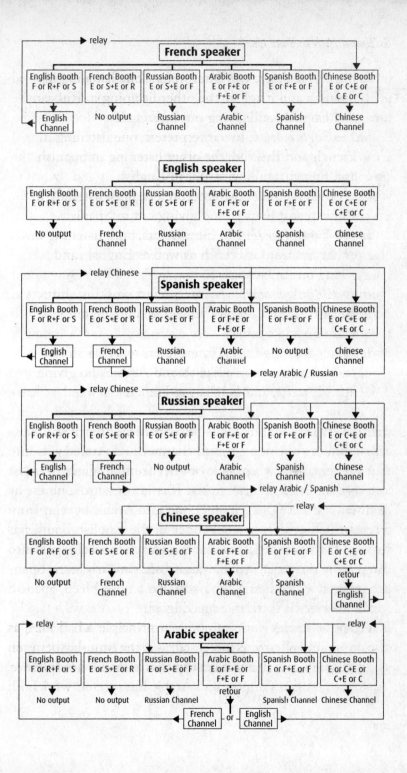

into their 'A' language and from it into English is not a good idea – working both ways at once more than doubles the mental stress involved. But the devices of relay (double translation) and *retour* (one interpreter working in two directions) are godsends for the UN officials whose task is to ensure the smooth running of the meetings. Without relay and *retour* the whole system would be vastly more expensive – and it's not exactly cheap as it is.

In the European Union, further refinements are used to ensure that meetings of a body with twenty-four official languages can be coped with. Full symmetrical interpreting under Nuremberg rules – that's to say, each translation direction being supplied by a single dedicated interpreter – would require a team of 552 interpreters, exceeding by far the number of delegates taking part in any meeting, and that's clearly not feasible. The system works like this:

When all participants in a meeting understand at least one of the EU's working languages (English, French, German or Italian) – and this is nearly always the case – then an asymmetrical language regime is used. 'Asymmetry' means that participants may speak in any of the official languages (as long as they let the interpreting service know which one ahead of time), but may listen in only one of the four working languages. Such a meeting would be said to have a '24:4' language regime. If each translation direction were served by a dedicated individual, that would require up to eighty interpreters per session, which is still far too many.

The number is further reduced by interpreters with two 'A' languages who can work into both, a device called *cheval*, but also, most crucially, by *retour* – interpreters who also work into their 'B' language. The greatest economy of all is of course made by relay. When the Lithuanian delegate speaks, an interpreter with Lithuanian 'B' provides a simultaneous German translation which the German–English, German–French and German–Italian interpreters use for their versions in the working languages (and in a 24:4 regime, no further language versions are required). In this example, the hub or pivot language is German; for other languages at the same imaginary meeting, the hub may be English, French or Italian, bringing the total number of actual bodies needed to service a meeting under '24:4' to a maximum of twenty-eight, and quite a lot fewer if (for example) the Portuguese-to-French interpreter also does Spanish when French is the hub language or the Swedish-to-German also does Danish when German is the pivot. Because all EU interpreters must have two 'B' languages, the use of asymmetric regimes together with *cheval*, *retour* and relay suffice to provide just about affordable simultaneous interpreting in Brussels and Luxembourg, and at the European Parliament in Strasbourg.[7]

At the UN, the system is often invisible to users. Interpreters are placed at the rear or the side of the assembly hall behind sound-proofed and tinted glass screens. You can attend a dozen meetings without even realizing the interpreters are physically present – so it's only natural they should get taken for granted. What's more insidious than the occlusion of the interpreting magic, however, is the impression that anything you say can be simultaneously heard in all other tongues. Conference interpreting, glamorous though it is, buries the real difficulties – and the real interest – of language transfer beneath sophisticated, almost circus-like tricks of the language trade. It makes people think that it's only a matter of time before we can all have a device to stick in our ear – the 'Babel fish' of the *Hitchhiker's Guide to the Galaxy* – to provide us with instant communication with all the peoples on earth.

Unlike most translators in written mode and a high proportion of consecutive interpreters, conference interpreters are rarely specialists in any particular field and come closest to being pure language professionals. Few domain-specific organizations are sufficiently large to justify having salaried interpreters on their books: only sixty-seven organizations in the world employ members of AIIC (the interpreters' professional body) as full-time staff, and only four (the UN in Geneva and New York and two of the International Criminal Tribunals in the Hague) employ more than ten. As a result, most of the 3,000 members of AIIC (and a roughly equal number of non-members) work freelance, and travel from conference to conference dealing with all sorts and kinds of topics. Fast-talking yet good listeners, interpreters must be both alert and relaxed, able to tolerate unspeakably boring harangues but also quick to pick up the gist when something entirely new comes on the agenda. They belong to a rare breed.

They might become even rarer, because there are several threats to the survival of the species. First, the precipitous decline in the teaching of foreign languages in the English-speaking world in the last fifty years means that there are ever fewer entrants to the profession with English 'A'. If you prevented boys from having bicycles, then the Tour de France would become a celebration of geriatric fitness in a decade or two, and then stop. If you don't teach native English-speakers two languages out of Spanish, Russian, Chinese, Arabic and French intensively to high levels while they are young, you will not have candidates for interpreter training within ten or fifteen years. There are many English–Spanish bilinguals, of course, but very few of them have another UN language to the requisite degree of fluency. If the requirement were lowered from two to one foreign language for English 'A', then the system could be run on relay and *retour* and staffing problems would be less acute. However, because ten applicants to a translators' school produce no more than five entrants, and because barely one third of those graduating will be found good enough to enter the profession, large investment in language education throughout the English-speaking world is urgently needed. Without it, the next cohort of our politicians and diplomats, businessmen and consultants, human rights campaigners, international lawyers and policy wonks may well be reduced to stuffing fish in both ears.

A second threat to maintaining current language practice in international organizations is that some states may become unwilling to finance simultaneous interpretation into languages that are ceasing to be global vehicular tongues – but the replacement of Russian (for example) may prove politically impossible for many decades yet, and nobody has a clear idea of what might replace French.

But the bigger threat looming on the horizon is something that's going on right now in research labs in New Jersey and elsewhere. Using the technology of speech recognition that allows a widely available word processor to generate text from speech, alongside the speech synthesis systems that power today's automated answering machines, the FAHQT target that current US science policy encourages could well become FAHQST – fully automated, high-quality speech translation. Experimental systems not very far from commercial release already produce running English text from Spanish speech. I may not live to see or hear it, but many of you probably will: automated interpreting for the secondary orality of predictable international diplomatic prose, for tourist inquiries at hotel reception desks, and maybe for other uses as well.

You will then enter the era of tertiary orality. It will be another world.

25. *Match* Me *If* You *Can*: Translating Humour

A relatively uncontentious way of saying what translation does is this: it provides for some community an acceptable match for an utterance made in a foreign tongue. This doesn't go very far, but as it applies equally well to conference interpreting, comic strips, legal contracts and novels, it's a reasonable place to start.

What it leaves open are three huge questions:

1. What makes a match acceptable?
2. Which of the infinite catalogue of qualities that any utterance has are those that a translation may or must make match?
3. What do we mean by 'match', anyway?

Those are the questions that translation studies have always sought to answer, sometimes under heavy academic disguise. 'Translation quality evaluation criteria', for example, is a label for answers to question 1. But whatever way you ask these three questions, the answers are not easy to provide.

All sorts of criteria may be involved in judgements made by different people at different times about the acceptability of a match – theoretical criteria, or practical, social or cultural ones, and no doubt, on occasions, purely arbitrary ones too (such as the translator is a famous prize-winner and *must* have got it right). Trying to rank these criteria or to distribute them to classes of situations where they might apply seems too complicated by half. It is perhaps more fruitful to work in from the outside edge, and to begin by looking at places where matches are commonly believed to be extremely difficult to find.

One area flagged by nearly all translation commentary as being match-poor is utterances that raise a laugh or a smile. Here's an old Soviet joke about Stalin:

> Stalin and Roosevelt had an argument about whose bodyguards were more loyal and ordered them to jump out of the window on the fifteenth floor. Roosevelt's bodyguard flatly refused to jump, saying, 'I'm thinking about the future of my family.' Stalin's bodyguard, however, jumped out of the window and fell to his death. Roosevelt was taken aback.
>
> 'Tell me, why did your man do that?' he asked.
>
> Stalin lit his pipe and replied:
>
> 'He was thinking about the future of his family, too.'[1]

Well, that's a translation (from Russian), and even in Russian it's a translation already, because exactly the same joke has been told over the centuries about other brutal potentates, starting with Peter the Great. We can safely assume that this joke-form can be preserved together with its point in any human language under two conditions that are only incidentally linguistic ones: the target language must possess an expression for 'thinking about your family' that can apply to two slightly different projects (to provide support for your spouse and children, and to protect them from persecution); second, that the listener understands or can guess that evil potentates punish disobedient underlings by persecuting their relatives. These two conditions may not be met in all cultures and languages in the world, but they are surely widely available. The 'untranslatability of humour' hasn't survived the very first dig of the spade.

Provided the two general conditions given above can be met, the jump-for-Stalin joke can be rejigged to fit a wide variety of other historical and geographical locales in the same language or any other, and still be the same joke. There are very many transportable, rewritable joke-patterns of that kind – including those politically incorrect ethnic disparagements of near neighbours that you hear in structurally identical form when the French talk about Belgians, Swedes about Finns, the English about the Irish, and so on.

Translating these kinds of circulating jokes means matching the pattern made by the interplay of presupposition and meaning that constitutes the point, and then rewriting all the rest to suit. An ability to recognize the match is not rare, and may be almost universal. But the ability to find a good match is one that only some people have. However, we don't have to go far to find humorous uses of language that work in a slightly different way.

A Brooklyn baker became deeply irritated by a little old lady who kept standing in line to ask for a dozen bagels on a Tuesday morning despite his having put a big sign in his window to say that bagels were not available on Tuesday mornings. When she got to the head of the line for the fifth time in a row the baker decided not to shout and scream, but to get the message through this way instead.

'Lady, tell me, do you know how to spell "cat" – as in "cat-echism"?'

'Sure I do. That's C-A-T.'

'Good,' the baker replies. 'Now tell me, how do you spell "dog" – as in "dogmatic"?'

'Why, that's D-O-G.'

'Excellent! So how do you spell "fuck", as in "bagels"?'

'But there ain't no "fuck" in "bagels"!' the little old lady exclaims.

'That's precisely what I've been trying to tell you all morning!'

There are different ways of saying what the point of this – admittedly paltry – joke is. It makes a character speak out loud a truth she had been unable to internalize. There's no reason to suppose that matches cannot be found in any language to make fun of some person in the same way. The overall point is made by playing on a difference between written and oral language: structurally similar plays can probably be found and constructed in any language that has an imperfectly phonetic writing system. But once we get down to the implementation of these two features, hunting for matches becomes much more difficult. The assimilation of the present participle of a taboo word to the stem of that word plus the preposition 'in' is only possible because in English the distinguishing mark of the first – the final consonant 'g' – is habitually dropped in colloquial speech. That's a low-level, local feature of a particular language, and it turns on the slight mismatch between its spoken and written forms. A structural match in any other language would most likely have to turn on a phonetically and grammatically different feature that may or may not allow the same point – making someone stupid say what they don't want to understand by diverting their attention from the issue through an intentionally deceptive spelling game.

What's usually considered to be at issue in humour of this kind is the capacity that all languages have for referring to themselves, and thus for playing games with words. Metalinguistic expressions – sentences and phrases that refer to some aspect of their own linguistic form – carry meanings that are by definition internal to the language in which they are couched. 'There ain't no "fuck" in "bagels" may be vulgar and silly, but it is a good enough example of a metalinguistic expression. It is not about bagels, only about the spelling and pronunciation of a word of the English language seen exclusively as a word and not as a sign. 'Plays on the signifier' are traditionally viewed as the dark corner of language where translation becomes a paradoxical, impossible challenge.

That would be a valid position if the criteria for an acceptable match obligatorily included matching the signifiers themselves. But they obviously do not. What a translation makes match never includes the signifiers themselves. It would not count as a translation if it did.

Just as only some jokes exploit the metalinguistic function of language, so not all self-referring expressions are funny. Especially not those used as example sentences by philosophers of language, such as:

1. There are seven words in this sentence.

It is no trouble to find a matching sentence in German:

2. *Es gibt sieben Wörter in diesem Satz.*

However, that particular trans-linguistic match is regarded as a happenstance – an arbitrary and irrational coincidence in a particular case. What's usually seen as problematic about sentences like (1) is that they cannot reliably be translated into other tongues, and they thus appear to contradict the axiom of effability – that any thought a person can have can be expressed by some sentence in any natural language and anything which can be expressed in one language can also be expressed in another (see p. 156).

The real problem with a sentence like (1) above is that it can't be translated into English either. This sentence consists of seven words' rephrases ('translates') (1), but by doing so it becomes counterfactual, which (1) is not. Likewise, rephrasing it in French produces an untruth if you think that translation means matching signifiers one by one with equivalents provided by pocket dictionaries:

3. *Il y a sept mots dans cette phrase.*

The main cause of problems is solutions, an American wit once declared, and the conundrums created by rephrasing self-referring sentences taken out of any context seem to be good examples of that. That's because (3) is not the only way you can express (1) in French. Indeed, it's just about the least plausible version you could come up with. A better match would be:

4. *Cette phrase est constituée par sept mots.*

But because philosophy is written by philosophers and not translators, the clash between (1) and (3) is taken to be a demonstration of a wider, general truth:

> Translation between languages cannot preserve *reference* (what a sentence is about), *self-reference* (what a sentence says about itself) and *truth-value* (whether the sentence is right or wrong) at the same time.[2]

This would explain in a nutshell why puns and plays on words and all those kinds of joke that exploit specific features of the language in which they are expressed cannot be translated. Because this is presented as a general assertion it can be disproved by a single persuasive counter-example. But the reason why it is wrong is not contained in any counter-example. The flaw in the axiom lies in its failure to say what it means by 'translate'. So here's my idea of a better approximation to the truth about translation:

> Arduously headscratching, intellectually agile wordsmiths may simultaneously preserve the reference, self-reference and truth-value of an utterance when fate smiles on them and allows them to come up with a multi-dimensional matching expression in their own language.

In Chapter Fifty-Two of Perec's *Life A User's Manual*, a depressed young man called Grégoire Simpson wanders round Paris and stares for hours at shop windows. He saunters into a covered arcade and gazes at the display of a jobbing printer's wares – dummy letterheads, wedding invitations and joke visiting cards. Here's one of them:

Adolf Hitler
Fourreur

Fourreur is the French word for 'furrier', but it is also an approximate representation of the way the German word *Führer* is pronounced in French. The joke is a metalinguistic and self-referring one, provided you know who and what Hitler was, know in addition that a furrier and a dictator are different things, and are able to subvocalize the French word as if it were a German sound and vice versa. What needs matching to make a translation of this joke is not any one of these particular things in French, but the relationship between them – the pattern of mismatched sounds and meanings between two tongues, one of which has to be German.

I came up with this:

𝕬𝖉𝖔𝖑𝖋 𝕳𝖎𝖙𝖑𝖊𝖗
German Lieder

It took a while to find, and it took a stroke of luck. It may well be not the only or the best possible translation of Perec's joke visiting card, but it matches well enough in the dimensions that matter. It plays a sound-game between English and German and it relies on the same general field of knowledge. It doesn't preserve all dimensions of the original – what ever does? – but it matches enough of them, in my honest but not very humble opinion, to count as a satisfactory translation of a self-referring, metalinguistic and interlingual joke.

Humorous remarks, shaggy-dog tales, witty anecdotes and silly jokes are only untranslatable if you insist on understanding 'translation' as a low-level matching of the signifiers themselves. Translation is obviously not that. The matches it provides relate to those dimensions of an utterance that taken together account for its principal force in the context in which it is uttered.

That still doesn't tell us what we mean by 'match'. But we're getting closer.

26. *Style* and *Translation*

Translations typically alter numerous features of the source in order to produce matches for those of its dimensions that count in the context it has. But there is one traditionally perceived quality of written and spoken language that is identified not with any particular dimension of an utterance, but with the overall relationship between them – its style.

Style is more than genre. Kitchen recipes are typically translated not into something as vague and undifferentiated as 'English', but into 'kitchen recipese', the genre constituted by the conventional features that kitchen recipes have in our tongue.

In like manner, you don't translate French poetry into 'English', but into poetry, as the American poet and translator C. K. Williams insists. Poetry is a characteristic social and cultural use of language and can therefore count as a genre in our sense, but it comes in many different forms. Beyond the genre, a poetry translator has to choose the particular style that he is going to use.

Twenty years ago Eliot Weinberger and Octavio Paz brought out a curious essay-cum-anthology entitled *Nineteen Ways of Looking at Wang Wei* – nineteen different English translations of a poem by a Chinese poet of the eighth century CE, 王維. Setting aside all their arguments about which of these 'ways of Wei' is to be preferred, what is quite obvious is that they represent nineteen different ways of writing poetry in English, nineteen 'styles' of fairly recognizable kinds

(Eliotish, Ashberish, free versish and so forth). Ten years later, Hiroaki Sato brought out *One Hundred Frogs*, a compilation of actually rather more than a hundred already published English versions of a famous haiku by Matsuo Bashô:

古池や蛙飛び込む水の音

> Furu ike ya
> kawazu tobikomu
> mizu no oto

> I
> The old pond
> A frog jumped in,
> Kerplunk!

> II
> pond
>   frog
>   plop!

> III
> A lonely pond in age-old stillness sleeps . . .
> Apart, unstirred by sound or motion . . . till
> Suddenly into it a lithe frog leaps.

If 'style' is the term that names the principal means of distinguishing the differences between these three versions of Bashô's haiku, then it means something that is not an individual property of, say, the poetry of Allen Ginsberg, John Masefield and Ogden Nash, but a collective property of poetry written in that style – in Ginsbergish, Masefieldish and Nashish, so to speak (one of them *was* written by Allen Ginsberg, in fact). Style in this sense is eminently imitable, and not just for comic effect. Students of musical composition develop their skills by writing in the manner of Mozart or Bach, and writers also practise at writing like Flaubert,[1] or writing like Proust.[2] The following pieces are *not* by William Wordsworth, T. S. Eliot or J. D. Salinger – but it does not take much more than vague memories of school to know which among them are Eliotish, Salingerish and Lake Poetish respectively:

There is a river clear and fair
'Tis neither broad nor narrow
It winds a little here and there –
It winds about like any hare;
And then it holds as straight a course
As, on the turnpike road, a horse,
Or, through the air an arrow

Sunday is the dullest day, treating
Laughter as a profane sound, mixing
Worship and despair, killing
New thought with dead forms.
Weekdays give us hope, tempering
Work with reviving play, promising
A future life within this one

Boy, when I saw old Eve I thought I was going to flip. I mean it isn't that Eve is good-looking or anything like that, it's just that she's different. I don't know what the hell it is exactly – but you always know when she's around. All of a sudden I knew there was something wrong with old Eve the minute I saw her. She looked nervous as hell. I kinda felt sorry for her

– even though she's got one of my goddam ribs, so I went over to talk to old Eve.

'You look very, *very* nice, Adam,' she said to me in a funny way, like she was ashamed of something. 'Why don't you join me in some apple?'

These examples could lead us to believe that the translation of style is an exercise in pastiche, the translator's task being the choice of an existing style in the target culture to serve as a rough match for the 'other'. Many literary translators go about their job in just that way. On reading a new work in French, for example, I certainly do run through in my mind the kinds of English style that might fit, and when starting on a new job, I often rifle through the books on my shelf to remind myself of the particularities of the 'style match' I have in my head. But this idea of style as a culturally constituted set of linguistic resources characteristic of an author, period, literary genre or school clashes with another widespread idea of what 'a style' is: the irreducible difference of any individual's unique forms of language. In brief: if style is 'inimitable', how come it can be imitated?

The muddle about what style is began in the gilded halls of the Académie française, an institution set up by Louis XIV to promote and defend the French language. In 1753, a natural scientist was invited to take his place as one of the forty 'immortals', as members are called. Georges-Louis de Buffon, an eminent botanist, mathematician and natural historian, gave an extraordinary acceptance speech that has since become known as the 'Discourse on Style'. In it he sought to reassure his audience – the thirty-nine academicians who had just elected him – that the promotion of a mere scientist to such elevated rank would not topple rhetoric from its proper place at the pinnacle of French culture. He may even have been sincere – but I wouldn't count on it. In his much-quoted but mostly misunderstood conclusion, Buffon emphasized that what mattered above all were the arts of language. Scientific discoveries, he declared, were really quite easy to make, and would quickly perish unless they were explained with elegance and grace. That was because mere facts are not human achievements – they belong to the natural world, and are therefore *hors de l'homme*, 'outside of humankind'. Eloquence, by contrast, was the highest evidence of human agency and genius: *le style est l'homme même.*

This meaning of 'style', as a synonym for elegance and distinction, continues to motivate most modern uses of the word and its cognates. Stylish clothes are those considered elegant by some group of people; to ski or to dance or to serve cucumber sandwiches in style is likewise to do these things with fashionable grace. Buffon's style is a social value. Nobody is free to construct his or her own idea of what is stylish, save by getting other people to agree. Similarly, stylish writing conforms to a shared notion, however vague, of what is fashionable, appropriate, socially elevated and so on, in the way you speak and write.

Matching posh for posh in translating between languages used by cultures with linguistic forms that correspond to hierarchical social structures is no sweat. Where the social structures of the source culture are more elaborate than those of the target, a degree of flattening occurs: the different social implications of *Estimado señor* and *Apreciado señor* at the start of a formal letter in Spanish, for example, can't be represented in English, which can only say 'Dear Sir'. To compensate for losses of this kind, which can be far more substantial when translating between cultures as unrelated to each other as Japanese and French, for example, the translator may invent target-language analogues for distinctions that belong to the social world of the original, and be accused variously of quaintness, condescension or fidelity to the source. But there are even less tractable issues involved when the social register of the language used in the source is low. There is a seemingly inevitable bias against representing forms of language recognized in the source culture as regional, uncouth, ill-educated or taboo by socially matching forms in the target tongue – presumably, because doing so risks identifying the translator as a member of just such a marginal or subordinated class. As a result, translation usually takes the social register of the source up a notch or two. The social dimension of 'style' doesn't flow easily from tongue to tongue.

Novelist Adam Thirlwell has argued that the meaning of the word 'style' changed in 1857.[3] In the convincing story he tells, 'style' flipped over, almost in one go, from being a description of the elegance of a whole manner of expression to being about just one sub-element in the composition of prose – the sentence. The culprits for this radical reduction of style were Gustave Flaubert, his novel *Madame Bovary*, and the many comments Flaubert made about sentences in his partly teasing letters to his girlfriend, Louise Colet. Since 1857 or thereabouts, Thirlwell argues, critics and readers have needlessly restricted their idea of a writer's style to those low-level features of grammar and prosody that can be exhaustively identified between a capital letter and a full stop. Henri Godin, writing about 'the stylistic resources of French' just after the Second World War, was quite certain that style and syntax are the same thing and reach their point of perfect harmony in the writing of ... Flaubert.

Because the grammatical forms, the sounds of individual words, and the characteristic voice rhythms of any two languages do not match (if they did we would call them the same language), the 'Flaubert shift' made style instantly untranslatable. Thirlwell's main aim is to show that this is nonsense – and that the novel is a truly international and trans-linguistic form of art.[4]

At some point in the course of the nineteenth century, the idea of style as 'the aesthetics of the sentence' got thoroughly muddled up with a completely different tradition that came to France and Britain from German universities. Scholars in departments of Romance Philology tended to justify the attention they paid to canonical writers on the grounds that their works represented special, innovative uses of language, distinct from the norms of the speech community, and were therefore important factors in the course of linguistic change. Poets, they argued, were not simply users of language, but the creators of it; a language was not a smooth and rounded whole, but a gnarled old potato marked by bumps and dents which speak the history of its creation. 'Style research', or *Stilistik*, pursued with fervour for a hundred years, and reaching its brilliant peak in the essays of Leo Spitzer (1887–1960), was an exciting but quite circular pursuit: the language of a 'great work' becomes a fine-grained map of the ineffable individuality of some great writer's 'self'; but the 'self' or the essence of, let us say, Racine is entirely constituted by what can be mapped through his language, subjected to a particular kind of analysis of his style. *Style* in this sense is inimitable by definition – that's the point of it. And if it can't be imitated in the same language, it's not even worth trying to translate it.

But it isn't true. Most of the features of language use that Spitzer identified as significant aspects of Racine's 'self', for example, can also be found in the language of Racine's contemporaries writing in the same literary genres. Yet the remarkable tenacity of the philologists' principle that every great writer has a manner that is unique and inimitable led people to reinvent the very history of the idea of 'style'. They went back to Buffon's famous 'Discourse', took his maxim that *le style c'est l'homme même* ('style is what makes us human'), lopped off the last word and recycled the remainder – *le style, c'est l'homme* – so as to prove that 'the style *is* the man'. As the noted Oxford scholar R. A. Sayce put it in his study of *Style in French Prose* (1953), 'details of style . . . reveal the deeper intentions and characteristics of a writer, and they must be dictated by some inner reason'.

'Style' thus has a very curious history. A sentence uttered in 1753 as a defence of literary eloquence came to be touted around as a pithy formulation of the idea that no two people speak or write in exactly the same way because no two speakers are the same person.

It's indisputable that every speaker of any language has an idiolect, a characteristic set of (ir)regularities that is not identical to the usage of any other person. Why this should be so is discussed in the last chapter of this book, but it should be obvious that there are no intellectual, psychological or practical obstacles to speaking in the same way as some other person (impersonators and pasticheurs do it all the time). But the fact of linguistic variation at individual level has some very practical applications – such as catching out forgers. Among the early applications of computers to the humanities were statistical programs for identifying the authorship of suspect documents. The programs themselves rested on rival theories about what 'style' was: typical patterns in individuals' use of verbs, or vocabulary, or other parts of speech, that were unfalsifiable by anyone else; or else that 'rare pairs' (two words occurring typically together) could be used to identify and distinguish different authors; or that the position in the sentence of common words was what gives the identity of the writer away. This last guess was called positional stylometry and was developed in the 1970s by A. Q. Morton and Sidney Michaelson at Edinburgh University. Results of their computer program were admitted as evidence in court in many cases, and also used to make scholarly hypotheses about the provenance of different parts of the Hebrew Bible.

Style in this individual sense cannot possibly be the object of translation. It would make no sense to try to simulate in English the statistically irregular positioning of, say, the negative particle *pas* in some French original.

Two interesting consequences ensue. If 'style' is such an individual attribute that it cannot even be controlled by the writer (thus allowing sleuths to catch forgers out), then every translator has a 'style' of that kind in his target language, and the style of all his translations must be more like itself than it can ever be like the style of the authors translated. I often wonder, in fact, whether my English versions of Perec, Kadare, Fred Vargas, Romain Gary and Hélène Berr – whose characteristic uses of French are manifestly quite different – are all, stylistically speaking, just examples of Bellos. By some accounts, they have to be: computational stylistics gives no quarter on that score. Secretly, though, I am quite happy that it should be so. After all, those translations are *my* work. But it will be known for sure only by a large computer program.

All the same, style can't be swept away just like that. Admittedly, we do not mean 'elegance', as Buffon did, when we talk about literature and translation, even if we still do when we talk about clothes or cucumber sandwiches. We do not mean statistical regularities in the way we place the indefinite article, though we do when we gratefully accept a court ruling on the incompatibility of the style of our uncle's alleged will with its claimed authorship.

We mean something else, not so difficult to express: *style* is the reason why a novel of Dickens is just Dickens's, why a piece of P. G. Wodehouse – even if it were written by somebody else – is still in its essence a piece of Wodehouse. Style is, if not the man, then the thing! It is what makes any work uniquely itself.

I also know a Dickens when I see one. But that's trivial. The question is: at what level is the Dickensianity of any text by Dickens located? In the words? the sentences? the paragraphs? the digressions? the anecdotes? the construction of character? or the plot? Because I, translator, can give you the plot, the characters, the anecdotes, and the digressions; I can even give you the paragraphs and most of the time I can give you a fair approximation to the sentences too. But I cannot give you the words. For that, you have to learn English.

For Adam Thirlwell, novelistic 'style' is the name of a holistic entity that comes somewhere between 'a writer's special way of looking at the world' and 'a writer's own way of writing novels'. Characteristic uses of sentence structures and sound patterns are certainly a part of the latter, and maybe of the former too – but only a part. Style in Thirlwell's sense – the most usable and purposeful sense – is something much larger. If it were not, it would disappear in translation. The circulation of novels between all the vehicular languages of the world and their incontestable conversations with each other demonstrate without a shadow of doubt that style does survive translation. The means that translators use to ensure this are no more than the common skills used in all translation tasks.

In sum, the widespread notion that style is untranslatable

is just a variant of the folkish nostrum that a translation is no substitute for the original. There is no more truth to it than there is in the idea that humour can't be preserved by rephrasing in the same or another tongue.

There is a difference between translating jokes and translating style, however. The first is typically done by concentrated effort; the second is better done by taking a slight distance from the text and allowing its underlying patterns to emerge by their own force in the process of rewriting in a second tongue. What they have in common is this: finding a match for a joke and a match for a style are both instances of a more general ability that may best be called a pattern-matching skill.

We're still short of an answer to the question of what we mean by match, but we're getting closer still.

27. *Translating* Literary *Texts*

In the English-speaking world, there are no job postings for literary translators, and few openings for beginners. Insofar as it is remunerated at all, literary translation is paid at piece rates equivalent to a baby-sitter's hourly charge. It is mainly pursued by people who have other sources of income to pay the rent and the grocer. There are a few exceptions, but literary translation into English is for the most part done by amateurs.

Yet it plays a central part in the international circulation of new literary work. The disparity between global role and local recognition is perhaps the greatest curiosity of the whole trade. Literary translation into any language has features that mark it off from most other kinds of language work. To begin with, it usually has liberal time constraints compared to work in commercial, legal or technical fields. It also engages the translator's responsibility in less daunting ways. Translation mistakes in court, in hospitals and maintenance manuals may cause immediate harm to others. Making a mess of a masterpiece certainly has consequences, but they don't threaten the translator or the client in comparable ways. Producing fluent prose to stand in place of a story told in German or Spanish is also more entertaining than writing an English-language summary of a Russian document on border issues in the Barents Sea. All these things make sense of the fact that the rewriters of foreign novels in English translation have low pay and low profiles. They don't have too hard a time.

It could hardly be more different in Japan. Shibata Motoyuki is without question the most famous translator from English in the country: his publisher puts out 'The Shibata Motoyuki Translation Collection' and bookshops set aside whole sections for it. His name does not just appear on the dust-jacket but is printed in the same type size as the author's name.

Japanese literary translators have much the same status as authors do in Britain and America. Many author-translators are household names, and there's even a celebrity-gossip book about them: *Honyakuka Retsuden 101*, 'The Lives of the Translators 101'.

Many other countries give translators greater symbolic and material rewards than America or Britain. In Germany, literary translators are usually granted a significant royalty on the books they translate; French literary translators too are better paid than their American counterparts. In the English-speaking world almost all literary translators have a day job to support their avocation, but in France, Germany, Japan and elsewhere you can use translating as your day job to finance a second calling – such as writing fiction of your own.

These discrepancies in the social and economic context of literary translation between the Far East, Continental Europe and the anglophone world reflect the asymmetry in the global flow of translations. The situational contexts of literary translation are so different when translating UP and translating DOWN – towards the centre, or towards the periphery, in Pascale Casanova's terms[1] – that they cannot fail to have broad effects on the way the task is done.

In cultures that lie on the periphery of the global circulation of literary works, what is wanted is access to the centre. The cultural standing of literary works in translation is determined in the first place by the simple fact that they give access to the foreign. In central languages, on the other hand, the foreignness of a new book is of no special importance. New writing from abroad has to win its place in the culture by other means. But as there is only one central language at the moment, the gulf in translation practice lies between English, and the rest.

Translating the new into English nearly always uses a fluent and relatively invisible translation style. This is obviously related to the fact that, like budding authors, literary translators of previously unknown work have a hard struggle finding a publisher to take them on. But, in practice, few books arrive in English as the direct result of a translator's efforts. Most international literature that is published has been picked by commissioning editors whose opinions are formed by pitches from international literary scouts, foreign publishers and gossip at book fairs around the world. Literary translators almost always get to hear about their next book when a publisher is already committed to bringing it out.

There aren't many publishing executives in Britain and the USA who read foreign languages other than French. One result of this almost embarrassing situation is that translation into French is, if not quite a precondition, then a very useful introduction for a work in any other language seeking entry to world literature.[2] The international careers of writers like Ismail Kadare and Javier Marías, for example, hinged at the start on their works being read in French translation by publishers in America and Britain. But many works are acquired for translation by editors relying exclusively on reports and 'buzz', and the English translator is often the only person in the chain who really knows very much about the book or its author at all. It's a daunting position, with responsibilities going far beyond the already difficult business of producing an acceptable and effective translation.

Retranslation of ancient and modern 'classics' takes place under a quite different set of real-world constraints. It gives rise to arguments about the translator's responsibilities that are distinct from those that rule the translation of new work.

Just after the end of the Second World War, Penguin brought out a new translation of Homer's *Odyssey*, by E. V. Rieu. It was an unexpected success. As the company's website records, the liveliness of Rieu's style 'proclaimed that this was a book that anyone – everyone – could, and should, read'. The classics were no longer restricted to the privileged few.

'Classic' here means Greek and Roman literature. Earlier translations had been done mostly to accompany the learning of Latin and Greek in the classier kind of schools, and so Rieu's colloquial version was a revelation for less privileged folk. Its success and the long series that followed also reflected an important social aspiration of post-war Britain – to give much greater educational opportunities to the broad public than it had ever had before. The early Penguin Classics were mostly of ancient and medieval texts, including Neville Coghill's famous rendering of Chaucer, but the series soon came to include literature ranging from Ancient Egypt to the closing years of the nineteenth century. A collective enterprise of that kind was sustained by a conscious and explicit culture of translation. 'It is the editor's intention to commission translators who can emulate his own example and present the general reader with readable and attractive versions of the great books in modern English, shorn of the unnecessary difficulties and erudition, the archaic flavour and the foreign idiom that renders so many existing translations repellent to modern taste.' Rieu's marching orders point firmly towards an adaptive translation style. At the start, he tried to recruit academics, but found that very few of them could write English of the kind he appreciated. He turned to professional writers like Robert Graves, Rex Warner and Dorothy L. Sayers, with personalities ranging from the scholarly to the idiosyncratic. But a stringent house style was imposed on these versions, and the result is that the first 200 Penguin Classics read as if they had all been written in the same language – fluent, unpretentious British English, circa 1950. It was a remarkable achievement. The series certainly did educate millions, and it is undoubtedly one of the historical sources of the strong preference in English-language translation for adaptive, normalizing or domesticating styles.

However, the social and cultural aspirations of these early retranslations are not necessarily those that motivate later retranslation projects. Save at special moments like 1945 (or the immediate aftermath of the Russian Revolution, when Maksim Gorky launched his 'World Literature' publishing house), retranslation is nearly always a strictly commercial affair.

Copyright is a modern invention, dating from 1708, but international copyright is even more recent. First sketched out in bilateral treaties in the 1850s, modern arrangements for the translation of literary works were first codified in the 1920s. The Berne Convention, which has since become the Universal Copyright Convention, doesn't allow a publisher to put out a translation without purchasing that right from the owner of the original text. But when a publisher does acquire the right to publish a foreign work in translation, he becomes the sole owner of the translated work for as long as the edition remains in print.[3] He has a monopoly in the target language – until the original work falls into the public domain.

International copyright protection is now set at seventy years from the author's death, or from first publication in the case of posthumous works. Marcel Proust died in 1922 and the last volume of *A la recherche du temps perdu* was published in 1927. Franz Kafka died in 1924 and his most famous works came out in 1925 (*The Trial*), 1926 (*The Castle*) and 1927 (*America*). English-language publishers of these perennial works lost their monopoly towards the end of the last century. Freud died in 1939, and so his works are now also 'free of rights'. Publishers generally seek to retain some part of their market share in these hardy perennials by commissioning retranslations. That's why over the last twenty years there has been a steady output of 'new' Prousts, Kafkas and Freuds.

The legal constraints on the international circulation of literary texts explain why there is only one translation available for most works first published since the First World War. Retranslation is not a practice that has any application to most of world literature created after the birth of the last generation but two.

A retranslator, whether working with older texts or with ones that have just become available at the seventy-year limit of protection, has to cope with ambiguous and conflicting demands. If the new translation is to be copyrighted as a new text, then it has to be measurably different from any other translation. The easiest way to ensure originality is not even to look at earlier versions, since the chance of any two translators coming up blind with the same target formulation is nil. On the other hand, a retranslator also needs to be able to explain why the new translation is better than the existing one, and to do that you have to read what is already there. The older version may help – it may be very useful indeed – but it always gets in the way of inventing a fresh solution to the trickier parts of the text. I don't envy retranslators of modern classics one bit. They have to steer a cliff-top path between inadvertent plagiarism and gratuitous change.

In some cases, a new translation is amply justified by the discovery or publication of the full or unexpurgated or corrected version of a text that had originally been brought out on the basis of a censored or imperfect manuscript (such is the case of Bulgakov's *The Master and Margarita*). In the case of work that has been intensively studied over several decades, a new translation may be able to incorporate readings and interpretations that were not available to the first. But the general principle that old translations need redoing 'every generation or two' is not well supported by these individual cases. It is supported with arithmetical exactitude by the law of international copyright and the commercial interests it creates.

Yet despite these major differences between translating and retranslating and between translating into English and into other tongues, the translation of literary works of all kinds has a feature that distinguishes it from all other translation tasks. We like to believe that a literary work, insofar as it really belongs to literature, is unlike all others – it is unique, not routine, and essentially just itself. This creates a real problem.

Translating serious non-fiction calls on skills and knowledge that literary translators don't need (knowledge of the field, for a start), but there's no special problem about knowing what linguistic norms the target text should meet. You naturally want to make a book about archaeology resemble other well-regarded books about archaeology in the receiving culture. When translating UP, the norms for non-fiction are those of original work in the same field done by speakers of the receiving language.

But difficult questions arise when the specific field of a non-fiction work is new or not easy to classify. There is perhaps no better example of the uncertain borderline between literary and informational translation than the works of Sigmund Freud.

Despite his worldwide fame Freud's complete works have been translated in full only into English, Italian, Spanish and Japanese. Based on the complete works published in German in London in 1942, James Strachey's English version is regarded by many as a masterwork of translation and by others as a betrayal of Freud. The long-running controversy over what kind of English should represent Freud's writing turns on the question of the genre to which Freud's writing should be attached. Does it belong to social science? Or is it more properly thought of as literary work?

Strachey took it for granted that psychoanalysis was a science. Scientific terminology in English traditionally relies on Latin and Greek roots to forge new words for new concepts. However, Freud himself wrote in a language that uses compounds of quite ordinary words in the natural and social sciences. Thus where in English we use bits of Greek for 'hydrogen' and 'oxygen', German uses only 'plain words': *Wasserstoff* is 'water-stuff', *Sauerstoff* is 'sour-stuff', but such terms are no less technical and precise than their Greek-based counterparts in English. Consequently, where Freud says *Anlehnung* ('leaning-on'), Strachey coins 'anaclisis', and for *Schaulust* ('see-pleasure') he invents 'scopophilia'. Many now common words of English – ego, id, superego, empathy and displacement, for example – were all first invented in James Strachey's translation of Freud, to replace the equally technical but less recondite neologisms of the original – *Ich*, *Es*, *Überich*, *Einfühlung* and *Verschiebung*.[4]

Strachey's approach is quite unexceptionable if Freud's writings are seen as contributions to social or medical science. We can test that in a back-translation exercise. What could Freud have written had he wanted to coin a term in German for the English neologism 'scopophilia'? The norms of German-language science writing of his era would have led him inevitably towards a compound noun like *Schaulust*.

If on the other hand works like *The Interpretation of Dreams* are assimilated not to science but to literary creation, then Strachey's English, which gives a version that is tonally and stylistically distant from the original, could easily be seen as a misrepresentation.

In France, a large and coordinated team has been engaged since the 1980s in producing the first 'Complete Works' in French. The enterprise aims to restore the German specificity of Freud, treating him less as the inventor of a new science than as a writer of a particular (and rather strange) kind of literary prose. Indeed, the team's leaders have declared that Freud didn't write German at all, but 'Freudish', 'a dialect of German that is not German but a language invented by Freud'. The result is widely regarded as incomprehensible in French – but then, if 'Freudish' isn't German, it wouldn't have been easy to read in the original either . . . [5]

The tangled disputes over Freud in French and English would not arise if it were clear how to categorize the field to which his work belongs. In most social science translation, the problem does not arise. Because it is believed in many places that the best work in social science is done in the US, translation of social science from English typically retains some linguistic features of the original, to authenticate the quality of the work. But in literature, there is no such collective agreement about where the 'top model' lies. Should a new foreign novel in translation conform to the manner and style of some existing writer of English prose? Some would say, of course not: what we want is something different from the familiar patterns of Philip Roth. Others say, of course it should! We want to read something that matches our existing conception of novelistic style in English prose. The book may have been written in Albanian or Chinese, but if it's a good novel, then it should sound like one – of the kind we know.

There is no resolution to this squabble. You could say that literary translation is easy because, in the last analysis, you can do what you like. Or you could say that literary translation is impossible, because whatever you do, serious objections can be raised. Literary translation *is* different from all other kinds. It serves readers in a quite special way. Modestly, often unwittingly, but inevitably, it teaches them on each occasion what translation is.

28. *What* Translators *Do*

Speakers of any natural language repeat themselves and others all the time, and to do so they use their natural facility to rephrase together with a well-filled kitbag of tools:

- they can replace one word with another of like meaning (synonymy)
- they can take one part of the expression and replace it with a longer and more elaborate one (expansion)
- they can take one part of the expression and replace it with either a dummy, an abbreviation, a short form, or nothing at all (contraction)
- they can take one part of the expression and move it to a different position, rearranging the other words in appropriate ways (topic shift)
- they can use the relevant tool from their language kit to make one part of the expression stand out as more important than the others (change of emphasis)
- they can add expressions that relate to facts or states or opinions implicit in the original in order to clarify what they (or their interlocutor) just said (clarification)
- but if they try to repeat exactly what has been said with the same tone, pitch, words, forms and structures, they do not succeed (unless they are also gifted, sharp-eared and well-trained impersonators, and probably employed in the music hall)

Translators do exactly the same things when they repeat the words of another, and the fact that their 'afterspeech' is in what we call another tongue makes no difference at all to the range of discursive devices they use.

But they use these tools to support an overriding aim which is not necessarily relevant to voluntary or inadvertent repetition in interaction in the same tongue. They seek to preserve the force of the original utterance – the overall meaning not only of what has been said, but the meaning that the saying of it has, and to do so in a way that is appropriate to the specific context in which the second formulation is to be heard or used. They are not trying to change anything – whereas when we repeat something without translating it, we usually intend to make some small or large difference to it.

Here's a tiny example of the kind of changes translators make in order not to change anything much at all. In the multilingual 'in-flight magazine' supplied to travellers on the Eurostar train, a page is devoted to graphics demonstrating the size and achievements of the whole enterprise of high-speed rail through the Channel Tunnel. One of the bubbles features the number '334.7 km/h', which is glossed in English as 'The record breaking top speed (208 mph) a Eurostar train reached in July 2003 when testing the UK High Speed 1 Line'. It is followed by the following French text:

> *Le record de vitesse d'un train Eurostar établi en juillet 2003 lors du test d'une ligne TGV en Grande-Bretagne*

The suppression of the 'miles per hour' speed in the French translation might be seen as simply conventional – but the obvious reason for its omission is that it is of no relevance to French readers, who do not generally know how far a mile is anyway. More interesting is the French assertion that 208 mph was the top speed of the train doing the test, whereas the English assert that the train's top speed broke a record. What record? Well, in Britain, just about every record – no train had ever gone faster on a UK track. But it's not a record for France, where TGVs have exceeded that speed many times. So for the French not to be frankly counterfactual, the translator has to rephrase and re-contextualize. However, the real subtlety in the re-contextualization is when the 'UK High Speed 1 line' becomes just 'a high-speed line in Great Britain' in French. French readers do not need to know the embarrassing fact that Britain still has only one such line, when the French have many, and so they had also better not be told the proper name of a piece of railway engineering that is unique exclusively in British terms. Now linked more closely than ever by a fast train, Britain and France still provide two quite different contexts of use for even the simplest expressions. Translations naturally rephrase the message to adapt it to its alternative context of use.[1]

Literary translators have a less clear idea of the 'context of use' of their work than translators of all other kinds. Actually, they don't know for sure that it will have any end-use at all. Many translated works (including many of great merit) sell pitifully small numbers of copies and disappear into a black hole. The only real 'client' of a literary translation is an imaginary reader – the Reader that each translator invents in his head.

That's the real reason why when it comes to the transmission of cultural goods translators tell themselves they are trying to produce an equivalent effect.

There are two difficulties with this commonly mentioned criterion of translation art: 'equivalent' and 'effect'.

Translations do have effects. They may make readers laugh or weep or rush to the library to find more books of the same kind. They can even have quite sinister effects, as the following historical anecdote shows.

In 1870, Otto von Bismarck, the German Chancellor, released a statement to the press about his sovereign's negative reaction to a request from the French ambassador that the German royal family should commit itself to never accepting the throne of Spain. The statement also reported that the Kaiser didn't want to talk to the French ambassador again and had sent him a message to stay away by the hand of the 'Adjutant of the day':

> *Seine Majestät der König hat es darauf abgelehnt, den franzö-sischen Botschafter nochmals zu empfangen, und demselben durch den Adjutanten vom Dienst sagen lassen, daß Seine Majestät dem Botschafter nichts weiter mitzuteilen habe.*

The 'adjutant of the day' – *Adjutant vom Dienst* – names a high-ranking courtier, an aristocratic aide-de-camp. But it happens to be almost identical to a word of French – *adjudant*. When Bismarck's statement was received in Paris it was instantly translated by the Havas news agency service and wired to all newspapers, which reprinted it in the 'special extra' that went on sale straight away. In the Havas version, *Adjutant* is not translated, but left in its original form. The effect of that one word was enormous. French *adjudant* means sergeant-major (warrant officer in the US). It therefore seemed that the French ambassador had been treated with grievous disre-spect by having had a message from the Kaiser taken to him by a messenger of such low rank. The French were outraged. Six days later, they declared war.

It's likely that the overall effect – the outbreak of war – was what Bismarck intended at that time, but it is implausible that he sought to achieve it by drafting a statement in such a way as to lead to its being misunderstood through the existence of a false cognate of a German word in French. After all, Bismarck didn't decide to leave *Adjutant* in German in French translation – the Havas agency did.

In life generally, and in translation in particular, we are not very good at calculating the effects that our words and actions will have.

When translating a crime novel by Fred Vargas I came across a comically grandiloquent passage of direct speech that recycled a famous line from Victor Hugo. To re-create what I thought would be an equivalent effect of misplaced hyperbole I substituted a barely altered quotation from a speech by Winston Churchill. It didn't work. A reviewer reprimanded me for inserting Churchillian language where the original had none. Can I blame her for not knowing what motivated the effect that I sought? Of course not. Using 'Churchill' for 'Hugo' was just an entertaining mind game. You can't require readers to notice that the switch was supposed to produce an equivalent effect, because there's no way of assessing whether it does that or not.

A similarly futile submission to the doctrine of equivalent effect can be found among the cans of sound recordings used by Jacques Tati for his Oscar-winning movie, *Mon Oncle*. Before it was released Tati conceived the ambition of producing an English-language version himself. He reshot several scenes that included public signage, painting over *École*, *Sortie* and so on with *School*, *Exit*, etc. It was then pointed out to him that the change of visible language would create confusion as to where the action was really located. His solution to that problem was to change the background music track of the English-language version to make it sound more French, and that's why the Tati archive contains cans labelled *ambiance française pour version anglaise* – 'French atmospheric music for the English version'. That didn't work either. Despite the care with which it was done, *My Uncle* never had an 'equivalent effect' because distributors and audiences loved the French original so much. The English version with its 'French effects' ran for a few weeks in a single cinema in New York, and then disappeared for fifty years.

Servile adherence to the ideology of equivalent effect can lead translators a merry dance and give rise to unforeseen effects – if they are seen at all. The investigator at the centre of an unfinished 'literary thriller' by Georges Perec called '*53 Days*' is looking into the disappearance of a thriller-writer by the name of Serval. He comes across Serval's last unfinished novel on the writer's desk, and is told by the typist that one chapter of it at least was copied out from another book. The investigator looks more closely at the two texts – Perec gives us the two-page original, which he invented – and notices that some of the words have been changed in the plagiarized version. Oddly, they are all twelve-letter words, and there are twelve of them. He writes them out in capital letters, and they naturally make two word-squares:

```
LAMENTATIONS      RESURRECTION
CALLIGRAPHIE      STENOGRAPHIE
SECHECHEVEUX      TAILLECRAYON
SACHERMASOCH      ROBBEGRILLET
MITRAILLEUSE      KALEIDOSCOPE
READERDIGEST      HEBDOMADAIRE
CARICATURALE      PAROXYSTIQUE
INTEMPORELLE      METAPHYSIQUE
FOOTBALLEUSE      OCEANOGRAPHE
HAMPTONCOURT      CHANDERNAGOR
QUELQUECHOSE      JENESAISQUOI
FORTDEFRANCE      SALTLAKECITY
```

The investigator stares at the two lists for a while, but as he can't see any sense in them, he puts them aside. End of chapter.

One day, when I had already started translating the novel, a graduate student burst into my office in Manchester to ask if I had noticed that the diabolical Perec had actually placed a huge clue in the word-list printed in the left-hand column above. Reading one letter per row from top left to bottom right in a diagonal line, you get the name of a mountain massif in south-eastern France which is also the first word in the title of a famous novel by Stendhal. I hope you can see. At the time, nobody – not even the editors and publishers of Perec's posthumous novel – had seen it. Bravo! I said to Heather, my sharped-eyed student. So what am *I* supposed to do?

What I did in mindless implementation of the idea of equivalent effect was this: I doctored the English translation of the pseudo-extract to make it include twelve twelve-letter words which, when written out as a list preserve reference, self-reference and truth value with respect to Perec's left-hand column:

<pre>
LAMENTATIONS
CALLIGRAPHER
FACUPROSETTE
SACHERMASOCH
MORTARBARREL
NEWYORKTIMES
EXORBITANTLY
CRAFTYARTFUL
HUNDREDMETRE
HAMPTONCOURT
CLEARLYGUESS
FORTDEFRANCE
</pre>

But having replanted the invisible clue, and feeling rather pleased with myself, I went one further, and invented a purely fictional list to stand in lieu of the twelve words that Serval had used to mask the original. These words had to fit plausibly into the same places in the plagiarized text, so my choices for List 2 had a retroactive effect on List 1 and consequently on the sentence formulations in the translation of the supposed source. Rome wasn't built in a day. But because the task was so mind-bendingly tricky I decided to give it a personal point which is not present in the French. Here are the two lists in English:

LAMENTATIONS	BENEDICTIONS
CALLIGRAPHER	PENCRAFTSMAN
FACUPROSETTE	KALEIDOSCOPE
SACHERMASOCH	CARLOFRUGONI
MORTARBARREL	DEDIONBOUTON
NEWYORKTIMES	SMITHSWEEKLY
EXORBITANTLY	TOOEVIDENTLY
CRAFTYARTFUL	STUPIDFUTILE
HUNDREDMETRE	TRAMPOLINING
HAMPTONCOURT	TRIPOLITANIA
CLEARLYGUESS	ALMOSTINTUIT
FORTDEFRANCE	NORTHDETROIT

Is the effect 'equivalent', after all that work? I'm not aware that my simulation of the game Perec played has had any effect on readers at all. Or else the fan mail is twenty years late.

An even more obvious trouble with the idea of an equivalent effect is that there's no scale available for measuring equivalence. 'Effects', especially holistic impressions left by extended works, can't be extracted from people and measured against each other. Nor can any one reader give an independent measure of the effects made on her by two language versions of the same text. That's because a reading of a text always happens in a language – not in between. The distinction between language A and language B is problematic enough but one thing is sure: there is no linguistic no-man's land in the middle, just as there is no mid-point between Dover and Calais where you can stand on the water and look on French and English from the outside at the same time.

A bilingual reader may have a perfectly trustworthy judgement of whether a translation communicates the same meaning as its source. But can such a person, however smart and subtle, ever reasonably say that this Baudelaire-in-German-translation has on her an effect equivalent to the effect that that Baudelaire-poem-in-French has? Such an assertion would be radically unverifiable – and in my view it is also a meaningless string of words. Baudelaire-in-French has a whole range of different effects on me at different times, and it surely has an even wider range of effects on the community of readers as a whole. Which one does the 'effect' of a translation aim to be the equivalent of?

The truth of literary translation is that translated works are incommensurable with their source, just as literary works are incommensurable with each other, just as individual readings of novels and poems and plays can only be 'measured' in discussion with other readers. What translators do is find matches, not equivalences, for the units of which a work is made, in the hope and expectation that their sum will produce a new work that can serve overall as a substitute for the source.

That's why Douglas Hofstadter's version of the poem by Clément Marot given at the start of this book is a translation of it. It matches many (but not all) of the semantic, stylistic and formal features of the source. You may not like it – that's your affair. But you cannot claim that it is not a translation on grounds that its overall effect, or one of its subunits, or some specific feature, is not 'equivalent' to the source.

A match may be found through all or any of the means that we have for rephrasing something in our own or any other tongue.

What counts as a satisfactory match is a judgement call, and is never fixed. The only certainty is that a match cannot be the same as the thing that it matches.

If you want the same thing, that's quite all right. You can read the original.

29. *Beating* the *Bounds*: What Translation is Not

What translators do includes all the things that speakers normally do when speaking their own tongues. But just because translation involves everything of that kind, not everything of that kind is usefully thought of as translation. Beyond its ability to call on all and any among the resources of natural languages, translation has features that are specific to it. What they are and what they have been is what this book tries to say.

Like language itself, translation has no rigidly fixed limits, and similarly fuzzy borderlines can be found in many other arts. A violinist may add his own cadenza, or modify a cadenza written by someone else, and still without question be the performer of Mendelssohn's Concerto in E. An actor may modify the lines of his role on some occasions and not others and still be performing the same part. In translation likewise the point where a reformulation ceases to count as a match for the source is open to negotiation within frameworks that vary widely between different traditions and genres.

In India, where Average West European ideas about translation have no roots, stories, myths, legends and religious texts have moved for millennia between different languages – under the guise of adaptations, or retellings of the source. In the West, poets have frequently taken possession of a source by using it as a springboard for a new creation in the same or another tongue. The lyrics Queneau wrote for a song that was sung by Juliette Gréco – '*Si tu t'imagines, fillette, fillette . . .*' – have a source in a poem by Ronsard, and could count as a translation from French into French, just as Robert Lowell's *Imitations*, explicitly modelled on poems in other tongues, can count as translations too, without ceasing to be genuinely new things.

To ask whether what Queneau did with Ronsard is a translation or something else is to ask a question about the meaning of words – specifically, the meaning of the word 'translation'. That's an inquiry that can lead us down many quaint historical, linguistic and cultural back alleys. In medieval times, for example, a 'translation' occurred when the relics of a saint were taken from one shrine to another (the Russian word перевод retains the same sense). In the ocean, a translation wave is one that transmits forward movement, and in law translation is the transfer of property. No end of other entertaining contexts for the word can be found: the way a ceiling crab walks (*translation latérale*, in French), direct passage from earth to Heaven (the translation of Enoch), and so forth. Roman Jakobson, a linguist of great renown, tried to sort the field out by dividing it into three. He distinguished translation between media ('transposition') from translation between different states of the same language ('intralingual translation'), and both of those from 'translation proper' – translation between languages. Jakobson's attempt at clarification actually introduced a great muddle which has to be tackled before the end of this book.

Many cultural practices have a broad structure which can be described, like translation, as consisting essentially of 'before' and 'after'. Knitting, cooking and the production of automobiles are processes that start with some source material (a ball of wool, edible ingredients or a range of separately manufactured parts) and end up with something that is radically different (a pullover, a meal or a car). English is flexible enough to allow us to say without risk of being seriously misunderstood that our partner has translated a few dozen tubes of dried durum wheat into a plate of spaghetti – or to say that by putting on a tuxedo I have translated myself into a toff – but users of English are wise enough to know that such statements have no relevance to translation itself.

In like manner, what a playwright does when he adapts a narrative text for performance on stage has no more relevance to translation than knitting does. Jakobson's proposal to regard switching media as a form of translation is a red herring, and it's not clear to me why he should ever have come up with it. But his many readers over the past decades have swallowed the bait, and treat stage and film adaptation of novels and other prose as particular instances of translation itself.

Making a movie calls on numerous skills and resources that have no connection to any of the things translators do or use. To call David Lean's *Dr Zhivago* a translation of Pasternak's novel is not only to disregard the specificity of film art, but to make such woolly use of the word 'translation' as to fit it to refer to any kind of transformation at all. Knitting included.

The popularity of the idea that everything is translation is no doubt a contemporary reflection of an ancient tradition of thought – in fact, an ancient tradition of thought about thought. It was obvious even to the Greeks that if words began as the proper names of things, then the many words which do not name things that can be seen in the world must be the names of mental states. Call them *ideas*. In fact, even for things that can be seen, the word does not name any one of them, but only that which allows all of them to be seen as instances of an idea. Thus 'tree' is not the proper name of this oak or that aspen, it names the idea of a tree – a mental representation of treeness that allows all actual trees to be recognized as such. In this way of thinking, all linguistic expressions are the external form of thoughts. What we do when we speak to each other is to transmit mental images through a process of translation, thus:

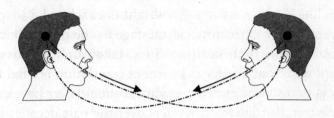

This diagram of 'telementation', or thought transmission, is actually taken from Saussure's *Course in General Linguistics*, which, despite its profound innovations, firmly maintained the long tradition of treating language as the dress of thought.

This visual representation of linguistic interaction does not in fact require A and B to be speaking the same language. As long as both A and B know languages L1 and L2, then the process of understanding speech that is displayed – translating a sound stream into a mental image, then producing a sound stream to represent a mental image for the interlocutor to translate inwardly in turn – would be exactly the same. You come to the same conclusion that language is thought in translation and thought is language translated if you extend the diagram to introduce Person C, a translator mediating between A and B speaking in different tongues. C would look exactly the same, with identical lines of transmission between mouth, ear and brain. Adding translation makes no difference to the model because the model already says that everything is translation already. As a consequence, Saussure's *Course* as well as the bulk of work on language that has taken place in its shadow pays no attention to translation between languages at all.

I don't know whether language is possible without thought – on the face of it, it must be, since so many people speak without thinking – and I wouldn't dare contribute to the unending argument about whether thought is possible without words. The sole contribution I feel confident of making is to say that assimilating all uses of language to translation on the grounds that all speech is a mental translation of thought seriously diminishes our capacity to understand what the practice of translation between languages is about.

To avoid such objections some scholars use the term 'transcoding' to refer to the transformation of work in one media into an altogether different thing (a play into a movie, a musical into a film, but most often a novel into anything else). It's a tactic that has even more damaging effects, since it leads people into thinking that all expressions can be treated as instances of some kind of code. Codes are clever and useful things, but as early adventures in machine translation proved without appeal, languages don't behave like codes at all. Turning a play into a movie has not the slightest analogy or connection with turning a coded message into another code, and to call it transcoding is to use a figure of speech based on not bothering to think what you might mean by code.[1]

The fellows of Oxford colleges inspect the properties the college owns in various parts of the country by annual outings when (in principle if not in fact) they circumperambulate the perimeter. It's called beating the bounds, and that's what we've now done with translation.

One of its sides is as unbounded as the line of a shore – tides rise and fall, and coasts can change shape. But other boundaries are clearly marked. Translation does not extend in every direction. Its own field is quite large enough.

30. *Under* Fire: Sniping at Translation

By always saying some other thing a second time, and saying it in a different way, an act of translation inevitably makes the new utterance your own. A journalist rephrasing an agency wire, a lawyer-linguist readjusting the expression of an opinion given by a judge at the European Court, a writer putting Pushkin into English verse or prose – translators of these and all other kinds possess the outcome of their work in a personal way. Translation cannot but be, in some measure, an appropriation of the source.

Possession, appropriation, making something your own – these are words from the language of the passions. What then of desire and its natural companions, jealousy and hurt?

It's a curious fact that much translation commentary in Western languages contains unmistakable signs of anger and hurt. Schoolmasters, book critics, even theorists routinely disparage other translators – bad translators, 'servile', 'mechanical', second-rate translators – with a range of insults that could easily be thrown about in a lovers' tiff. You have a tin ear! You write dull, wooden, clunky prose! You have taken one liberty too many! What makes you think such licence is allowed? What you have done, young man, is called betrayal! Ignoramus! Cheat! Commoner! Thief!

In 1680, John Dryden, in his thoughtful translator's preface to Ovid's *Epistles*, cast anathema on a rival translator, Spence, for having replaced 'the fine raillery and Attic salt of Lucian' with the 'gross expressions of Billingsgate'.[1] How uncouth!

The philosopher Schopenhauer denigrated those 'people of limited intellectual abilities' who 'use only worn-out patterns of speech in their own language, which they put together so awkwardly that one realizes how imperfectly they understand the meaning of what they are saying . . . so that [their translations are] not much more than mindless parrotry'.[2] Oafs!

'One of the main troubles with would-be translators is their ignorance,' sniped Vladimir Nabokov. Examples he quotes are introduced by him as 'dreadful', 'incredibly coy' and 'grotesquely trite'.[3]

Ortega y Gasset summed up a view that has been expressed without serious interruption since the beginning of the whole debate: 'Almost all translations done until now are bad ones.'[4]

It seems implausible that anyone would ever make such a statement about any other human skill or trade. Let's just try it out: 'Almost all fire fighters up to now have been bad ones', 'Almost all mathematical proofs devised up to now are bad ones', 'Almost all novels written before mine are second rate', 'Almost all women I met before you were dreadful'. If you said any of these things except the last, you would be out of your mind – and the exception is granted only because we permit a degree of insanity in what we say about affairs of the heart. Translators, whose working lives are not sexy in the least, use the language of love to talk about their work. How strange!

But these circumstances make it not strange at all that lay people don't have a high regard for translators. When it comes to defending the profession, translation commentators lead the field in throwing most of its work in the direction of the garbage dump.

Most people encounter translation at school in foreign language lessons. Success in learning a foreign tongue comes at that gratifying moment when, all of a sudden, you find you are able to read and perhaps even think in the foreign tongue without the need to translate in your head. At that point you leave translation behind. It's a second-rate support for those who've not studied hard enough. And if you go on to study the classical or foreign languages at a higher level, using translations becomes almost taboo.

It's a curious paradox. The disparagement of translation emanates most powerfully from those very circles where the ability to translate (at least, in the technical sense) is most likely to be found. It is reinforced in many universities by departments of modern languages that grudgingly permit the teaching of literature in translation only if it's restricted to a separate programme in comparative literature. Of course, their colleagues in history, English, philosophy, sociology, anthropology and even mathematics use translated works all the time. But modern language departments don't seem to notice that at all.

Not all translation commentary is negative, but the range of terms available for complimenting a translator on her work is remarkably small. When book reviews pay any attention at all to the translation of a translated work under review and don't use the opportunity to trot out one or more of the false platitudes we've tried to demolish in other chapters of this book, they recycle one of a small set of standard words of praise: fluent, witty, racy, accurate, brilliant, competent and stylish. You would have to comb through a great quantity of book reviews to find any nods towards translators that step outside of this set and its quasi-synonyms. Translation quality evaluation criteria are hard to establish, as we pointed out; critical language to express such evaluations seems even harder to find.

When you are using translation as a language-learning device, what you want to know when you've done one is whether you got it right. Since few members of the English-speaking community ever get much further than that in acquiring a foreign language, what most people want to know, when they have a translation in front of them, is the same as what they needed to know at school. We are taught to value 'rightness' very highly when we are young, and teachers exploit the competitive spirit to make children internalize the concept. Being wrong is a shameful thing, and the aspiration towards getting the right answer stays with us for a long time. It acts as a focus for self-esteem, and for many other feelings, often passionately held. When a lay reader asks of a translation, 'But is it right?' a question of almost moral importance is implied. But it is the wrong question. If it could be abandoned entirely, then many of the passions that make translation commentary such a vituperative business would abate and maybe one day disappear.

A translation can't be right or wrong in the manner of a school quiz or a bank statement. A translation is more like a portrait in oils. The artist may add a pearl earring, give an extra flush to the cheek or miss out the grey hairs in the sideburns – and still give us a good likeness. It's hard to say just what it is that allows viewers to agree that a portrait captures the important things – the overall shape as well as that special look in the eye. The mysterious abilities we have for recognizing good matches in the visual sphere lie near to what it takes to judge that a translation is good. But the users of a translation, unlike the friends of a portraitist's sitter, don't have full access to the model (they would barely need the translation if they did). That's probably why translation raises such passionate responses. There's no choice but to trust the translator. When it comes to speech and writing, and for reasons that are by now I hope quite clear, people are an untrusting lot.

31. *Sameness*, Likeness *and* Match: Truths About Translation

For a repeated utterance in a different natural language to count as a translation of the source, it must give the same information and have the same force. It may make explicit information that is unstated in the source (by inserting it into the text or by adding footnotes); and it may also, but less frequently, omit information because it is assumed to be too widely known among intended readers to merit the same prominence given to it in the source. But within these areas of tolerance, sameness of information and force is a widely respected norm for the translator's art.

It's worth remembering that these are not the only features of an utterance that could in principle be preserved in a repetition of it in some other tongue. It would not be hard to reproduce the exact pattern of commas and full stops when moving a text between, say, English and French, but nobody bothers to do that. (I did once work briefly with an author who insisted that his punctuation was an inalienable feature of his style, but this only confirmed my initial impression that he was slightly mad.) A competent translator with a lot of time on her hands could easily preserve the word and character count of a source by paragraph, sentence or line, but these kinds of sameness are not considered relevant to the translator's task.[1] Nor does the notion of sameness extend to the selection or distribution of the letters of the source – though there is an exception in Douglas Hofstadter's replacement of the title of Françoise Sagan's *La Chamade* by *That Mad Ache*. In the translation of poetry and song lyrics, sameness in the syllable count, line by line, may be accepted as a constraint, and approximate sameness in length of script is a requirement for strip cartoon legends, for road signage, and museum and exhibition captions. But these are all regarded as special cases. Everywhere else, the requirement of sameness stops at information and force.

In speech translation, tone, pitch, gestures of the face and hands, and the stamping of feet are thrown to the winds, even though they transmit major clues as to how the speech is to be understood.

In all the many other dimensions and levels of an utterance in speech or writing the criterion of translation is not to be the same, but to be like.

A is like B only in respect of C. This is a way of saying that when a thing is compared to some other thing, the act of comparing rests on a third term that is neither A nor B. What makes *soupe de poisson* like chowder? The comparator (called *tertium comparationis* in the old rhetoric) could be soup (but that would be a poor kind of likeness), or seafood (that's richer, both are soups made from fish), or the fact that they are both eaten hot, or that they are both available in tins, or that there are tins of both on that shelf. The 'likeness' of *soupe de poisson* and chowder is a variable, and its value varies in accordance with the comparator used or implied in any given context of use.

The dimensions of an utterance where likeness is the relevant criterion of translation are of many different kinds. Register, tone, rhythm, style and wit can only ever be said to be like each other in respect of something external to the text itself. For example, to judge that writing iambic pentameters in English is like Racine's use of the twelve-syllable line is to base likeness on the social and cultural values of poetic forms in two different environments. In both English and French verse, these are the commonest, most frequently used forms, and thus like each other in that respect. But they are not like each other in any other way. Writing twelve-syllable lines in English to represent French verse, on the other hand, is like the original only in respect of the number 12, but quite unlike it in respect of the underlying rhythms of English, which is a stress-timed language, and of French, which is not.

By choosing which dimensions to connect in a relationship of likeness and the extent to which the likeness is made visible, a translation hierarchizes the interlocking, overlaying features of the original. To that extent at least, translations always provide an interpretation of the source. It's more obvious in literary texts with relatively few practical constraints, but the same underlying situation holds for all acts of translation between languages.

The nub of the question is this: given that a translation preserves the information and the general force of the original, in what respect is it possible to say that its manner or style or tone is like those features of its source?

Georges Perec wrote in a wide variety of styles, but a characteristic feature of all his writing is that important information is placed at the very end, making you realize that up to that point you hadn't understood the main import of the sentence or paragraph – or even the novel. At the level of sentences and paragraphs it is easier to do this in French than in English literary prose, which typically introduces new information in a different manner. Nonetheless, by exploiting the notorious flexibility of English sentence structure and bending it a fair bit, I respected Perec's 'late release' technique as far as I could. By the very fact of doing so I offered an interpretation of Perec's style, but the likeness of my prose to his is a tightly focused and fragile thing. Because I had to take greater liberties with English than he did with French, my writing is not 'like' Perec's at all in respect of linguistic norms.

No translation is the same as its source, and no translation can be expected to be like its source in more than a few selected ways. Which dimensions are selected depends on the conventions of the receiving culture, the nature of the field involved, or even the whim of the commissioner of the translation. But any utterance is such a multidimensional and many-faceted thing that no translator is ever short of a little elbow-room. To put it the other way round, no set of social, practical, linguistic or generic constraints ever determines completely how a translation is to be done.

If meaning and force are kept the same and if in a limited set of other respects a translation is seen to be like its source, then we have a match. Translators are matchmakers of a particular kind. It's not as simple as the marriage of content and form. Just as when we match faces and portraits, we rely on multiple dimensions and qualities to judge when a translation has occurred.

Children's puzzle books exploit and psychologists study our ability to recognize and manipulate the distinct but overlapping relations I've called same, like and match.

Translators use that ability in the specific fields of speech and writing in a foreign tongue. Not all of them are great at their job, and not many have the time and leisure to wait for the best match to come. But when we say that a translation is an acceptable one, what we name is an overall relationship between source and target that is neither identity, nor equivalence, nor analogy – just that complex thing called a good match.

That's the truth about translation.

32. *Avatar*: A Parable of Translation

On a recent visit to India, where I was trying to learn more about translation, I took an afternoon off to go to the movies, and watched a faded copy of what I believe is the most expensive film ever made. To my delight and surprise, *Avatar* turned out to be a parable about translation, and that's why I bring it in at the end of this book.

The hero of James Cameron's science-fiction fantasy is a human transformed by a laboratory technique into another being – nine foot tall, with a prehensile tail and amazing sky-diving skills. His task is to penetrate the society of same-looking beasts causing trouble for a galactic mining company, and then to send back to his controllers the information they need to get the local inhabitants out of their way. He is still a human being under his impressive new shape.

But now he has become a Pandoran in outward appearance, our hero becomes Pandoran in other ways too. He goes native, so to speak, and becomes loyal to the community that has now accepted him as one of its own. These strange beings are fighting to remain themselves and to pursue the lives they have always had. Our hero makes their right to be different his own.

But respect for difference is clearly intended in the film to be an expression of a *human* value. So is our hero one of them, or still, at bottom, one of us? Is the mining company the vector of humanity – or are the awkward beasts in its way the true embodiment of our aspirations and souls?

The movie doesn't quite answer the question at the end. It

is the question that translation sets and must also leave open. How can a hugely modified transmogrification of some utterance – incorporating on occasions the verbal equivalent of a nine-foot-long tail – still remain, at some fundamental level, what it was?

Like Cameron's fantasy, the practice of translation rests on two presuppositions. The first is that we are all different: we speak different tongues, and see the world in ways that are deeply influenced by the particular features of the tongue that we speak. The second is that we are all the same – that we can share the same broad and narrow kinds of feelings, information, understandings and so forth. Without both of these two suppositions, translation could not exist.

Nor could anything we would like to call social life.

Translation is another name for the human condition.

Afterbabble: In Lieu of an Epilogue

In most intellectual disciplines the stories of the Hebrew Bible are no longer used as sources or tools for thought. Translation studies is an exception. Scholars and essayists in this field continue to pay extravagant attention to the account of the origin of linguistic diversity given in the Bible.[1] It's far from obvious that their time is well spent.

The Tower of Babel comes from a story told in Genesis 11. The first verse states that in the beginning 'the whole earth was of one language, and of one speech'.

This is not very plausible. Nothing we know or can observe about human linguistic behaviour makes it likely that there ever was a single form of speech.

The rest of this section of the Bible, Genesis 11.ii–ix, offers an account of how the ancestors of the Jewish people got from their hypothetical state of linguistic unity to the condition of diversity which manifestly characterized the part of the world they lived in some three to four thousand years ago.

The voluminous tradition of Babel commentary weaves religious, philosophical, historical, cultural, archaeological and philological speculations around the story told in Genesis. Do these verses contain a trace of historical events? Or should we read them rather as a fable designed to account for the way things are, or the way they were long ago? For the purposes of this book, it does not matter whether there really was a ziggurat honouring the Assyrian god Marduk near the place now called Babil (in Iraq), or whether it was visited by Herodotus, or when it fell down. For an understanding of language and translation, it doesn't matter if or how the Bible story is related to the Sumerian *Incantation of Nudimmud*. Nor does it make any difference whether we pick from the welter of Babel commentaries those which assume that linguistic diversity is a Dreadful Mess (the vast majority, in fact), those that claim it has a Silver Lining, or those few who argue that it is a Very Good Thing.[2]

What matters is whether we allow verse one to close our minds to other ways of imagining the origin of human speech. Cynics might say that's what religious texts are supposed to do. But translation is not a matter of faith. It's much more interesting than that.

The supposition of an original common form of speech has been taken to mean that intercomprehensibility is the ideal or essential nature of language itself. Such an assumption makes translation a compensatory strategy designed only to cope with a state of affairs that falls short of the ideal. It licenses, indirectly but no less strongly, all the many attempts there have been to devise languages that for some if not all purposes improve upon those that we have.[3]

This contentious foundation of the Babel story acquired implicit if unintended support in the nineteenth and twentieth centuries from the scholarly work of historical linguists. They sought to group languages into 'families' and to reconstruct the hypothetical progenitors of these cousin-tongues, as well as the rules by which each had received its inheritance. The discovery of a family likeness between Sanskrit, Greek, Latin and Old Persian opened a new vista into the past, towards a single source for a whole spectrum of languages spoken between northern India and the Atlantic Ocean.

These exciting advances made it easy to see the historical

derivation of modern languages like a cascade trickling down
the mountainside of time, branching out into streams and
rivers. At the now inaccessible top of the hill, there must have
been a single source – Proto-Indo-European, for the great
family that joins the languages of northern India to many of
those of the West; and, at an even more remote altitude, Nostratic, the supposed ancestor of Indo-European and other
language groups of Europe and Asia; and, high above that,
'proto-World', the language of ante-Babel, the original and
unitary human tongue.

Some saw the underlying meaning of linguistic change and
diversification through spectacles borrowed from Darwinism.
For them, the growth in complexity from single-cell life forms
to the magnificent machinery of humankind served as a model
for understanding the 'evolution of language', from the rough-
and-ready speech of hunter-gatherers to the refinements of
the French Academy. Others saw language change as a per-
petual fall from the economy and mystery of the ancient
tongues to the confusing multiplicity you can hear in the
street. But behind these scholarly (and often schoolmasterly)
pursuits lay a single barely questioned assumption – that all
languages are, at bottom, the same kind of thing, because, at
the start, they *were* the same thing. In fact, there was rather
better evidence of the contrary. The Babel story may say that
in the beginning all language was one – but what it shows is
that, for a single people in the third or second millennium
BCE, linguistic diversity was a major fact of life.

However, if we accept the proposition that all languages are
instances of the same kind of thing, we have to ask: what is it
that makes them the same? The most influential answer to
this question in the twentieth century has been: a grammar.

The idea that a grammar is the common property of all

human languages looks like a hypothesis – something you could test against data, then either abandon or refine. But that's not the main way in which it has actually been used. Characteristically, the 'grammaticality hypothesis' is an axiom, a circular foundation stone. The axiom 'explains' why animal and mechanical signalling systems are not languages. Since traffic lights and the barking of dogs seem to have either no discernible rules of combination or no ability to create new combinations, they have no grammar, and because all languages have a grammar in order to count as languages, dog barking and traffic lights are not languages. QED.

In a similarly circular way, the axiom of grammaticality pushes to the edge of language study all those uses of human vocal noises – ums, hums, screams, giggles, mumbles, stammers, exclamations and interjections, alongside ellipses, nonsense words, gargles, cooing, baby-talk, pillow-talk and so forth – that don't decompose neatly into nouns, verbs and full stops.

Even leaving out the whole range of 'ungrammatical' and 'non-linguistic' uses of vocal sounds, the variability and range of the things that the grammars of actual languages regulate make it very hard to see what it can mean to say that a grammar is what all languages have in common. Inevitably, it prompts a second question: what is it that all grammars have in common?

It is hard to find an existing grammatical category that is common to all forms of human speech. Many languages do without determiners such as 'a' and 'the' (Russian and Chinese, for example). Many languages do without gender (spoken Finnish makes no distinction between 'he', 'she' and 'it'). Numerous major and minor languages in the world do not mark number (Chinese, again, has no special form for dual or plural). It's fairly obvious that you don't really need adjectives – even in English, you can use 'tomato' or 'beetroot' if you want to call something red; prefixes allow you to distinguish between big and small versions of the same thing (English *minibus*, French *hyper-marché*), just as suffixes do in Italian (*uomaccio*, 'big man'), Latin (*homunculus*, little man) and Russian (левчик, 'little lion'). The Argentinian wit Jorge Luis Borges thought up a language without nouns – where verbs and adverbs sufficed for all expressions. 'It moons bluely' is all you would need to refer to the presence of a blue-tinted moon in the sky. Aspect is only properly grammaticalized in some languages (Russian, for example) and tense is clearly redundant even in languages that have it. 'I go to Paris tomorrow' is perfectly good English, just as *Napoléon entre dans Moscou en août 1812* is normal French, with the explicit expressions of time ('tomorrow', '1812') making the grammatical marking of time unnecessary. Only some languages have evidentials; vast numbers of them have no prepositions and many others have no agglutinations. The concept of case is virtually absent from English (it subsists in the distinction we still make between *he* and *him*, *she* and *her* – and that's about it) and totally alien to Chinese.

And so it goes on. Mood is not part of English grammar (we use separate words, such as *may*, *should*, *ought* and so forth), but it provides Albanian with an elaborate set of resources for expressing all sorts of affective qualities, including admiration. Vowel harmony is a basic feature of Hungarian: you say *a moziba* if you went to the cinema, but *az étterembe* if you went to the restaurant, because the 'o' and 'i' sounds of the first require the suffix *ba* to match them, and the 'é' and 'e' sounds of the second call for the suffix to be *be*. Nothing like that happens in the vast majority of the world's languages.

The hunt for what all grammars share – 'Universal Grammar'

– has been going on for a long while, and has got about as far as the search for the Holy Grail.[4] However, at one level, the answer is obvious, because it is definitional: all grammars regulate the ways in which free items may be combined to make an acceptable sentence.

The trouble with that is obvious: 'sentence' is a grammatical concept to begin with. Sentencehood is not an observable quality of acts of natural speech. It's not just in the poetry of Mallarmé that we have difficulty in knowing where to put the full stop. Just listen to your children! They *never* finish their sentences properly.

It is true that we can make sentences in any human language. But it is just as true that most of our actual uses of speech do not involve anything that looks much like a grammatical sentence. When we write, of course, we usually try to write in sentences. But not always.

The second major problem with the axiom of grammaticality – with the idea that what makes a language a language is its having a grammar – is that no living language has yet been given a grammar that accounts for absolutely all of the expressions (including sentences) that are uttered by speakers of that language. The 'grammar of English' – or any other language – has not yet been completed, and it's a fair guess that it will always remain a work in progress.

Flaws of this magnitude in aerodynamics or the theory of probability would not have allowed the Wright Brothers to get off the ground or the National Lottery to finance the arts.

The Achilles heel of a linguistic theory that places grammar at its core could be put like this. Since universal grammar remains elusive and no exhaustive grammar of any single form of speech has yet been devised, every speaking subject on this planet knows something that grammar does not.

So let us put the Bible story and school-learned wisdom aside. Let us also suppose that there is something about every form of human behaviour that we recognize as a language that all languages have in common. What is it? What is it that unambiguously identifies some set of sounds made by humans as a language?

It's a huge question, and it's hard to know where to begin. But let us try to do so without any presuppositions. One of the first things we can easily observe has to do with our hands.

There is no form of language in the world that is ever spoken aloud without accompanying hand movements. Indeed, the greater the effort of concentration on live speech, the more the speaker needs to move his or her hands. Try watching the conference interpreters behind their glass screens in Luxembourg or Geneva. Although absolutely nobody is supposed to be looking at them, all of them – whether they are speaking German, Estonian, Arabic or Dutch – gesticulate wildly, simply in order to keep the flow of speech up to speed. Hand movement is a profound, unconscious, inseparable part of natural speech.

We could therefore start from the reliable and repeatable observation that natural speech is a partly but obligatorily manual activity.[5] Here's an obvious exception that proves the rule. In most languages, television newscasters do not gesticulate at all, but keep their hands on or under the desk, or use them only to shuffle the papers in front of them. That is because they are only pretending to talk to you. What they are actually doing is reading words written on the teleprompter screen. Similarly, a lecturer who moves his hands is almost certainly ad-libbing – actually talking to you, in the forms of natural speech. One who is reading written lecture notes aloud characteristically keeps his hands to his side, or on the desk. Speaking is not the same thing as reading aloud from written text.

Conversely, delicate finger-work of a non-linguistic kind almost always prompts movement of the lips. Have you watched anyone threading a needle? Few people can do it without pursing or twisting their mouths.

What links hand and mouth? The most obvious connection is feeding. The hand – of humans, but also of many other primates – is used to take food to the mouth, which is also the organ of speech.

Eating and speaking are two separate activities that have a great deal in common. They both involve hand and mouth. Moreover, they use almost all of the same muscles. That is perhaps why trying to do both at the same time is regarded as uncouth. For infants and young children, whose muscular control is not yet fully developed, it can also be quite dangerous.

Speaking can be seen in this light as a parasitic use of organs whose primary function is to ensure survival. But what then was the original function of this wonderful, additional, alternative use of lips and tongue and of the muscles that control breathing and swallowing? In what way did it correlate to other uses of hands and arms?

There are considerable variations in the communicative force of hand and arm use among different cultures and communities, but they are not nearly as extensive as the bewildering range of different sounds, words and grammatical structures among the languages of the world. A slap on the back, a shrug of the shoulders and a punch in the gut don't have exactly the same meaning the world over, but they are far more 'transportable' than any word or sound I can make. Even a cry for help, a burst of laughter, or a squeal of pain is less intercomprehensible between different language cultures than a touch on your arm.

Articulated language, however and whenever it emerged, in one group of our ancestors or among many, added a communicative channel that was radically different from hand use. It was far less transportable than the resources available up to that point. That is likely to have been the reason why it caught on.

In most domains of life we are well aware that what a thing was invented for and what is actually done with it bear no necessary relationship to each other. The umbrella may have been designed to protect us from the rain, but on one notorious occasion one such device was used to assassinate a dissident on Waterloo Bridge. Matchsticks owe their existence to a wish to make ignition widely and cheaply available, but they are also very serviceable toothpicks. What a thing is 'for' and what it can be used to do must be kept apart. It is very odd that almost no serious thinking about language and translation has ever bothered to observe this basic rule.

The plain fact of linguistic diversity suggests very strongly that speech did not arise in order to communicate with members of other groups of like beings. If that is what it was for, our ancestors got it badly wrong. They should have dropped it on the spot.

Similarly, there is no particular reason to think that language first arose in order to allow members of the same group to communicate with each other. They did that already – with their hands, arms, bodies and faces. Many species clearly do. You can watch them at it in the zoo.

'Communication' is what we think we do when we speak or write, largely because that is what we have been taught at school. But when we watch and listen to humans 'behaving linguistically', as spectators at the human zoo, what we see and hear is something altogether different.

Like other uses of lips and hands, such as smiling, stroking, pouting and punching, vocal noise establishes bonds between people who need or wish to be linked together in some way – for mutual support, to establish rank or to declare hostility, for example. From that perspective, the baby-sitter who coos at an infant in a cot is performing a language act of the same general kind as the ambitious student who greets me with a rising tone on the last syllable of 'good morning, sir'. If these acts are communicative, then we must redefine communication not as the transmission of mental states from A to B (and even less as the transmission of 'information') but as the establishment, reinforcement and modification of immediate interpersonal relations. But it would be better to say: that's not communication, that's language. Language is a human way of relating to other humans.

Among the larger primates such functions are carried out through the much-studied practice of grooming. Grooming bonds mother and child, it bonds males in hierarchical rank (the 'pecking order'), it establishes bonds between males and females prior to copulation, and it generally binds together the entire clan or group of cohabiting animals. But it is a time-consuming business. There is a point of population growth where it can't easily serve its purpose any more. Robin Dunbar has suggested that a group of fifty-five animals is just about as large as a grooming-based community can get before it has to split up. When it does, no cross-grooming is possible: you belong to either the old group or the new one. You do not pick fleas off the fur of chimps that are not of 'your kind'.[6]

There is a striking fit between this picture of social construction among primates and the way people actually talk. Articulated language allows the group size to increase greatly, but not infinitely. The way any individual talks is part of his identity as a member of a specific community, defined by region, area, city, maybe even street, and certainly by clan or family. What's called dialectal variation, which is just another aspect of linguistic diversity, performs a similar structuring function to the grooming habits of chimpanzees. To put this broad understanding in a nutshell: language is ethnicity.

Ethnicity in this sense has nothing to do with lineage, heredity, race, blood group or DNA. It means: how a social group constitutes and identifies itself.

The bewildering variety of diction that can be heard among the inhabitants of the British Isles gives a spectacular demonstration of the fine-grained group-membership function of the way people speak. Different sounds are used to communicate membership of communities based in Essex, Norfolk, the three Ridings of Yorkshire, Teesside, Edinburgh, Aberdeen, Orkney, Shetland, Lewis, Glasgow, Liverpool, Manchester, Birmingham, North Wales, South Wales, Somerset, Scilly, Solent and Kent, and in addition the diction of London, now called Estuarine, is audibly divided in two, depending on whether you live on the north or south bank of the Thames's muddy maw. On top of this, specific phonologies override or else merge with these regional markers to locate the speaker in the pecking order of British society, from the 'Mayfairditsch' of wealth and privilege to the related but not identical speech of those educated at private schools (called public schools), public schools (called grammar schools), and the rest. Some of course learn to speak not from their classmates but from listening to the BBC (which I think must have been the case for me) and signal thereby their allegiance to an idea of 'educated speech' as the dialect of (cultural) authority. In Britain, you just can't escape the messages about region and class that come from anyone who opens his or her mouth.

In the musical *My Fair Lady*, based on G. B. Shaw's stage play *Pygmalion*, which itself rewrites a far more ancient myth,

Professor Higgins asks: 'Oh! why can't the English teach their children how to speak?' We must answer: Oh, but they do, Professor Higgins. They teach them to declare themselves to be Geordies and Aberdonians, Etonians and lads on the Clapham omnibus, ladies from Morningside or fishermen from Newquay. If you are British, you just can't not notice. Alongside its role as a planetary interlanguage in print, English speech – like any other – is a highly pixellated way of telling people who you are.

That is something that all forms of human speech share, and it is perhaps the only thing that is truly universal about language. Every language tells your listener who you are, where you come from, where you belong. Linguistic diversity, including the subtle differentiation in diction within intercomprehensible forms of speech, is the mechanism by which this primordial social function is performed.

The differential function of speech goes even further than that. No two individuals make exactly the same sounds, even when they are speaking the same local variant of a language. All my mother-in-law ever needed to say when she rang was *Allo! c'est moi!* A waste of breath, I would think every time. But the unreflecting purpose of her phatic expression was only partly to 'establish the channel'. What it did was confirm an interpersonal relationship based on the irreducible difference between her and me. Every act of speech does just that – whatever you say.

Individual diction and forms of speech do not vary because they need to for any physical, intellectual or practical reasons – impersonators demonstrate that it is possible to adopt the voice-print of someone else if you train yourself hard enough. Individual speech varies because one of the fundamental and perhaps original purposes of speaking is to serve as a differentiating tool – to differentiate not only where you come from, what rank and clan or street-gang you belong to, but to say 'I am not you but me'.

Babel tells the wrong story. The most likely original use of human speech was to be different, not the same.

In parts of the world that are sparsely populated and where travel is made perilous by physical obstacles – high mountains, waterless deserts or thick jungle – linguistic diversity is extremely high. That is because the various indigenous communities of Papua New Guinea, the great Australian plains and the Amazon basin do not often come into contact with each other. Even in a wealthy country like Switzerland, the physical obstacles to contact between its many high valleys over the centuries have left their mark in the continued cohabitation of four main languages. But in other parts of the world where geography is more conducive to travel, and thus to contact, interchange, trade and war, linguistic diversity is much reduced. Languages merge when people do.

Let us therefore abandon the old image of linguistic diversity as a picture of rivulets splitting and dividing as they course down the mountainside from a single glacier-tip. We should see it rather as the always provisional result of a multiplicity of springs, wells, ponds and snowmelts furrowing down into valleys to meet and merge in broader, deeper rivers. English is once again a fairly extreme example – its identifiable sources include the Germanic language of the Angles and Saxons, the French learned by the Norman soldiers who overran the island in 1066, together with ample helpings of Latin, a dash of Danish, a sprinkling of Celtic, and bits and bobs from at least a hundred languages around the world. Just at the moment it seems to be bursting its already wide banks and spilling into many other streams. But it's not really anything to worry about. There is no greater likelihood of all languages being gobbled up by English than of the Amazon and the Volga flowing into the same sea. In any case, as we have seen, the primordial mechanism of linguistic differentiation makes English no less a tool for marking difference than any other tongue.

It follows from this that translation does not come 'After Babel'. It comes when some human group has the bright idea that the kids on the next block or the people on the other side of the hill might be worth talking to. Translating is a first step towards civilization.

Hundreds of thousands, maybe millions of years elapsed between the emergence of speech-sounds to perform the social bonding functions of grooming and the invention of alphabetic script. In the course of that for ever hidden eon, human communities found that they could do vastly more things with speech than just keep their families, clans and tribes in good order.

Translation deals with most of those other things. It does not and cannot attempt to perform or mimic or replicate the interpersonal functions of human speech. As we noted in an earlier chapter, translators do not match dialect for dialect when translating between established languages. 'Hallo, darling', 'Yalrite?' and 'Wotcha, mate' are forms of greeting that declare the speaker to be, respectively, a fashionista, a Glaswegian and a Londoner. They may serve as translations of *bonjour, monsieur*, but the task they perform, involuntarily and obligatorily, is to claim membership of *that* community and not any other. It makes no sense to imagine transporting the ethnic, self-identifying dimension of any utterance. Absolutely any other formulation of the expression, in the same or any other dialect or language, constructs a different identity.

If you're looking for the ineffable, stop here. It's blindingly obvious. It's not poetry, but community, that is lost in translation. The community-building role of actual language use is simply not part of what translation does.

But translation does almost everything else. It is translation, more than speech itself, which provides incontrovertible evidence of the human capacity to think and to communicate thought.

We should do more of it.

Caveats and *Thanks*

As I've tried to write about translation between natural languages I've not mentioned the use of the word as a technical term in mathematics, logic and some branches of computer science. That would be a different book.

I've also failed to say anything about the uses and pitfalls of translation in the military, in war zones and in hospitals. I plead ignorance. There is surely a lot to be learned from the courageous language mediators who work in these fields.

Readers familiar with translation studies may notice other omissions. Some of them are intentional. George Steiner's *After Babel* is still in print, and my reasons for not commenting further on Walter Benjamin's essay 'The Task of the Translator' can be found in *Cambridge Literary Review* 3 (June 2010), pp. 194–206.

Many of the brains I have picked are mentioned in footnotes and references, but other people and institutions have given me hints, memories, insights and material in less formal ways. I hope I have not missed out any of my treasured and sometimes involuntary helpers, present and alas in some cases past, who receive here the expression of my sincerest thanks: Ruth Adler, Valerie Aguilar, Esther Allen, Srinavas Bangalore, Alex Bellos, Nat Bellos, George Bermann, Susan Bernofsky, Jim Brogden, Olivia Coghlan, Karen Emmerich, Michael Emmerich, Denis Feeney, Michael Gordin, Jane Grayson, Tom Hare, Roy Harris, Susan Harris, James Hodson, Douglas Hofstadter, Susan Ingram, Adriana Jacobs, David Jones,

Graham Jones, Patrick Jospin, Joshua Katz, Sarah Kay, Carine Kennedy, Martin Kern, Judy Laffan, Ella Laszlo, Andrew Lendrum, Perry Link, Simone Marchesi, Heather Mawhinney, Ilona Morison, Sergey Oushakine, Claire Paterson, Georges Perec, Katy Pinke, Mr Pryce, Kurt Riechenberg, Anti Saar, Kim Scheppele, Bambi Schieffelin, 'Froggy' Smith, Jonathan Charles Smith, Lawrence Venuti, Lynn Visson, Kerim Yasar, Froma Zeitlin; The Library of the École de Traduction et d'Interprétation (ETI), University of Geneva; the staff and resources of the Firestone Library, Princeton; the speakers and listeners at the Translation Lunches at Princeton since their inception in 2008; and the four cohorts of students from the classes of 2008 through 2013 who by taking the TRA 200 'Thinking Translation' course obliged me to think, a lot.

Notes

1. What is a Translation?

1 Douglas Hofstadter, *Le Ton beau de Marot: In Praise of the Music of Language*, Basic Books, 1997, p. 1a.

2. Is Translation Avoidable?

1 Harish Trivedi, 'In Our Own Time, on Our Own Terms: "Translation" in India', in Theo Hermans (ed.), *Translating Others*, St Jerome, 2006, Vol. 1, pp. 102–19.

2 Claire Blanche-Benvéniste, 'Comment retrouver l'expérience des anciens voyageurs en terres de langues romanes?', in Virginie Conti and François Grin, *S'entendre entre langues voisines: vers l'intercompréhension*, Chêne-Bourg: Georg, 2008, pp. 34–51. On lingua franca, see John Holm, *An Introduction to Pidgins and Creoles*, Cambridge UP, 2000.

3 Different authorities give different figures, ranging from 5,000 to 7,000. We're using the higher estimate, but the actual figure doesn't really matter for the argument of this book.

4 These figures, taken from Wikipedia, include non-native users of the languages concerned. Because many people speak two or more of the world's major languages, the total population of the 'top thirteen' may exceed the total population of the world. Figures for total native or first-language speakers show a different picture: Mandarin Chinese 863 million, Hindi 680 million, English 400 million, Spanish 350 million, Arabic 280 million, Russian 164 million, Japanese 130 million, German 105 million, French 80 million, Turkish 63 million, Urdu 60 million, Indonesian 17 million, Swahili 10 million, total 3.2 billion, or just over half the world's population.

5 One obvious answer is: Portuguese. But despite its importance for

large and far-flung communities in Europe, South America and
Africa, its role as a vehicular language is minimal.

6 J. N. Adams, *Bilingualism and the Latin Language*, Cambridge UP,
2003, gives a detailed portrait of the relations between Latin and the
other languages of Rome and its possessions. Many texts discussed
by Adams show Latin in contact with other languages, but none of
his material could be classed even approximately as a Latin translation of a non-Latin text.

7 Georges Perec, 'Experimental Demonstration of the Tomatotopic
Organization in the Soprano', in *Cantatrix Sopranica et autres écrits
scientifiques*, Paris: Seuil, 1991.

8 According to Claude Hagège, *Dictionnaire amoureux des langues*,
Paris: Plon, 2009, p. 109, Konstantin Päts, the last president of independent Estonia, also made a broadcast in Latin in August 1939, for
the same reasons.

9 Elisabeth and Jean-Paul Champseix, *57, Boulevard Staline. Chro-
niques albanaises*, Paris: La Découverte, 1990.

10 Adapted from Georges Perec, *Life A User's Manual*, transl. David
Bellos, Vintage, 2009, p. 110.

3. Why Do We Call It 'Translation'?

1 Michael Emmerich, 'Beyond Between: Translation, Ghosts, Metaphors', posted online at wordswithoutborders.org, April 2009.

2 Bambi B. Schieffelin, 'Found in Translating: Reflexive Language across
Time and Texts in Bosavi', in Miki Makihara and Bambi B. Schief-
felin (eds.), *Consequences of Contact: Language Ideologies and Sociocultural
Transformations in Pacific Societies*, Oxford UP, 2007, pp. 141–65.

3 From Andrew Chesterman, *Memes of Translation*, John Benjamins,
1997, p. 61.

4 From the *Book of Rites*, after 206 BCE, as quoted by Martha Cheung
in *Target* 17:1 (2005), p. 29.

5 Taken respectively from the first Chinese dictionary, second century
CE; Kong Yingda, seventh century CE; Jia Gongyan, also seventh
century; and a Buddhist monk, Zan Ning, as quoted (and translated)
by Martha Cheung in *Target* 17:1, pp. 33, 34.

6 For the time being, I am using 'translation' to refer to interlingual communication of all kinds, spoken and written. Interpreting, which deals exclusively with speech, is the subject of Chapter 25.

7 'A small man's son is astounded by the food market', from Luis d'Antin van Rooten, *Mots d'heures, Gousses, Rames*, Grossman, 1967.

4. Things People Say about Translation

1 See Leo Spitzer, *Essays on Seventeenth-Century French Literature*, Cambridge UP, 1983, pp. 253–84, for the whole story.

2 Quoted in Lev Loseff, *On the Beneficence of Censorship: Aesopian Language in Modern Russian Literature*, Munich: Otto Sagner, 1984, p. 78.

3 Lev Loseff, 'The Persistent Life of James Clifford: The Return of a Mystification', *Zvezda*, January 2001 (in Russian).

5. Fictions of the Foreign

1 Lawrence Venuti, *The Translator's Invisibility: A History of Translation*, Routledge, 1995, p. 20 and passim.

2 Jean Rond d'Alembert, 'Observations sur l'art de traduire', in *Mélanges de littérature . . .* , Amsterdam: Chatelain, 1763, Vol. III, p. 18. My translation.

3 *Dangerous connections: or, letters collected in a society, and published for the instruction of other societies*. By M. C**** de L***, London, 1784.

4 Fred Vargas, *Have Mercy on Us All*, transl. David Bellos, Harvill, 2003.

5 Directed by David Ka-Shing for the Yellow Earth Theatre and Shanghai Dramatic Arts Center, performed in Stratford-upon-Avon, London and Shanghai in 2006.

6 Friedrich Schleiermacher, 'Über die verschiedenen Methoden des Übersetzens', a paper read in 1813 to the Royal Academy of Sciences in Berlin, in a new translation by Susan Bernofsky, in Lawrence Venuti, *The Translation Studies Reader* (2nd edn), Routledge, 2004. An earlier and more widely available translation by Waltraud Bartscht omits several passages.

7 From Chapter Two of Jacques Derrida's *Of Grammatology* (1967), transl. Gayatri Chakravorti Spivak, Johns Hopkins UP, 1974.

8 Mariagrazia Margarito, 'Une valise pour bien voyager ... avec les italianismes du français', *Synergies* 4 (2008), pp. 63–73.

9 Antoine Volodine, 'Écrire en français une littérature étrangère', *chaoïd* 6 (2002).

10 David Remnick, 'The Translation Wars', *The New Yorker*, 7 November 2005.

11 Ibid. See also Gary Saul Morton, 'The Pevearsion of Russian Literature', *Commentary*, July–August 2010, which takes a much harsher line.

12 Mariusz Wilk, *The Journals of a White Sea Wolf*, transl. Daniusa Stok, Harvill, 2003, uses the device to great effect.

6. Native Command

1 In some countries the children of immigrant parents are not even granted a nationality. Statelessness can be seen as the 'zero condition' of what is acquired by the fact of being born – and also an infringement of international conventions on fundamental rights.

2 G. T. Chernov, *Osnovy sinkhronnogo perevoda* ('Foundations of Simultaneous Interpreting'), Moscow: Vysshaia shkola, 1987, pp. 5–8.

3 Lynn Visson, *Sinkhronni perevod s russkogo na angliski*, Moscow, 2007, pp. 15–16; see also Lynn Visson, 'Teaching Simultaneous Interpetation into a Foreign Language', *Мосты* 2.22 (2009), pp. 57–9.

7. Meaning is No Simple Thing

1 From *LINGUIST- List* 2.457, 3 September 1991.

8. Words are Even Worse

1 Roman Jakobson, 'On Linguistic Aspects of Translation', in Reuben Brower (ed.), *On Translation*, Oxford UP, 1959, p. 232.

2 This is just a simple explanation of Zipf's law, which says that the frequency of any word is inversely proportional to its rank in the

frequency table. Thus the most frequent word will occur approximately twice as often as the second most frequent word and three times as often as the third most frequent word. As a result, just 135 different words account for half of all the word occurrences in an English-language corpus of about 1 million words.

3 Leonard Bloomfield, *Language*, H. Holt & Co., 1933, p. 140.

4 It may be not arbitrary at all from a historical point of view: the two words 'light' come from quite different origins, whereas all the meanings of 'head' come from a single source.

5 Additional sub-rules apply to alphabetic sequences that include the symbols - and * (as in 'back-up' and the proprietary name 'E*Trade'); in some language there are additional typographical marks like ¿¡ but these and other features found in languages with alphabetical or syllabic scripts don't alter the structure of the rules or the basic idea of what a word is – for a computer.

6 Hayley G. Davis, *Words: An Integrational Approach*, Curzon, 2001, has many hilarious examples of English-speakers' utter confusion about what a word is.

7 Anna Morpurgo Davies, 'Folk-Linguistics and the Greek Word', in George Cardon and Norman Zide (eds.), *Festschrift for Henry Hoenigswald*, Tübingen: Narr, 1987, pp. 263–80.

9. Understanding Dictionaries

1 Jonathon Green, *Chasing the Sun: Dictionary-Makers and the Dictionaries They Made*, Cape, 1996, pp. 40–41.

2 Jan Assmann, 'Translating Gods: Religion as a Factor of Cultural (Un)Translatability', in Sanford Budick and Wolfgang Iser (eds.), *The Translatability of Cultures: Figurations of the Space Between*, Stanford UP, 1996, pp. 25–36.

3 Information from Christoph Harbsmeier, *Language and Logic in Traditional China*, forming volume VII.1 of Joseph Needham's *Science and Civilisation in China*, Cambridge UP, 1998, pp. 65–84; and Endymion Wilkinson, *Chinese History: A Manual*, Harvard UP, 1998, pp. 62–94.

4 Philitas of Cos, Ἄτακτοι γλῶσσαι, *Átaktoi glôssai* or 'Disorderly

Words', explains the meanings of rare Homeric and other literary words; the oldest surviving full Homeric lexicon is by Apollonius the Sophist, from the first century CE. The first Sanskrit word-list, *Amarakośa*, was written by Amara Sinha in the fourth century CE.

5 Georges Perec, *Life A User's Manual*, transl. David Bellos, Vintage, 2009, pp. 287–8.

10. The Myth of Literal Translation

1 According to Naomi Seidman, 'One would be hard put to name a major defence of word-for-word translation before the modern period.' *Faithful Renderings: Jewish–Christian Difference and the Politics of Translation*, Chicago UP, 2006, p. 75.

2 George Steiner, *After Babel*, 3rd edn, Oxford UP, 1998, p. 251.

3 Nicolas Herberay des Essarts, translator's preface to *Amadis de Gaule* (1540), ed. Michel Bideaux, Champion, 2006, p. 168, my translation.

4 Octavio Paz, *Un poema di John Donne: Traducción literara y literalidad*, Barcelona: Tusquets, 1990, p. 13.

5 Quoted by one of Kelly's former colleagues at Ottawa University on a blog named 'Unprofessional Translation'.

6 Mark Twain, *The Jumping Frog, in English, then in French, then clawed back into a civilized language once more by patient, unremunerated toil*, Harper and Brothers, 1903, pp. 39–40.

7 Michael Israel, 'The Rhetoric of "Literal Meaning"', in Sean Coulson and Barbara Lewandowska-Tomaszczyk, *The Literal and Non-Literal in Language and Thought*, Frankfurt: Lang, 2005, pp. 147–238.

8 See Dominique Jullien, *Les Amoureux de Schéhérézade: Variations sur les Mille et Une Nuits*, Geneva: Droz, 2009, for a discussion of the cultural issues surrounding Mardrus's translation.

9 Quoted in ibid., p. 107, my translation.

10 André Gide, in *La Revue blanche*, XXI:475 (January 1900), quoted in Jullien, *Amoureux de Schéhérézade*, p. 110.

11 J.-C. Mardrus, letter to the editor in *Revue critique d'histoire et de littérature* XLI.26:515 (June 1900), quoted in Jullien, *Amoureux de Schéhérézade*, p. 85.

11. The Issue of Trust

1 Roy Harris, *The Origin of Writing*, Duckworth, 1968, p. 177. Writing has been invented four times: by the Maya, in pre-Columbian America; in China; in Ancient Egypt; and in Mesopotamia. All modern writing systems derive from just two of these inventions, and all alphabetic scripts from just one.

2 The term 'primary orality' was coined by Walter Ong, SJ. See his *Orality and Literacy*, Methuen, 1987.

3 Universal literacy was first achieved in most Western European countries at some point between 1860 and 1920. In other parts of the world it is even more recent than that; and in many of them it remains a long way off.

4 Leo Tolstoy, *War and Peace*, transl. Rosemary Edmonds, Penguin Books, 1957, p. 1153.

5 In practice, when relations are cordial, the ancient protocol is often abandoned, and the two translators take it in turn to translate both ways in twenty-minute shifts, just as they would when working in more public encounters. But for discussions on major topics between heads of state and of government, there can be no question of having only one translator present.

6 Ismail Kadare's *Palace of Dreams* is an ironic fiction about Ottoman dream-records with some basis in historical fact.

7 See E. Natalie Rothman, 'Interpreting Dragomans: Boundaries and Crossings in the Early Modern Mediterranean', *Comparative Studies in Society and History* 51.4 (2009), pp. 771–800, for far more detail than is possible here.

8 *Ziggurat* (a pyramidal temple) is generally reckoned to be the only other word of Akkadian in English, but it came into the language only in the nineteenth century.

9 *The Blinding Order* and *The Three-Arched Bridge* complement *The Palace of Dreams* in this respect.

10 French started to be used in this role in the seventeenth century, and in the nineteenth it displaced Italian entirely.

11 The example is from Bernard Lewis, *From Babel to Dragomans: Interpreting the Middle East*, Oxford UP, 2004, p. 29.

12 Ibid., p. 27.

13 George Abbott, *Under the Turk in Constantinople*, Macmillan, 1920, p. 46, quoted in Judy Laffan, 'Navigating Empires: "British" Dragomans and Changing Identity in the Nineteenth-Century Levant', unpublished Ph.D. thesis, University of Queensland.

14 Abbott, ibid.

15 Published with Françoise Sagan, *That Mad Ache*, transl. Douglas Hof stadter, Basic Books, 2009.

16 See Allan Cunningham, '*Dragomania*: The Dragomans of the British Embassy in Turkey', *Middle Eastern Affairs* 2 (1961), pp. 81–100.

12. Custom Cuts

1 Stephen Owen, 'World Poetry', a review of Bei Dao's *The August Sleepwalker*, transl. Bonnie McDougall, *New Republic*, November 1990.

2 For a list of foreign film stars and their established German voices, see the 'Synchronsprecher' website.

3 *Le Monde*, 7 August 2010, p. 14.

4 Vladimir Nabokov, 'Introduction', in *Eugene Onegin: A Novel in Verse by Aleksandr Pushkin*, Routledge, 1964, Vol. 1, pp. vii–ix.

5 Vladimir Nabokov, 'The Servile Path', in Reuben Brewer (ed.), *On Translation*, Harvard UP, 1959, pp. 97–110.

6 Georges Perec, interview with Marcel Benabou (December 1965), in *Review of Contemporary Fiction XIII*. 1 (1993), p. 19.

13. What Can't be Said Can't be Translated

1 See http://www.packingtownreview.com/blog/, postdated 2 December 2007.

2 Thom Satterlee, in *Delos* (1996), pp. 46–52, finds a kind of source in an essay by Ezra Pound, 'How I Began' (1913), but which claims the opposite: 'I would know what was accounted poetry everyday, what part of poetry was "indestructible," what part could not be lost in translation.'

3 Ludwig Wittgenstein, *Tractatus Logico-philosophicus* (1921), Proposi tion 74: *Wovon man nicht sprechen kann, davon muß man schweigen*.

4 English-language philosophers since Willard van Orman Quine have treated this issue at length. My position reflects that of Donald Davidson as I understand it from the commentary provided by J. E. Malpas in 'The Intertranslatability of Natural Languages', *Synthese* 78 (1989), pp. 233–64.

5 Romain Gary, *White Dog* (1970), Chicago UP, 2004, p. 51.

6 Marshall Sahlins, *The Western Illusion of Human Nature*, Prickly Paradigm, 2008, takes this argument much further. Christine Kenneally, *The First Word: The Search for the Origins of Language*, Penguin, 2007, gives an up-to-date report on current research that is fast undermining the distinction between 'language' and 'signal' and between human and non-human communication.

7 Mark E. Laidre and Jessica L. Yorzinski, 'The Silent Bared-Teeth Face and the Crest-Raise of the Mandrill (Mandrillus sphinx): A Contextual Analysis of Signal Function', *Ethology* 111 (2005), pp. 143–57. A standard introduction to the field of animal sign systems is Thomas A. Sebeok, *How Animals Communicate*, Indiana UP, 1977.

14. How Many Words Do We Have for Coffee?

1 Laura Martin, '"Eskimo Words for Snow": A Case Study in the Genesis and Decay of an Anthropological Example', *American Anthropologist* 88.2 (1986), pp. 418–23, explained and defended by Geoffrey Pullum in *The Great Eskimo Vocabulary Hoax and Other Irreverent Essays on the Study of Language*, Chicago, 1991.

2 Inuit languages are agglutinative and typically express what would be complex expressions in English by suffixes and prefixes added to the stem-word. As a result, Inuits have uncountably many 'words' for everything. Each word-form contains indicators of qualities and roles that in English would be expressed by many separate words. It's as pointless to say that some Inuit language has twenty or sixty or eighty words for 'snow' as to say that Hungarian has seventeen words for 'Anna'.

3 Published in *The Works of Sir William Jones*, London: Robinson and Evans, 1799.

4 Wilhelm Freiherr von Humboldt, *Prüfung der Untersuchungen über die Urbewohner Hispaniens vermittelst der vaskischen Sprache*, 1821.

5 Wilhelm Freiherr von Humboldt, *Über die Entstehung der grammatischen Formen und ihren Einfluss auf die Ideenentwicklung*, 1822.

6 See Lera Boroditsky's report on this language at http://www.edge.org/3rd_culture/boroditsky09/boroditsky09_index.html.

7 Edward Sapir, 'Abnormal Types of Speech in Nootka' (1915), in *Selected Writings in Language, Culture and Personality*, ed. David G. Mandelbaum, U. of California Press, 1956, pp. 179–96.

8 Hilary Henson, *British Social Anthropologists and Language*, Clarendon Press, 1974, p. 11.

9 Mildred L. Larson, *Meaning-Based Translation*, University Press of America, 1984, p. 158.

10 E. J. Payne, *History of the New World Called America*, Clarendon Press, 1899, Vol. 2, p. 103, quoted in Henson, *British Social Anthropologists*, p. 10.

11 See Michael Coe, *Breaking the Maya Code*, Thames & Hudson, 1999.

15. Bibles and Bananas

1 Figures from Philip Noss (ed.), *A History of Bible Translation*, Rome: Edizioni di Storia et letteratura, 2007, p. 24.

2 Eugene Nida and Jan de Waard, *From One Language to Another: Functional Equivalence in Bible Translating*, Nelson, 1986.

3 Edesio Sánchez-Cetina, 'Word of God, Word of the People', in Noss, *A History of Bible Translation*, p. 395.

4 Daud Soeslo, 'Bible Translation in Asia–Pacific and the Americas', in Noss, *A History of Bible Translation*, pp. 165–6, 175.

5 Eugene Nida, *Fascinated by Languages*, John Benjamins, 2003.

6 Richard Rohrbaugh, *The New Testament in Cross-Cultural Perspective*, Cascade, 2007, quoted in Dietmar Neufeld (ed.), *The Social Sciences and Biblical Translation*, Society of Biblical Literature, 2008, p. ix.

7 Neufeld, *Social Sciences and Biblical Translation*, p. 3.

8 Leora Batnitsky, 'Translation as Transcendence: A Glimpse into the Workshop of the Buber–Rosenzweig Bible Translation', *New German Critique* 70 (1997), pp. 87–116.

9 Gott sprach zu Mosche/Ich werde dasein, als der ich dasein werde./ Und sprach:/So sollst du zu den Söhnen Jifsraels sprechen:/ICH BIN DA schickt mich zu euch/Und weiter sprach Gott zu Mosche:/ So sollst du den Söhnen Jifsraels sprechen:/ER,/der Gott eurer Väter/der Gott Abrhamas, der Gott/Jitzchaks, der Gott Jakobs/ schickt mich zu euch./Das ist mein Name in Weltzeit/das mein Gendenken,/Geschlecht für Geschlecht.

16. Translation Impacts

1 Friedrich Schleiermacher, 'Über die verschiedenen Methoden des Übersetzens', transl. Susan Bernofsky, in Lawrence Venuti, *The Translation Studies Reader* (2nd edn), Routledge, 2004.

2 Martha Gellerstam, 'Fingerprints in Translation', in Gunilla Anderman (ed.), *In and Out of English: For Better, for Worse*, Multilingual Matters, 2005, from whom the following material is taken.

3 Preston M. Torbert, 'Globalizing Legal Drafting: What the Chinese Can Teach Us about *Ejusdem Generis* and All That', *The Scribes Journal of Legal Writing* (2007), pp. 41–50.

4 All the information in the following paragraphs is borrowed and summarized from Bambi Schieffelin, 'Found in Translating: Reflexive Language across Time and Texts in Bosavi', in Miki Makihara and Bambi B. Schieffelin (eds.), *Consequences of Contact: Language Ideologies and Sociocultural Transformations in Pacific Societies*, Oxford UP, 2007, pp. 141–65.

5 *The Good News Bible* (1966), Mark 2:6–10.

6 Quoted by Scott L. Montgomery, *Science in Translation*, Chicago, 2000, p. 68.

17. The Third Code

1 Lawrence Venuti, *The Translator's Invisibility: A History of Translation*, Routledge, 1995.

2 Sara Laviosa, *Corpus-Based Translation Studies. Theory, Findings, Applications*, Rodopi, 2002.

3 Mairi McLaughlin, '(In)visibility: Dislocation in French and the Voice of the Translator', *French Studies* 61.2 (2008), pp. 53–64.
4 Exceptions include Rosemary Edmonds's *War and Peace*, Penguin Books, 1957, in which Platon Karataev speaks a generic folk dialect of English vaguely indebted to Yorkshire.
5 See Ineke Wallaert, 'The Translation of Sociolects: A Paradigm of Ideological Issues in Translation?', in Janet Cotterill and Anne Ife (eds.), *Language Across Boundaries*, British Association for Applied Linguistics, 2001, pp. 171–84.

18. No Language is an Island

1 Simon Gaunt, 'Translating the Diversity of the Middle Ages: Marco Polo and John Mandeville as "French" Writers', *Australian Journal of French Studies* XLVI.3 (2009), 235–48.
2 Claude Lanzmann and Simone de Beauvoir, *Shoah: The Complete Text of the Acclaimed Holocaust Film*, Da Capo, 1995, provides an English translation of the subtitles only. Cross-linguistic interactions can only be studied by watching the film.
3 Cyril Aslanov, *Le Français au Levant*, Champion, 2006, resurrects the often-forgotten 'Empire of French' that spread from Sicily and Cyprus to the (French-speaking) Kingdom of Jerusalem between 1100 and 1400 CE.
4 Gaunt, 'Translating the Diversity of the Middle Ages', p. 237.
5 Leo Tolstoy, *War and Peace*, transl. Rosemary Edmonds, Penguin, 1957, p. 417.

19. Global Flows

1 The figure is remarkably stable for other major or central languages. Gisele Sapiro ('Globalization and Cultural Diversity in the Book Market', *Poetics* 38.4 (2010), pp. 419–39) logs forty-two source languages for literary translations published in France between 1984 and 2002. A relatively new American adventure in literary translations on the web – WordsWithoutBorders.org – has widened the net to

include over seventy source languages, but it has yet to affect book publishing in traditional form to any significant degree.

2   For a brief exposition of the dollar delusion, see Michel Onfray's article 'Les deux bouts de la langue', *Le Monde*, 10 July 2010.

3   See Gideon Toury, 'Enhancing Cultural Change by Means of Fictitious Translations', available online at http://spinoza.tau.ac.il/~toury/works.

4   Rasa'il Ikhwan al-Safa, III (Cairo, 1928), p. 152, quoted in Bernard Lewis, *From Babel to Dragomans: Interpreting the Middle East*, Oxford UP, 2004, p. 31.

5   Katharina Rout, 'Fragments of a Greater Language', in Susan Ouriou (ed.) *Beyond Words: Translating the World*, Banff Center Press, 2010, pp. 33–7.

6   Jessica Ka Yee Chan, 'Translating Russia into China: Lu Xun's Fashioning of an Antithesis to Western Europe', paper given at the MLA Conference, Philadelphia, Pa, 2009.

7   Arnold B. McMillin, 'Small is Sometimes Beautiful: Studying "Minor Languages" at a University with Particular Reference to Belarus', *Modern Language Review* 101.4 (October 2006), pp. xxxii–xliii.

8   Anonymous leader, *Yomiuri Shimbun*, 23 June 1888, translated by Michael Emmerich.

9   'The Wu Jing Project: A New Translation of the Five Chinese Classics into the Major Languages of the World; an International Project Sponsored by the Confucius Institutes Headquarters, Beijing, China', project description kindly supplied by Martin Kern.

20. A Question of Human Rights

1   There are two English translations: *Course in General Linguistics*, transl. Wade Baskin, Peter Owen, 1960; and *Course in General Linguistics*, transl. Roy Harris, Duckworth, 1983. The second is to be preferred.

2   See Rosemary Moeketsi, 'Intervention in Court Interpreting: South Africa', in Jeremy Munday (ed.), *Translation as Intervention*, Continuum, 2007, pp. 97–117.

3   Like Japanese, however, it does have unofficial status. The German Translation Section, funded jointly by the German, Swiss, Lichten-

stein and Austrian governments, provides German-language services at UN headquarters in New York.

4   Quoted in Sir Frederick Pollock, *A First Book of Jurisprudence for Students of the Common Law*, Macmillan & Co., 1896, p. 283.

5   Karen McAuliffe, 'Translation at the Court of Justice of the European Communities', in Frances Olsen, Alexander Lorz and Dieter Stein (eds.), *Translation Issues in Language and Law*, Palgrave, 2009, pp. 99–115 (p. 107). My emphasis.

21.   *Ceci n'est pas une traduction*

1   The separate Directorate-General for Interpretation also has a huge budget – it is the largest interpreting service in the world by far.

2   Karen McAuliffe, 'Translation at the Court of Justice of the European Communities', in Frances Olsen, Alexander Lorz and Dieter Stein (eds.), *Translation Issues in Language and Law*, Palgrave, 2009, p. 105.

3   *Lubella* v. *Hauptzollamt Cottbus*, quoted in Lawrence Solan, 'Statutory Interpretation in the EU: The Augustinian Approach', in Olsen, Lorz and Stein, *Translation Issues in Language and Law*, p. 49.

4   See Solan, 'Statutory Interpretation in the EU', pp. 35–53.

22.   Translating News

1   Susan Bassnett and Esperanca Bielsa, *Translation in Global News*, Routledge, 2009, is the principal source of information and examples given in this chapter.

23.   The Adventure of Automated Language Translation Machines

1   See Michael Gordin, *Red Cloud at Dawn: Truman, Stalin, and the End of the Atomic Monopoly*, Farrar, Straus, Giroux, 2010, for a well-documented account of the intelligence-gathering machinery of the period.

2   Warren Weaver, 'Translation', in W. N. Locke and A. D. Booth (eds.), *Machine Translation of Languages: Fourteen Essays*, MIT Press, 1955, p. 15.

3   Weaver, 'Translation', quoted in *MT News International*, 22 (July 1999), p. 6.

4   Yehoshua Bar-Hillel, 'A Demonstration of the Nonfeasibility of Fully Automatic High Quality Translation' (1960), in *Language and information*, Addison-Wesley, 1964, p. 174.

5   http://www.youtube.com/watch?v=_GdSC1Z1Kzs.

6   http://www.whitehouse.gov/administration/eop/nec/Strategyfor AmericanInnovation/, section 3.D.

24. A Fish in Your Ear

1   Martine Behr and Maike Corpataux, *Die Nürnberger-Prozesse: Zur Bedeutung der Dolmetscher für die Prozesse and der Prozesse für die Dolmetscher*, Munich: Meidenbauer, 2006, pp. 25–30.

2   Richard W. Sonnenfeldt, *Witness to Nuremberg*, Arcade, 2006, p. 51.

3   Francesca Gaiba, *The Origins of Simultaneous Interpretation: The Nuremberg Trial*, U. of Ottawa Press, 1998, p. 110.

4   Provisional Rules of Procedure of the Security Council (1946), Rule 42.

5   Annelise Riles, 'Models and Documents: Artefacts of International Legal Knowledge', *The International and Comparative Law Quarterly* 48.4 (October 1999), p. 819.

6   Denis Peiron, 'La France à court d'interprètes', *Le Monde*, 8 March 2010, raised a cry of alarm at the shortage of French candidates for language jobs in the European Union; Brigitte Perucca, 'Un monde sans interprètes', *Le Monde*, 19 March 2010, reports that barely 30 per cent of candidates for interpreter posts in all international organizations pass the first-stage tests.

7   The Council of Europe is distinct from the European Parliament, though it also sits in Strasbourg. Its official languages are English and French, but it provides German, Italian and Russian interpreting as 'additional working languages' at its own expense.

25. Match Me If You Can

1 Arvo Krikmann, *Netinalju Stalinist* – Интернет-анекдоты о Сталине – *Internet Humour about Stalin*, Tartu: Eesti Kirjandus-muuseum, 2004, joke No. 11, quoted by Alexandra Arkhipova, 'Laughing About Stalin', paper given at a conference on 'Totalitarian Laughter', Princeton, May 2009.

2 For a fuller discussion of this thorny field of study, see W. D. Hart, 'On Self-Reference', *Philosophical Review* 79 (1970), pp. 523–8.

26. Style and Translation

1 Georges Perec, *Things* (1965), takes his exercise in Flaubert to an unusual pitch of intensity by incorporating a dozen or so sentences that really are by Flaubert.

2 Jean Rouaud, *Fields of Glory*, transl. Ralph Manheim (1998), is a good example of how an imitation of Proust's 'inimitable' French style can be represented *as such* in another language.

3 Henri Godin, *Les Ressources stylistiques du français contemporain* (1948), 2nd edn, Blackwell, 1964, pp. 2, 3.

4 Adam Thirlwell, *Miss Herbert*, Cape, 2007.

27. Translating Literary Texts

1 Pascale Casanova, *The World Republic of Letters*, transl. M. B. DeBe-voise, Harvard UP, 1999.

2 Spanish could plausibly take over the role of 'first inter-language' in literary translation, but I see no sign of that happening yet.

3 English-language rights may be acquired for the entire world and they are then called WELR (World English Language Rights) or else for one or another of its territories – 'UK and Commonwealth' or 'North America', sometimes further subdivided into 'USA' and 'Canada'.

4 See Mark Solms, 'Controversies in Freud Translation', *Psychoanaly-sis and History* 1 (1999), pp. 28–43.

5   Elisabeth Roudinesco, 'Freud, une passion publique', *Le Monde*, 7 January 2010.

28. What Translators Do

1   *Eurostar Metropolitan*, June 2010, p. 5. The changes make it clear that this sentence was translated from English into French, and not vice versa. A back-translation of the French would probably give 'Top speed reached in July 2003 by a Eurostar train during testing of a high-speed line in the UK'.

29. Beating the Bounds

1   Roman Jakobson and Abraham Moles proposed an influential Communication Model in which the role of natural language is played by something they called a *code*. They didn't really mean a code as such, but the metaphor has stuck.

30. Under Fire

1   John Dryden, 'On Translation', in Rainer Schulte and John Biguenet, *Theories of Translation: An Anthology of Essays from Dryden to Derrida*, Chicago, 1992, p. 31.

2   Arthur Schopenhauer, *Parerga und Paralipomena* (1800), extract translated by Peter Mollenhauer as 'On Language and Words', in Schulte and Biguenet, *Theories of Translation*, p. 34.

3   Vladimir Nabokov, 'Problems of Translation: *Onegin* in English', *Partisan Review* 22.5 (Fall 1955), reprinted in Schulte and Biguenet, *Theories of Translation*, pp. 137, 140.

4   José Ortega y Gasset, 'La Miseria y el esplendor de la traducción', *La Nación* (Buenos Aires), June 1937, transl. Elisabeth Gamble Miller, in Schulte and Biguenet, *Theories of Translation*, p. 98.

31. Sameness, Likeness and Match

1   For a counter-example where the character-count is respected in translation line by line, see Chapter 51 of Perec's *Life A User's Manual*, and above, p. 135, version 12.

Afterbabble

1   A small selection: Walter Benjamin, 'The Task of the Translator' (1923), in Rainer Schulte and John Biguenet, *Theories of Translation: An Anthology of Essays from Dryden to Derrida*, Chicago, 1992; George Steiner, *After Babel*, Oxford UP, 1975; Paul Zumthor, *Babel ou l'inachèvement*, Paris: Seuil, 1997; Daniel Heller-Roazen, *Echolalias*, MIT Press, 2005; Jacques Derrida, 'Des Tours de Babel', in *Psyché: L'Invention de l'autre*, Paris: Galilée, 2007.

2   For example, François Ost, *Traduire: Défense et illustration du multi-linguisme*, Paris: Fayard, 2009. Ost's long first chapter runs through many of the possible interpretations of the Babel story.

3   See Arika Okrent, *In the World of Constructed Languages*, Pennsylvania UP, 2008, for a witty and accessible account of the long history of language improvement schemes.

4   That is not to say that neo-grammarians have been wasting their time. The epic adventure of transformational grammar that began in 1957 remains for many people more stimulating than all the legends of the Arthurian Cycle put together.

5   For a fuller discussion of gesture in the evolution of language, see Christine Kenneally, *The First Word: The Search for the Origins of Language*, Penguin, 2007, pp. 123–38.

6   The classic statement of the evolutionary relationship between grooming and language is Robin Dunbar's *Grooming, Gossip and the Evolution of Language*, Faber, 1996. Although Dunbar remains committed to monogenesis (a single origin for all varieties of speech), his work provides numerous valuable insights that have been borrowed in simplified form in various places in this book.

Permissions and Acknowledgements

p. 6 (English translation of Marot) Reproduced with the kind permission of Professor Douglas Hofstadter.

p. 14 (Scientific pastiche), from *Cantatrix Sopranica et autres écrits scientifiques*, 1991, Éditions du Seuil, Paris, © Georges Perec; published in the UK as *Cantatrix Sopranica: Scientific Papers of Georges Perec*, 2008, Atlas Press, London.

p. 18 (Anadalam 1), from *La Vie mode d'emploi* (ed. Magné), 1978, Hachette-Littératures, p. 141, © Georges Perec; published in the UK as *Life A User's Manual*, 2008, Vintage, p. 110, © David Bellos, reprinted by permission of The Random House Group Ltd; and in the USA as *Life A User's Manual* New ed., 2009, David R. Godine publishers, p. 125, © David Bellos.

p. 19 (Anadalam 2), from *La Vie mode d'emploi* (ed. Magné), 1978, Hachette-Littératures, p. 142, © Georges Perec; published in the UK as *Life A User's Manual*, 2008, Vintage, p. 110, © David Bellos, Reprinted by permission of The Random House Group Ltd; and in the USA as *Life A User's Manual* New ed., 2009, David R. Godine publishers, p. 125, © David Bellos.

p. 22 (Japanese translation terms) from Michael Emmerich, 'Beyond Between: Translation, Ghosts, Metaphors', posted online at wordswithoutborders.org, April, 2009, reproduced with the kind permission of Professor Michael Emmerich.

p. 28 Finnish translation of the sight poem courtesy of the translator, Reijo Ollinen, originally quoted in Andrew Chesterman, *Memes of Translation*, John Benjamins, 1997, p. 61.

p. 32 (French version of Humpty Dumpty) from Luis d'Antin van Rooten, *Mots d'Heures, Gousses, Rames*, Grossman, 1967.

p. 44 (Gibberish song from Charlie Chaplin's *Modern Times*, 1936) courtesy of the Chaplin estate, Copyright © Roy Export S.A.S. All rights reserved.

p. 50 from *De La Grammatologie*, Jacques Derrida, © Editions de Minuit; published in English as *Of Grammatology*, Jacques Derrida. Translated by Gayatri Chakravorty Spivak. © 1998 The Johns Hopkins University Press. Reprinted with permission of The Johns Hopkins University Press.

p. 54 (letter from Estonian translator) reproduced with the kind permission of Anti Saar.

p. 84 (Leonard Bloomfield) from Leonard Bloomfield, *Language*, H. Holt & Co., 1933, p. 140.

p. 100 (Perec's word-killer) from *La Vie mode d'emploi* (ed. Magné), 1978, Hachette-Littératures, p. 341, © Georges Perec; published in the UK as *Life A User's Manual*, 2008, Vintage, p. 287–88, © David Bellos, Reprinted by permission of The Random House Group Ltd; and in the USA as *Life A User's Manual* New ed, 2009, David R. Godine publishers, p. 327, © David Bellos.

p. 121 From *War and Peace*, by Leo Tolstoy, translated by Rosemary Edmonds, © Penguin Classics

p. 133–135 (*shunkouliu*) Reproduced with the kind permission of Professor Perry Link, University of California at Riverside.

p. 136 (Asterix 1) © 2011 Les éditions Albert René / Goscinny-Uderzo.

p. 137 (Astertix 2) © 2011 Les éditions Albert René / Goscinny-Uderzo.

p. 145 (Israeli 'Onegin stanza') from *Another Place, a Foreign City*, by Maya Arad, copyright © by Xargol Books Ltd., Tel-Aviv, 2003; translated into English by Adriana Jacobs and reproduced with her kind permission.

p. 147 (Nabokov on translation) from *Eugene Onegin: A Novel in Verse* by Aleksandr Pushkin, translated and with a commentary by Vladimir

Nabokov, Routledge, 1964, Vol. 1, pp. vii–ix., © Princeton University Press.

p. 146 (Sybil) from *La Disparition*, Georges Perec, 1969, Editions Denoël, in the translation, *A Void*, by Georges Perec, translated by Gilbert Adair, published by Harvill Press, p 107–108. Reprinted by permission of The Random House Group Ltd.

p. 157 (Pete the Strangler) from *White Dog*, Romain Gary, 1970. Reprinted courtesy of the author's estate and The University of Chicago Press, 2004, p. 51.

p. 218 (the perfect language) from *From Babel to Dragomans: Interpreting the Middle East*, Bernard Lewis, Oxford University Press, 2004, © of and reprinted with permission from The British Academy.

p. 222 (Japanese newspaper editorial) translation reproduced with the kind permission of Professor Michael Emmerich.

p. 257 (Warren Weaver) from Warren Weaver, 'Translation', in *Machine Translation of Languages*, by William N. Locke and A. D. Booth (eds.), published by The MIT Press.

p. 258 (Warren Weaver) *ibid.*

p. 260 (FAHQT) from 'A Demonstration of the Nonfeasibility of Fully Automatic High Quality Translation', Yehoshua Bar-Hillel, (1960), in *Language and Information – Selected Essays on their Theory and Application*, Addison-Wesley Publ./Jerusalem Academic, 1964, p. 174.

p. 289 (Joke visiting card 1) from *La Vie mode d'emploi* (ed. Magné), 1978, Hachette-Littératures, p. 341, © Georges Perec; published in the UK as *Life: A User's Manual*, 2008, Vintage, p. 287–88, © David Bellos. Reprinted by permission of The Random House Group Ltd; and in the USA as *Life A User's Manual* New ed., 2009, David R. Godine publishers, p. 327, © David Bellos.

p. 290 (Joke visiting card 2) from *La Vie mode d'emploi* (ed. Magné), 1978, Hachette-Littératures, p. 341, © Georges Perec; published in the UK as *Life A User's Manual*, 2008, Vintage, p. 287–88, © David Bellos. Reprinted by permission of The Random House Group Ltd; and in the USA as *Life A User's Manual* New ed, 2009, David R. Godine publishers, p. 327, © David Bellos.

p 292 (Haikus) from *One Hundred Frogs: From Matsuo Basho to Allen Ginsberg*, by Hiroaki Sato, 1995, Weatherhill, Shambhala Publications Inc., Boston, MA, © Allen Ginsburg, © James Kirkup, and © Curtis Hidden Page.

p. 293 (Wordsworth pastiche) by Catherine M. Fanshawe, extracted from *The Faber Book of Parodies*, Simon Brett (ed.), 1984, Faber & Faber.

p. 293 (T. S. Eliot pastiche) from *The Sweeniad*, by Myra Buttle (aka Victor Purcell), Secker & Warburg, 1958. Extracted from *The Faber Book of Parodies*, Simon Brett (ed.), 1984, Faber & Faber.

p. 293 (J. D. Salinger pastiche) from *Adam & Eve & Stuff Like That*, by Ed Berman. Extracted from *The Faber Book of Parodies*, Simon Brett (ed.), 1984, Faber & Faber.

p. 317 (*53 Days*) from *53 Jours*, Hachette-Littératures, 1989, © Georges Perec; published in the UK as *53 Days*, by Georges Perec, translated by David Bellos, published by Harvill Press, 1994, p. 61. Reprinted by permission of The Random House Group Ltd; and in the USA as *53 Days*, David R. Godine publishers, p. 61, © David Bellos.

Every effort has been made to contact the copyright holders prior to publication. If notified, the publisher undertakes to rectify any errors or omissions at the earliest opportunity.

Index

A la recherche du temps perdu 307
Abkhaz 233
abstract thought, and classical
   languages 169
accent 206
ad-libbing 345
Adair, Gilbert 146, 147
Adieu Gary Cooper 38
adjective generalizing 230
aesthetics of the sentence 297
after-speaking 32, 313
AIIC 280
Akkadian 95, 125, 172, 213
Albanian 64, 161, 208, 343
Alembert, Jean d' 41–42
Alexander the Great 214
Alpijskaja Balada 221
Alsatian language 167
America 307
Americanisms 173, 195, 196
Amoritic 95
Anadalams 18–19
analogy-based substitution 180
Anglo-Saxon 214, 351
animal language 157–58, 159, 347–48
anisomorphism of languages 82, 229
Another Place, a Foreign City 145
ante-Babel language 341
The Arabian Nights 111–13
Arabic 10, 11, 13, 65, 88, 111, 112, 113, 122,
      123, 124, 125, 172, 176, 178, 193, 209,
      216, 217, 218, 220, 223, 274, 275, 276,
      280
Arad, Maya 145, 147
Aramaic 141, 173, 176, 179, 193

Aristarchi, Stavraki 128
Armenian 174, 176
Asia Pacific Christian Mission 190
Asmat 180
Asterix the Gaul 136–37, 147
asymmetric regimes 278, 279
asymmetry of translations 209–23,
      278
Atxaga, Bernardo 221
audio-books 140
Augerau, Véronique 141
Augustinian approach to EU law 245,
      248
Austin, J.L. 72–73, 75
Austro-Hungarian empire 211
authentic foreignness 49
authentic Frenchness 51
automatic translating machines
      269–73
Avatar 337–38
Average West European 69, 169–70,
      322
axiom of effability 149–59, 169, 287,
      353
axiom of grammaticality 342, 344
Azeri 125, 212

Babel commentary 339–41
Babelfish 279–80
back-translation 51–52, 108, 195, 309
Balzac, Honoré de 205–06
Bar-Hillel, Yehoshua 260–61
Bartleby the Scrivener 144
Bashô, Matsuo 292
basic units of language 92

BASIC-E (British-American-Scientific-International-Commercial English) 15
Basque 161, 162, 167, 168
BBC English 349
Belgium 228
Bell, Anthea 137, 147
Bengali 49, 206, 217
Benjamin, Walter 155, 354
Bergman, Ingmar 139
Berman, Antoine 155
The Berne Convention 306
Berr, Hélène 299
Bible translation 104–08, 155, 173–78, 181–86, 187, 190–92, 245, 299, 339–40
bilingual glossaries 94, 97
bilingualism in early societies 121
Bismarck, Otto von 315
Bloomfield, Leonard 83–84
Boeinglish 262
Bosavi 190–92, 193
Breton 167
British English 195, 196, 306
Brooks, James 31
Brückner, Christian 140
Buber, Martin 183, 184, 185
Buddhism 29
Buffon, Georges-Louis de 294–95, 298
Bykau (Bykov), Vasil 221
Byrne, Gabriel 140

calques 179, 192
Castilian 8–9
The Castle 307
The Castle of Otranto 37
CAT (computer-aided translation) 261–62
category-terms 24–25
Caucasus 212
Cawdrey, Robert 98–99, 100
celebrity journalism 187
Celentano, Adriano 43
Celtic 161, 351

Chabon, Michael 206, 207
La Chamade 333
Champollion, Jean-François 156
Chaplin, Charlie 44, 47
Charlemagne 240
Chatterjee, Upumanyu 206
Chaucer 305
cheval 278
China 15, 28, 29, 65
Chinese dictionaries 96–97
Chinese 10, 11, 16, 29–30, 65, 122, 130–33, 139, 182, 189–90, 209, 216, 217, 219, 220, 265, 274, 275, 276, 280, 281, 291, 292, 342
Chomsky, Noam 74
Chronicle in Stone 39–40
chuchotage (whisper translation) 141, 268
Churchill, Winston 316
Chuvash 49, 221
clarification 312
class presumption 189
classics 305
Clifford, James 37–38
Coghill, Neville 305
The Colbert Report 142
Cold War 256–57
colonial expansion 162–66, 211, 212
colloquial speech 286
colour terms 81–82
Columbus, Christopher 8–9
Commission générale de terminologie et de néologie 177
Condé, Maryse 222
conference interpreters 266, 274, 275, 279, 345, see also translators
Confucius Institute 223
Contact languages 9, 15, 16, 124, 178, 190
Context Group of the Society of Biblical Literature 183
contraction 274, 312
Coptic 174, 176
copy-editing 204

copyright 306–07
Course in General Linguistics 225, 325–26
court interpreters 228, 268–73, 275
Coverdale, Miles 176
cribs 116
Crowe, Russell 140
cultural substitution 180–82
Cyprus 228
Cyprian language 92
The Czar's Madman 220
Czech 203, 204, 211, 215

Daghestani 212
Danticat, Edwidge 222
Dangerous Liaisons 42
Danish 211, 237, 351
de Niro, Robert 140
*Déclaration des droits de l'homme et du
    citoyen* 229–30, 231
*Déclaration Universelle des Droits de
    l'Homme* 231
Dempe, Dagmar 140
determiners 342
DG Translation 239
dialects 199, 204, 349
dialogue 188
Díaz, Junot 206
Dickens, Charles 300
dictionaries 82–83, 91, 94–103, 259
Dictionnaire de l'Académie 97
The Different Methods of Translating 47
differentiation by speech 350–51
Dios Habla Hoy Bible translation
    175–76
Discourse on Style 294, 298
La Disparition 146
Distinctive feature analysis 89, 90
dominant languages 218–19
Donovan, General "Wild Bill" 272
double translating 276, 278
down translation 172, 173, 177, 182, 185
Dr Strangelove 47
Dr Zhivago 324

dragomans 125, 126–30
dragomania 130
Dryden, John 143, 328
dubbing 139–40
Duhamel, Marcel 173
Duino Elegies 153
Dutch 178, 184, 211, 216, 237
Dutch East India Company 178
dynamic equivalence 174–75
Dzhabayev, Dzhambul 213

effability 149–59, 169, 287, 353
effects 314–21
Egyptian hieroglyphs 156
Elamite 95
eloquence and style 295
Emmerich, Michael 24
emphasis, change of 312
English, August 206
English language 10–16, 22–24, 32,
    42–43, 53, 59–60, 65, 72–73, 75, 79,
    88, 91, 115, 122, 126, 127, 136, 145, 152,
    153, 168, 169, 172, 177, 178, 187–90,
    194, 195–99, 202, 206, 207, 209,
    210, 212, 214, 216, 217, 222–23, 230,
    233, 234, 237, 241, 248–49, 264, 268,
    269, 274, 275, 279, 280–81, 304, 306,
    309, 310, 316, 317, 324, 334, 349–51
English legal language 234
English-soundingness 51
Epistles 328
equivalence 174–75
equivalent effects 314–21
Erasmus 176
Eskimo vocabulary 160, 162, 166, 170
Esperanto 15
Estienne, Robert 98
Estonian 54
Estuarine 349
ethics 41
ethnic disparagements 285
ethnicity 349
ethnocentric violence 41, 56

Eugene Onegin 142–46
European Court of Justice (ECJ) 236, 241–49
European linguistic nationalism 167
European Union
    languages within 237–49
    official languages 241, 278
    translating in 278
European Union Treaty 237
Eurostar 313, 314
evidentials 164, 168, 191, 193
evolution of language 341
expansion 312
explorer-linguists 165

facing-page translation 116–17
FAHQT (fully automated high-quality translation) 260–63, 281
Farsi 65, 152, 264, 265
features of meaning 89
felicity, conditions of 73
53 Days 317
figurative meanings 109–10
Filene-Finlay Speech Translator 269–73
films
    and meaning 68–71, 337–38
    translation 138–41, 324
Fingal 36–37
Finnish languages 27–28, 217, 222, 228
Fish *see* Babelfish
The Five Classics 223
Flaubert, Gustave 296
foreign language teaching 280
foreign-soundingness 41–57
foreignisms 46, 55, 179
foreignizing 45–56, 185
formal equivalence 174
formality in conversation 70
Foucault, Michel 239
French 4, 10–12, 38, 42, 44, 46, 48, 51–54, 59, 60, 64, 65, 68, 79, 86, 88, 98, 103, 108, 109, 111, 114, 120, 122,

140–41, 150, 152, 162, 167, 168, 172, 176, 177, 185, 187, 190, 194, 197–99, 202–05, 207, 209, 211, 216, 217, 218, 220, 221, 223, 230, 231, 233, 234, 237, 240, 241, 242, 244, 265, 268, 269, 274, 275, 276, 279, 288, 289–90, 299, 304, 310, 316, 317, 334, 351
Freud, Sigmund 307, 309–10
Freudish 310
Fritsch, Thomas 140
Frost, Robert 152
functional equivalence 174

Gaelic 204, 215, 251
Gary, Romain 38, 157–58, 299
Gascon 167
Ge'ez 174, 176
Generic Immigrant Romance 44–46
Geneva conventions 234–35
Genji Monogatari 221
genres 77–79
geographical varieties of English 196
Georgian 174, 212
Gerard of Cremona 193
German 11, 12, 13, 25, 27, 42, 46–47, 48, 49, 53, 68, 88, 91, 114, 120, 140, 152, 153, 162, 172, 176, 183, 184, 185, 187, 203, 204, 209, 211, 216–20, 223, 230, 231, 233, 235–36, 237, 240, 241, 265, 268, 269, 279, 287, 289–90, 309, 310, 351
Germanness 49
gesticulation 345–46
gibberish 43, 44, 47
Gide, André 112
Ginsberg, Allen 292–93
globalization 54–55, 188
Goddard, Paulette 44
Godin, Henri 296
The Gold Bug 199–200
The Golden Gate 145
Google Translate (GT) 262–67

Index

Göring, Hermann 272
Gothic 161
GPDs (general purpose dictionaries) 95–96, 99–100
grammar
  and abstract entities 169
  axiom of grammaticality 342, 344
  breaking rules of 260
  common feature in language 341–42
  and culture 167
  differences between languages 342–43
  gender terms 230–31
  in legal decisions 245–47
  in legal translation 230–32
  Universal Grammar 343–44
grammaticality hypothesis 342, 344
The Great Escape 68–69, 71
The Great Eskimo Vocabulary Hoax 160, 161, 166, 170
Greek 11, 45, 52, 92, 98, 105, 107, 114, 116, 124, 130, 150, 161, 162, 164, 169, 172, 173, 175, 176, 177, 185, 187, 193, 194, 214, 218, 219, 220, 237, 259, 309, 340
grooming among primates 348
group-membership function of language 349

habitual patterns of thought 168
Habsburg empire 211, 218, 243
Hakkenden 221
hand-mouth links 346
Harris, Roy 120
Harvill Press 208
headline language 76–77
Hebrew 9, 107, 125, 141, 145, 175, 176, 177, 178, 183, 184, 195, 215, 220, 223, 265, 299, 339
hieroglyphs 156, 240
Hindi 8, 10, 49, 52, 88, 206, 209, 216, 223
historical semantics 86
Hitchhiker's Guide to the Galaxy 280

Hofstadter, Douglas 4–5, 129, 151, 179, 320, 332–33
homogenization of languages 187, 229, 233, 247
homonyms 86, 87
homophonic translation 32, 33, 108
homophones 32, 33, 87, 108
Hopi 163–64, 167, 169–70
Hörn, Stefan 272
Höss, Rudolf 272
Hoxha, Enver 17
Hugo, Victor 316
human rights legislation 229–33
Humboldt, Wilhelm von 161, 162, 165, 167–68
humour 283–90
Hungarian 59, 60, 92, 140–41, 172, 343
Hurritic 95
Hushaphone 269
hypernyms 23
hyponyms 23

Icelandic 176, 264, 265
ideas, classification of (Roget) 101
idiolect 298
immersion 114
imperfect matching 82
indeterminate speech flow 120
Index Translationum 209
India 8, 10
individual diction 350
Indonesian 11
ineffable 149–59, 353
Ingush 212
intentional alteration 74
intercomprehensibility 340
interlingua 259
international copyright 306–07
International English 196–97
international languages 274
international law 224–36
international rules of combat 234–35

382

international scientific English 14
internationalism 54
The Interpretation of Dreams 310
interpreters *see* translators
Inuit 160, 166
invariant core 259
Irish 237
isograms 135, 317
isolation 17–20
Italian 8, 11–12, 43, 52–53, 117, 124, 125,
 126, 140, 152, 176, 185, 202, 216, 217,
 222, 231, 237, 241, 309
Italianness 49
It's Complicated 78–79

Jackson, Robert H. 272
Jacobs, Adriana 145, 146
Jakobson, Roman 81, 323, 324
Japanese 10, 17, 22–23, 24, 25, 75, 150, 182,
 193, 195, 216, 217, 220, 221, 292, 303,
 309
Jerome, Saint 104–08, 176
Jesuit dictionaries 97
Johnson, Charles 144, 145, 147
Johnson, Samuel 95
Jones, Sir William 161, 162
The Jumping Frog of Calaveras County
 108–09

Kadare, Ismail 39–40, 64, 126, 208, 299,
 304
Kafka, Franz 307
Kannada 8
Katz, Jerrold 156
Kazakh 212
Kelly, Louis 105–06
Khrushchev, Nikita 204
King James Bible 177, 178, 183, 184, 187
King Lear 43
kitchen recipese 291
Klebsch, Klaus-Dieter 140
koiné 107, 173, 239
Kross, Jaan 220

Kuuk Thaayorre 163

L1 (source language) 57, 64, 65, 67, 181,
 202, 207, 217, 222, 325
L2 (target language) 57, 64, 65, 66, 67,
 116, 177, 178, 181, 202, 207, 325
L3 202–08
language
 alternation 207
 articulated 346–48
 barrier 30
 change 194
 clarification 312
 as code 257–58, 317–19
 as communication 347–48
 contraction 274, 312
 databases 13
 drafters 241–42
 emphasis change 312
 as ethnicity 349
 as exclusive to humans 159
 expansion 312
 fiction in EU 241
 group-membership function 349
 hierarchy 177, 194
 match 283, 290
 natural language processing 90
 origins 341
 parity in European Union 237–49
 sounds 32
 sounds identifiable as 345
 superiority 219
 synonymy 312
 teaching
  simulated environments 115
  translation based 113–14
 and thought 326
 topic shift 312
 turners 191
language-acquisition device 61
language-boys 114, 124
language-elimination 13
language-imposition 13

languages
anisomorphism of 82, 229
basic units of 92
Biblical origins of 84
bond with mentality 161, 162, 164, 165
classical 169
colloquial speech 286
communicating without 20
culturally dominant 215
and culture 194
decline of 9–10
dialects 199, 204, 349
different registers of 84
dominant 217
equality of 167
in European Court of Justice (ECJ) 236, 241–45
European standard 167
in European Union 237–49
geographically isolated 351
international 53
and isolation 17–20
main world 10
as mother tongue 57–67
newspaper headline 76–77
number of 9
publishing style 91
rank order of 172
regional dialects 199
in regular translation 208
and scientific discovery 12
small languages 53–54
spoken speech language 269
thinking in 167
of truth 177
unification of 11–16, 343–44
as untranslatable 155–56
unusual 162–63
vehicular 10, 13, 16, 107, 208–09, 281
see also individual languages by name

Lanzmann, Claude 203
Larsson, Stieg 188
late release 335
Latin 9, 11, 15, 22, 26, 58–59, 98, 105, 114, 116, 130, 162, 169, 172, 173, 175, 185, 193, 204, 212, 215, 218, 219, 241, 251, 309, 340, 351
lawyer-linguists 244
League of Nations 235
lectoring 141–42
left dislocation 198
legal definitions 225, 227
legal translation 189, 224–36, 273
legislation
Ancient Egyptian 240
human rights 229–33
The Letters of a Portuguese Nun 37
lexical translation 144
Life A User's Manual 18, 289
Lifshitz, Emmanuel 37–38
likeness 333–34
Linear B 92
Lingua franca 9, 27
linguistic borrowing 33
linguistic diversity 341, 347, 351
linguistic interaction 325
linguistic sign 225–26, 236
linguists 9
lip-synchronization 43, 139–40
literacy level 113
literal translation 103–17, 312–21
literary works 34–40, 224, 302–11, 334
Lithuanian 279
live speech *see* oral translation
The Lives of the Translators 101 303
loan words 33
Luther, Martin 176, 184, 187

MacAuliffe, Karen 236
Macbeth 39–40
MacPherson, James 37
Madame Bovary 199–200, 296

Makine, Andreï 37
Malay language 18–19, 152, 178, 180, 184, 223
Malayalam language 217
Malta 243
Mandarin *see* Chinese
Les Mangeurs d'étoiles 38
Manhattanese 163
Mankel, Henning 188
Marathi 8, 49
Mardrus, Joseph-Charles 111–12
Marías, Javier 304
Marot, Clément 4, 5, 151, 320
Masefield, John 292
The Master and Margarita 308
matching 283, 290, 294, 312–21, 334–36
Mauss, Marcel 18
Mavrokordato, Alexander 126
Mawhinney, Heather 318
Maya 167
meaning 67–80
   invariant core of 259
   and sound relationship 150
The Meaning of Meaning 21
Mei Ying-Tso 96
Melville, Herman 144
Meschonnic, Henri 185
Mesopotamia 95, 125, 214
metaphor 87
metonymy 87
Michaelson, Sidney 299
mind grooves 168, 169
Modern Greek *see* Greek
Mon Oncle 316
Morton, A.Q. 299
mother tongue 57–67
Motoyuki, Shibata 303
Les Mots français selon l'ordre des lettres ainsi que les fault escrire & tourner en latin 98
mouth/hand links 346
mouthing 32

multi-level pattern matching 147
multilingual glossaries 94
multilingualism 9, 17
Murad II, Sultan 126
musical composition 293
My Fair Lady 349–50
mysterium 105–06, 108

Nabokov, Vladimir 142–44, 146, 329
Nash, Ogden 292
nationalities (in USSR) 212
nationality 63–4
Native American languages 164, 165, 166, 167, 169–70, 228
native speaker competence 63
native speakers 57–67
natural language processing 90
news agencies 251–55
news translations 250–55
newscasters 345
Newspeak 239
Nida, Eugene 174–75, 178, 179, 181, 182, 184, 185
Nineteen Eighty-Four 239
Nineteen Ways of Looking at Wang Wei 291
nomenclaturism 83–85, 100
Nootka 163
Normans 214, 234, 351
Norwegian 211
Nostratic 341
Nupela Testamen 190–91
Nuremberg International Military Tribunal 235–36, 268–73, 275, 278

Odyssey 305
Ogden, C.K. 21
Old French 241
Old Gothic 174, 176
Old High German 241
Old Persian 340
One Hundred Frogs 292
oral mediation 118

Index

oral translation 118–32, 202–03, 268–82
orientation change 274
Ortega y Gasset, José 329
Ottoman Empire 123, 127, 243
Ottoman Turkish 123, 125, 218

Papavrami, Tedi 64
Papua-New Guinea 27, 170
paraphrasing 144
Paz, Octavio 104, 109, 117, 291
Penguin Classics 305–06
Penguin Parallel Texts 117
Le Père Goriot 205–06
Perec, Georges 18–19, 100, 144, 146, 289,
    299, 317–18, 334–35
performative verbs 73–74, 76
Persian 123, 161, 174, 176, 219, 264, *see
    also* Old Persian
person-switching 202–04
Peterson v. *Weddel & Co., Ltd.* 245–46
Pevear, Richard 55–56, 64
Peythieux, Philippe 141
Phanariots 124, 128, 129
phonology 43
Picard 167
pivot languages 219–23, 264, 265
pizza-language 55
plain translation 134
poetry 149–54, 156, 291–95, 297, 322–23,
    333–34
Polanski, Roman 139
Polish 141, 152, 203
Polo, Marco 202, 204
polysemy 87
Portuguese 8, 178, 211, 212, 237
positional stylometry 299
posthumous copyright 306–07
prepositional verbs 91
primary orality 119
printing 202
Professor Marten's Departure 220
Proto-Indo-European 341
Proto-World 341

Proust, Marcel 306–07
Provençal 167
pseudo-translations 35–9, 213
Pygmalion 349–50

quasi-native competence 62
Quprili, Grand Vizier 126

Racine, Jean 297
rare pairs 298
re-contextualizing 314
reference 288
regional dialects 199–200, 349, 352
Reina-Valera Bible translation 175
relay 276, 278, 279
rephrasing 288, 312–13, 314
retour 278
retranslation 176, 305, 307
Richards, I.A. 15
Rieu, E.V. 305–06
Rilke, Rainer Maria 153
Roget, Peter Mark 101–02, 103
Roget's Thesaurus 101–02, 103
Romans 11, 26, 98, 114, 141, 211, 214,
    259
Roosevelt, Eleanor 231
Rosenzweig, Franz 183
Rosetta Stone 156, 239
Russian Federation 10
Russian 10, 12, 16, 25, 33, 45, 46–47,
    55–56, 64–65, 81, 82, 115, 117, 122,
    152, 154, 172, 205, 212–13, 217, 220,
    221, 223, 232, 233, 256, 268, 274, 275,
    276, 280, 342
Ruthenian language 211
Ruyl, Albert Cornelius 178, 180,
    184–85

Sagan, Françoise 333
sameness 332–33
Sanskrit 11, 98, 161, 172, 178, 217, 340
Sapir, Edward 167–68, 169
Sapir-Whorf hypothesis 168

Sato, Hiroaki 292
Saussure, Ferdinand de 225–27, 248, 325–26
Sayce, R.A. 298
Schleiermacher, Friedrich 47–48, 177, 187
Schopenhauer, Arthur 329
science and language 12–13
scientific English 14
scriptism 120
Sebokht, Severus 193
self-reference 288
semantic expansion 179
semantics 86, 87, 89
sense-for-sense translation 105, 134
sentencehood 344
Septuagint 107, 173, 176
Serbo-Croat 211
Seth, Vikram 145, 147
sexist language 130–31
Shannon, Claude 257
The Shibata Motoyuki Translation Collection 303
Shoah 203
shunkouliu 133–36
Siberia 212
sight-poem 27–28
sign language 31
sign, linguistic 225–26, 236
signifier 225–26
The Simpsons 141
simultaneous interpreting 268–82
sincerity 190
Singin' in the Rain 43
single-word substitution 108–09
skip-reading 106
slaves 114, 122, 124, 132
Slovak 211
Slovene 211
small languages 53–54
Smetona, Antanas 15–16
social correctness 130–31, 296
social register of language 296

social science translation 309, 310
Sonnenfeldt, Richard 272
sound/meaning relationship 150
sounded-out translation 135
source languages 215–16, 341
source-text language (L1) 57, 64, 65, 67, 181, 202, 207, 217, 222
South African official languages 228
Spanglish 31, 206
Spanish 8–9, 10, 48–49, 65, 117, 122, 140, 150, 177, 211, 212, 216, 217, 221, 222, 223, 231, 237, 274, 276, 280–81, 309
spelling standardization 98
Spitzer, Leo 297
Steiner, George 103, 155
stems, 92–93
Stilistik 297
Strachey, James 309
Strasbourg Oath 240–41
Strategy for American Innovation 267
Streep, Meryl 140
strip cartoons 136
Style in French Prose 298
style match 294
style research 297
style and translation 291–301, 304, 334
sub-linguistic mental units 89
substitution 180
subtitling 138, 139
Sumerian 26, 94–95, 101, 125, 172, 213–14, 218
suppression 313
Swahili 11, 216
Swedish 12, 176, 188, 190, 207, 209, 211, 214–15, 216, 222, 231
symptomatic meaning 68–72
synonymy 312
syntactic calque 177, 192
Syntactic Structures 74
Syriac 11, 172, 173, 176, 177, 185, 193
Szabó, Istvan 139

Index

A Table Alphabeticall of hard usual English Wordes . . . 99

Tagalog 61, 65

Tamil 8, 65, 216

target culture 185

target language (L2) 57, 64, 65, 66, 67, 116, 177, 178, 183, 202, 207, 296

target-language modification 177–78

targums 141, 176

Tartu 53

Tati, Jacques 316

telementation 325

telephone, invention of 268

television newscasters 345

tercüman 125

Thesaurus 101–02, 103

third code 197–98, 201

Thirlwell, Adam 296, 297, 300

thought
    habitual patterns of 168
    transmission 325

title-making 78–79

Tok Pisin 27, 190–92, 193

Tolstoy, Leo 120–21, 205, 206

tones in Chinese 227

topic shift 312

Torah 173

Torbert, Preston 189–90

Tractacus Logico-Philosophicus 154

Trader/Translator 129

Tranglish 196

transcoding 326

translatedness of news 254

Translating Means Translating Meaning 175

translation
    alternatives to 7–8
    apparent impossibility of 81, 83
    back-translation 51–52, 108, 195, 309
    boundaries 326–27
    by language volume 217
    as commercial venture 306
    copyright 306
    definitions of 323
    double 276, 278, 279
    down 172, 173, 177, 178, 182, 185
    as education aid 116
    equivalent effects 314–21
    in EU 238, 278, 279
    facing-page 116–17
    faithfulness 131
    flow 208–23
    foreign-soundingness 41–57
    in France 303
    gender terms 229–30
    in Germany 303
    and globalization 54–55, 188
    and improvement 202–05
    invisibility 197
    in Japan 303
    job opportunities for 243, 302
    as language-learning device 330–31
    lexical 144
    likeness 333–34
    literal 103–17
    literary 302–11
    meaning of 21–33
    mechanical 256–57
    methods 51–52, 108, 130–33
    mother tongue 57–67
    nationality of 217–18
    as opposite of empire 212
    oral *see* oral translation
    Ottoman 125
    and poetry 151–53
    political 122
    quality evaluation criteria 283–84, 330
    re-translators 307
    relay 276, 278, 279
    reliability of 118, 121–22, 124, 127–32

retour 278
role of 118
sameness 332–33
Schleiermacher's methods of 47–48
sense-for-sense 105, 134
share by world languages 209–33
simultaneous interpreting 268–82
sound/homophonic 32, 33, 108
and style 291–301
as substitute for original text 34–40
terminology for 28–29
as transfer of meaning 25–26, 30
translation relations 171–86
types of 22–23
UN 204, 233, 273, 275–78, 279
up 172, 175, 182
variability of 5
whisper-translation 141
word-for-word 103–17
see also individual languages
translations-in-English 196
translators
  AIIC 280
  as celebrities 303
  conference interpreters 266
  criticism of 328, 329–31
  English-language 219, 223, 303, 306
transnational law 254
The Travels of Marco Polo 202–03, 204, 205, 215
Treaty of Rome 237, 238
The Trial 307
Trique 165
trisyllibic verse 151
truth-value 288
Tschinag, Galsan 220
Turkish 11, 123, 124, 126
Turkmen 212
Tuscan 204
Twain, Mark 108–09

Ugaritic 95
UNCHR (UN Commission for Human Rights) 233
UNESCO 209, 210, 216, 217
United Bible Societies 175
United Nations 64–65, 122–23, 204, 209, 210, 216, 217, 231, 233, 273, 275–78, 279, 281
Universal Copyright Convention 306
Universal Grammar 343–44
up translation 172, 175, 182
Urdu 8, 10
USSR 64–65, 212–13, 221

Vargas, Fred 42, 299, 316
vehicular languages 10, 13, 16, 107, 208–09, 281
Venetian 204
Venice 124
Venuti, Lawrence 197
Verbatim 123
vertical axis of translation relations 171–86
vocabulary imports 177
vocal emphasis 197–98
Volapük 16
Volokhonsky, Larissa 64
vowel harmony 343

Waard, Jan de 175
Waley, Arthur 182
Walpole, Horace 37
War and Peace 120–21, 205
Weaver, Warren 257, 258, 260, 263
Weinberger, Eliot 291
whisper translation (chuchotage) 141, 268
Whorf, Benjamin Lee 163
Williams, C.K. 291
Wittgenstein, Ludwig 154
Wodehouse, P.G. 300
Wolof 65

word
    lists 165
    meaning of 119–20
    occurences 82–83
    rectangle 135
Word Magic 21, 24, 113
word-for-word translation 103–17,
    137
World-Wide-Science.org 13
wording 115–17
World Charter of Human Rights
    231

Wu Jing Project 223

Yade, Rama 233
Yiddish 59, 60, 195, 202, 203, 206
The Yiddish Policeman's Union 206,
    207
Yomiuri Shimbun 221
Yoruba 49
Young, Thomas 156

Zamenhof, Lejzer 15
Zulu 233

Ψάρι εί
αυτό μέ
στο
αυτί σο

U *has gots*
fish in ur eer?!11

Translayshun
and da Meening
of stuffz

Kako si
on korva

Tu ce, ai pest
in ureche

Che hai, un pesce
nell'orecchio?

Ĉu
tiu
estas
fiŝo
en via
orelo?

?

Что это у вас в
ухе? Рыба?

Tu ce, ai peste
in ureche?

ער א פיש
ין דיין
ר